A Penguin Special
Your Disobedient Servant

Leslie Chapman was born in 1919 in Windsor and joined
the Civil Service at the age of twenty as an executive
officer in the Office of Works. War broke out soon
afterwards and as a Territorial he was at once called up.
In 1945, invalided out of the army, he returned to the
Ministry of Works. In 1967, aged forty-seven, he was
promoted to regional director. He retired at his own
request in 1973.

Leslie Chapman

Your Disobedient Servant

Penguin Books

Penguin Books Ltd, Harmondsworth,
Middlesex, England
Penguin Books, 625 Madison Avenue,
New York, New York 10022, U.S.A.
Penguin Books Australia Ltd, Ringwood,
Victoria, Australia
Penguin Books Canada Ltd, 2801 John Street,
Markham, Ontario, Canada L3R 1B4
Penguin Books (N.Z.) Ltd, 182–190 Wairau Road,
Auckland 10, New Zealand

First published by Chatto & Windus Ltd 1978
Published with revisions in Penguin Books 1979

Copyright © Leslie Chapman, 1978, 1979
All rights reserved

Made and printed in Great Britain by
Richard Clay (The Chaucer Press) Ltd,
Bungay, Suffolk
Set in Monotype Times

Contents

6 *Contents*

Introduction to the First Edition

Civil servants in this country have just one loyalty – to the public, which in practice means to the democratically elected representatives of the public. Such obligations as they may assume towards the Civil Service as an organization, and to their colleagues within it, can be permitted only to the extent that these in turn serve the public interest. In no circumstances can that interest be served adequately if instructions from Ministers are ignored, modified or delayed.

I have learned by experience that only if the deficiencies of the Civil Service are made public is there any prospect of change for the better. The last few months have produced signs of progress but these have not stemmed from parliamentary or government action. They were solely the consequence of comment by the Press, radio and television. The publication of this book seeks to take that process a stage further.

Leslie C. Chapman
August 1977

Blockley,
Near Moreton-in-Marsh
Gloucestershire

Introduction to the Second Edition

This book was first published in May 1978 and its appearance created something of a furore. One of the issues it dealt with which was in consequence publicly debated was the extent to which the suppression of official information generally and the operation of the Official Secrets Act in particular can be used to conceal inefficiency and negligence in the public service. Such concealment must bear down heavily on all democratic processes, including the functioning of any Parliamentary Select Committees involved in scrutiny of the activities of the public sector. The consequences may be no less serious even where misleading or inaccurate information is given inadvertently and in good faith. Responses since the first publication to the challenge on one such issue (see Chapter 8) are dealt with in Chapter 22 of this edition.

One of the most disturbing features of these events is that it has taken a book, two television documentary programmes, several Parliamentary questions and considerable newspaper coverage to bring into the open an admission that inaccurate evidence had been given to Parliament and the Public Accounts Committee. It has taken a further session of that Committee to establish that it was indeed misled by the evidence presented to it. There is no certainty that even this much would have been achieved without the huge publicity. Today, four and a half years after I retired from the service and three years after the misleading evidence was given to the PAC, there is still much to be done, and more disquieting matters to be investigated.

In July 1978 the Government published a White Paper proposing a wholesale reform of Section 2 of the Official Secrets Act. While this is welcome and sensible (see Chapter 18) it is no substitute for the statutory right of citizens to have access to official information. It will be necessary to ensure that the

Government, in its own words, treats this reform only as 'a necessary preliminary to greater openness in Government' and not as the last word.

In this edition the material of the first edition remains substantially unaltered apart from minor revisions and the addition of Part IV and Appendixes 8–14.

November 1978

Publishers' Note

Penguin Books and Chatto & Windus wish to make it known that Mr Chapman has declined to accept payment of any kind for *Your Disobedient Servant*.

Part I

The Wasting Sickness

1 General Case History

I joined the Civil Service in March 1939 as a twenty-year-old junior executive officer, and except for the war years stayed in it until I retired at my own request on 1 January 1974. From 1967 onwards I held a senior management post in what was then the Ministry of Public Building and Works and is now the Property Services Agency, a part of the Department of the Environment.

This book describes what happened when, during that time, I sought, in a variety of ways, to reduce waste and extravagance. It describes also the reasons why these efforts, like those of many others before me in the public sector, met with only limited success and it sets out the changes which I believe need to be made to bring about improvements. My subject is the very limited one of waste in government service and especially in the Civil Service. This is not the kind of waste that stems from government spending on projects which, though well-intentioned, seem so often to end in disaster. I am writing about waste in the old-fashioned sense – the waste involved in having ten men where five are enough, in using fuel to heat empty buildings, and in spending money to keep land idle and useless. It is waste that stems from inefficiency and mismanagement.

The first six chapters give an account of how some economies came to be made in one part of a government department. By implication these chapters suggest that, given time and determination, substantial savings are possible throughout the Civil Service. They also indicate that the shortcomings revealed here cannot be dismissed as the occasional mishaps that can occur in even the best-run organizations.

The next three chapters, Part II, take the story on to see what the wider reactions were to those economies, and how effectively first the departmental, then the Civil Service, and then the Parliamentary machinery of scrutiny, surveillance and direction worked in practice. Again, by implication, you will be invited to conclude that these procedures either worked too slowly or did not work at all.

With a few minor exceptions, the facts used for Parts I and II are taken from material published officially or published and not challenged. The contents of the Comptroller and Auditor General's Report, the proceedings before the Public Accounts Committee and the Public Accounts Committee's findings are important to the development of the argument and the reader needs to be sure that quotations and summaries are fair and accurate. On the other hand, constant reference to basic documents destroys continuity. I have therefore made the text self-contained and reproduced in full the documents concerned as appendixes.

I believe that the reader will deduce from Part II that the procedures for safeguarding the taxpayers' interests do not work well and that this is due to weaknesses inherent in the system rather than to failures by individuals. Part III makes proposals for changes which I think could overcome at least some of these weaknesses. These proposals are limited in the same sense as the subjects covered by the first two parts are limited – that is, they relate to the control of expenditure in areas where policy is settled, and only the efficiency of execution is in question. Parliament and the Treasury, Ministers and accounting officers, have obligations and powers which go far wider than this in the control of expenditure, and the control of expenditure in turn is only a part of their responsibilities.

It is estimated that the public sector in this country disposes of over one half of the community's total resources, and some estimates put the figure closer to three quarters. It is unlikely that this figure will be substantially reduced in the near future. Whether public spending on this scale is considered to be good or bad, it affects every citizen in more ways than any other form of government activity – except war. If inefficiency and waste exist to the extent I have suggested, then either less is available for goods and services or there is more taxation than is necessary. Moreover, the malignant effects of waste in public spending cannot be counted in financial terms only. There are consequences also for the mood of the general public. Taxpayers will put up with heavy taxation if they think their money is being well spent. Employees in the essential public services – policemen, teachers and nurses, for example – will accept low rates of pay if no more money seems to be available. These attitudes will go sour, however, if either of these groups sees evidence of a lot of public money being wasted. I believe the cost of effective measures to eradicate this waste would be justified if the only benefit was to eliminate this risk.

There are plenty of excellent textbooks available which describe accurately the theory of government financial control. I have deliberately avoided making use of them because I wanted to present only opinions and remedies based on my own experience. When I have thought it desirable to bring in supporting evidence, this, too, has been taken from others speaking from first-hand experience.

Criticisms of the public service are not new and a number of recent ones are examined in more detail later in this book. For the moment it is enough to note that what *is* new is the rapid increase in the volume of these criticisms and, perhaps more important, the status and experience of the people making them.

The standard civil service responses to criticism are as follows: first, dead silence; do nothing. By tomorrow or the next day the newspaper or the politician will fix their attentions elsewhere. This is an effective defence and many senior civil servants are temperamentally suited to practise it.

Second, courageous silence. This may be used if the first kind of silence does not work. The objective here is to give the impression that only because the full story *cannot* be told is the criticism being left unchallenged. If an impression can be given of tight-lipped, unflinching acceptance of unjust treatment from that very public which this reticence protects, so much the better. No simple matter when the complaint is of too much money spent on sewage plants or football pitches, but in conjunction with the Official Secrets Act it can be managed; and when defence or security matters are involved, however remotely, it is easy.

Third, 'we are not perfect, but we are willing to learn'. This line is comparatively new but is increasingly common. It is particularly suitable for radio and television interviews, providing they are not the kind where journalists and such are allowed to spoil things with questions. It requires a relaxed approach (to show that on the whole all is well) coupled with fleeting recognition that the situation could be better – even though not significantly.

These methods, combined with the knowledge that the Official Secrets Act prevents many unwelcome disclosures and can be manipulated, if necessary, to obscure and blur the remainder, have enabled the Civil Service, in the past, to shrug off most attempts to change it. It is against this background that this book has been written.

2 Some Statistics

In early 1967 I took up my appointment as regional director of the Southern Region of the Ministry of Public Building and Works. In order to understand my story, you need to know first something about the civil service machine, and where I, and my part of the organization, fitted in.

Government departments have specialized functions. Most of these relate to a particular service to the public – the collection of taxes, or the administration of education, for example. A few, like the Stationery Office, are mainly concerned with providing a service to the other departments: the Stationery Office does indeed provide the Civil Service with all its pens, paper, and typewriters. The Ministry of Public Building and Works was one of this second group, having as its main function the provision of accommodation. It had been created in 1962–3 by amalgamating the Ministry of Works with the works departments of the Royal Navy, the Army and the Air Ministry. As a result of this merger, the new department was responsible for practically all government works and building services, with the exception of roads, schools and hospitals, though where these services were provided exclusively for the armed services, they also were the responsibility of the Ministry of Public Building and Works.

The service given by the department was a comprehensive one. It provided all the accommodation needed by other government departments (the client departments), either by building specially for them, or by leasing or buying accommodation in existing buildings. Thereafter the department was responsible for all building maintenance work and many interior services such as heating, lighting, furnishing and decorating. Major new buildings were for the most part designed at headquarters and built by specially appointed contractors. Most building maintenance work and a large part of the building of small works was delegated to the department's regional organization, which also was responsible for most of the interior services.

The merger necessitated a good deal of reorganization, and by the time things had settled down the UK organization consisted of a headquarters based in London, seven regional directorates in England, a Scottish office and a Welsh office. The last two were very similar in size and responsibilities and organization to an English region.

The London headquarters had a Minister and a Parliamentary Secretary. The civil service head was the permanent secretary, whose most senior subordinates were deputy and under secretaries. The under secretaries were for the most part heads of directorates responsible for particular blocks of work or specialized services – building research; finance; overseas works services; establishments, and so on. At the time of my appointment, regional directors were responsible directly to the permanent secretary, but in practice worked closely with under- and assistant secretaries at headquarters. Figures 1 and 2 (pp. 19–21) give some further explanation of the organization, and the significance of these civil service gradings.

My region covered the counties of Hampshire, Berkshire, Buckinghamshire, Dorset and Oxfordshire and was about average in terms of size and responsibilities, although we had rather more of the glossy establishments such as staff colleges than other regions. One big continuing programme of work for Southern Region, as for the other regions, Scotland and Wales, arose from the provision of offices for all the other government departments. Each town of any size has its Department of Social Security, Department of Employment, tax offices, Post Offices and all the other outposts of the government administrative machine. In addition to these local offices there were representatives of the higher levels of administration: the area and regional offices and in some cases offshoots of these other departments' national headquarters. These departments also needed training facilities ranging from one-room local centres for typists to major educational and instruction establishments such as residential colleges, together with a variety of other buildings from

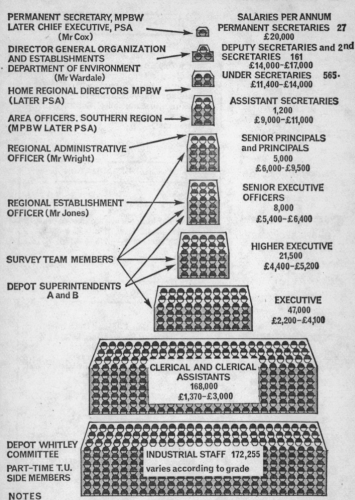

PERMANENT SECRETARY, MPBW
LATER CHIEF EXECUTIVE, PSA
(Mr Cox)

DIRECTOR GENERAL ORGANIZATION
AND ESTABLISHMENTS
DEPARTMENT OF ENVIRONMENT
(Mr Wardale)

HOME REGIONAL DIRECTORS MPBW
(LATER PSA)

AREA OFFICERS. SOUTHERN REGION
(MPBW LATER PSA)

REGIONAL ADMINISTRATIVE
OFFICER (Mr Wright)

REGIONAL ESTABLISHMENT
OFFICER (Mr Jones)

SURVEY TEAM MEMBERS

DEPOT SUPERINTENDENTS
A and B

SALARIES PER ANNUM
PERMANENT SECRETARIES **27**
£20,000

DEPUTY SECRETARIES and 2**nd**
SECRETARIES **161**
£14,000-£17,000

UNDER SECRETARIES **565·**
£11,400-£14,000

ASSISTANT SECRETARIES
1,200
£9,000-£11,000

SENIOR PRINCIPALS
and PRINCIPALS
5,000
£6,000-£9,500

SENIOR EXECUTIVE
OFFICERS
8,000
£5,400-£6,400

HIGHER EXECUTIVE
21,500
£4,400-£5,200

EXECUTIVE
47,000
£2,200-£4,100

CLERICAL AND CLERICAL
ASSISTANTS
168,000
£1,370-£3,000

DEPOT WHITLEY
COMMITTEE

PART-TIME T.U.
SIDE MEMBERS

INDUSTRIAL STAFF **172,255**
varies according to grade

NOTES

1 To the general service grade numbers shown must be added approximately 316,000 specialist non-industrials

2 Figures below Under Secretary are rounded

3 Civil Service Department figures as at 1 July 1977 were
Non-industrial 567,445
Industrial 172,255

4 Salaries are rounded

5 Figures for grades used in the text are totals. Figures used in this diagram do not include 316,000 specialists (see above, note 1)

Figure 1

MPBW: HQ (London)

MINISTER
↓
PARLIAMENTARY SECRETARY
↓
PERMANENT SECRETARY

RESPONSIBLE FOR

Divisions dealing with administration and policy. Civil Engineers; Mechanical and Electrical Engineers; Quantity Surveyors; Estate Surveyors; Architects; Building Surveyors; Supplies (furniture, fuel, transport); Contracts; Finance; Accounts; Establishments (personnel)

RESPONSIBLE FOR

REGIONAL DIRECTOR
(grades varied between home and overseas)

DIRECTOR FOR WALES

UNDER SECRETARY FOR SCOTLAND

RESPONSIBLE FOR

REGIONAL ORGANIZATION

HOME   OVERSEAS

Cambridge, Birmingham, | Gibraltar, Cyprus,
Leeds, Hastings, Bristol, | Malta, Germany,
Reading, Manchester | Hong Kong
Cardiff, Edinburgh

RESPONSIBLE FOR

READING (SOUTHERN)

REGIONAL DIRECTOR

RESPONSIBLE FOR

Administration; Civil and Mechanical and Electrical Engineering; Estate Surveyors; Quantity Surveyors; Architects; Building Surveyors; Supplies; Contracts; Establishments

RESPONSIBLE FOR

AREA HQ

AREA OFFICERS
(SUPERINTENDING GRADE PROFESSIONAL)

RESPONSIBLE FOR

Bournemouth, Aldershot, Abingdon, each having civil engineers, quantity surveyors, mechanical and electrical engineers, contracts, administration

RESPONSIBLE FOR

DEPOT SUPERINTENDENTS
(TECHNICAL OFFICER GRADES A and B)

RESPONSIBLE FOR

DEPOT HQ (11 to each area)

Technical supervisory staff, clerical support staff, industrial staff

RESPONSIBLE FOR

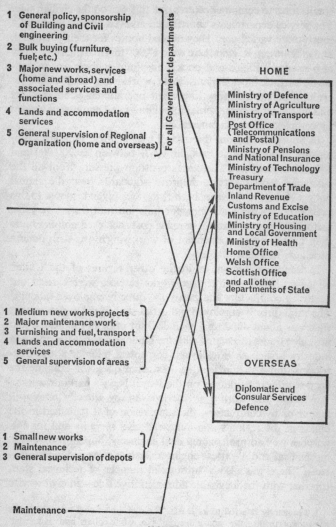

1 General policy, sponsorship of Building and Civil engineering
2 Bulk buying (furniture, fuel; etc.)
3 Major new works, services (home and abroad) and associated services and functions
4 Lands and accommodation services
5 General supervision of Regional Organization (home and overseas)

For all Government departments

HOME

Ministry of Defence
Ministry of Agriculture
Ministry of Transport
Post Office (Telecommunications and Postal)
Ministry of Pensions and National Insurance
Ministry of Technology
Treasury
Department of Trade
Inland Revenue
Customs and Excise
Ministry of Education
Ministry of Housing and Local Government
Ministry of Health
Home Office
Welsh Office
Scottish Office
and all other departments of State

1 Medium new works projects
2 Major maintenance work
3 Furnishing and fuel, transport
4 Lands and accommodation services
5 General supervision of areas

OVERSEAS

Diplomatic and Consular Services
Defence

1 Small new works
2 Maintenance
3 General supervision of depots

Maintenance

NOTES

Regional organizations varied considerably. Southern Region is shown here.
MPBW: HQ organization was changed substantially 1968-1973.
Staff gradings in the left-hand column are explained in Figure 1.

Figure 2

small stores to computer centres. All this was on the civilian side. The service departments contributed an even greater load and a much more varied one. They needed houses for their personnel, and in Southern Region there were 17,000 married quarters. They also needed airfields and docks, hospitals, schools, roads, railways, barrack blocks, giant stores, workshops, small public recruiting offices and very important operational establishments and all the other paraphernalia, buildings and equipment needed by complex defence organizations.

In Southern Region, the overall cost of these building maintenance services alone was, in 1967, between £9,000,000 and £10,000,000 a year. There was constant pressure from all the customer departments to improve standards, and the annual budget had for some years been rising steadily in response to this pressure, even after allowing for inflation (not then a very big factor). Efforts to stem these rising costs achieved nothing more than temporary postponement of work which was then done a little later at greater expense.

In Southern Region, as in the other regions of the United Kingdom, these maintenance works services were carried out partly by contractors and partly by 'directly employed labour'.[1] The total directly employed industrial staff in the region at that time was about 4000, and included not only all the skilled and unskilled trades associated with the building and civil engineering industries, such as bricklayers, carpenters, plumbers and electricians, but also some rather less usual ones, for example the deep-sea divers employed on the Royal Navy's harbour works.

Whether the work was carried out by directly employed labour or by contractors, the supervision of it remained in the hands of the region's non-industrial civil servants and for this purpose we had professional civil engineers, building surveyors, mechanical and electrical engineers, estate surveyors and architects. There was also a substantial number of technical staff, together with the inevitable administrative side – in civil service

---

1. Frequently referred to as DEL. The division of civil servants in the same department into 'non-industrial' (i.e. white-collar) and 'industrial' is an anachronism overdue for scrapping. Similar divisions within the non-industrial grades, known as 'classes', have already been largely abolished.

terminology the clerical and executive grades. There were altogether about 1700 non-industrial staff, most of them directly or indirectly concerned with maintenance work.

The territorial organization of the Southern Region was broadly similar to the other regions of the United Kingdom and consisted of a regional headquarters located at Reading, area offices at Abingdon, Aldershot and Bournemouth, and about thirty-three depots divided equally between the areas.[2] The regional headquarters comprised about 400 non-industrial civil servants, the area offices had very roughly 200 each, and the remaining non-industrial civil servants and all the industrial staff were attached to the depots. The area officers were superintending grade professionals, and they were usually either civil engineers or mechanical and electrical engineers, although other professions were entitled to compete for these posts. Nearly all the depot superintendents were technical officers. Regional directors' posts in the UK were open to all but were mostly held by administrative staff (Figures 1 and 2).

This large and expensive organization tried to keep in reasonable working order (though rarely to the complete satisfaction of its customers) the government estate which I have already described, together with some of the machinery and ancillary services associated with the buildings. Not only was this organization large and expensive, it was, despite changes in departmental structure and title,[3] and even greater changes in building technology, doing very much what it had always done and doing it very much in the same way.

There are, of course, always two ways of looking at an organization which has served its clients and the public adequately for many years. One approach is to apply the injunction sometimes addressed to the maintenance technician, 'If it works, please don't mend it.' Alternatively, one can take the view that such an organization which has remained largely unchanged for

2. Regional and area headquarters were offices only. Depots resembled builders' yards, with a few small offices, a store, garages and sheds.

3. In 1970 the Ministry of Public Building and Works was merged with the Ministry of Housing and Local Government and Ministry of Transport to become the Department of the Environment. In 1972 it was hived off to form the Property Services Agency (PSA).

decades is open to suspicion, particularly when that organization is insulated from competitive pressures. Given that the world around us in 1967 had changed substantially in the past twenty-five years, it seemed to me then that this second attitude was the one to adopt. Some searching inquiries were needed to make sure that all was well.

I had another reason for seeking further diagnosis. By and large the estimate of costs of building maintenance for the Southern Region, as for the other regions, which eventually found its way into the department's estimates for approval by Parliament, was based almost entirely on what had been spent for similar purposes in preceding years.

It was true that a variety of instructions existed which were supposed to make provision for detailed calculation, but in practice estimates were always prepared by people working against the clock. Unless there was some very striking and compelling reason for doing otherwise (which there never was in my experience), this year's estimates, with minor adjustments, looked like last year's expenditure.

These minor adjustments, which were made at a variety of levels, including, finally, discussions between my department and the Treasury, included global additions and subtractions to the budget which reflected financial policy considerations rather than the costs of the work actually needing to be done. For example, it might be conceded in a given year that to take account of inflation it was necessary to add 5 per cent to last year's overall budget. The department, arguing that the 5 per cent would only be adequate to hold its position, would also try to get extra money to cover rising standards, arrears of work and new programmes. Depending on the national financial position, the Treasury would either concede the increases, wholly or in part, or even occasionally refuse any extra. The result would be no more than last year's (and earlier years') budget provisions titivated up to reflect this year's financial and political expediencies. Its connection with real need was extremely tenuous. And yet it could be argued that the system *seemed* to work. No one could prove conclusively that any one estimate was right or wrong, and all concerned could persuade themselves that while the final figures could have been a little better they would certainly have been much worse but for their own contribution.

In such circumstances (this applies to a wide range of activities in the public sector) it is easy to create an unchanging, self-perpetuating organization. The expenditure for 1966 produces, with minor variations, the estimate for 1967. The estimate having been approved, the money is spent, and this in turn produces the estimate for 1968. To all outward appearances a busy group of skilled people is performing an essential and long-standing public service. This may indeed be the case. On the other hand it may as easily be wasting its time and the public's money.

For the organization which I inherited in 1967 there was here a double hazard. A large part of my maintenance budget related to wages for directly employed industrial labour. There had been a tacit understanding between the department and the trade unions, going back over a number of years, that there should be no substantial reductions in the number of directly employed industrial staff. It was not suggested, of course, that staff should be kept on if there was inadequate work for them to do. Rather it was understood that if work by any chance fell off (and nobody very seriously expected this to happen), reductions would be made in the use of contractors. Nevertheless, the effect of this hard core of continuing expenditure was to heighten the risk of self-perpetuation in the estimates.

The obvious first step in order to determine the truth of the situation was to stop dealing in terms of global estimates and regional budgets, to try to establish where the money was actually being spent and to see what was being bought. In the past there had been occasional inspections and appraisals of this kind carried out either by the department's headquarters (sometimes in conjunction with Treasury representatives) or at regional level. All these inspections had produced reassuring results but I believed that what was needed was a much more penetrating detailed fact-finding examination than had been carried out hitherto. Early in 1967, therefore, I appointed two of the senior professional officers in the region to carry out a survey of maintenance expenditure and to advise whether we needed to change our rate of spending (up or down) to produce the results which would give the best value for money. Where preceding surveys had taken a day or two I wanted this one to be carried out, if not regardless of time, at any rate with more importance attached to the quality and accuracy of the findings than to the speed with which they were produced.

The two officers concerned were relieved, as far as possible, of other duties and they spent about six weeks, not quite full-time, in fact-finding visits or interviews and in producing their report. Both men were well qualified professionally and had had long experience within the department and outside it. They were competent and conscientious and were aware of the importance we attached to the results of this inspection.

In the light of this, and having regard to the results of later surveys, the summary of their findings contains a lesson which has implications elsewhere in the public sector. In no case did they find 'a single penny' spent that was not essential to the preservation of the fabric of the buildings, complying with the minimum requirements for safety, the observance of bye-laws and similar obligations. In view of what followed, I remember that one phrase very clearly. Indeed the report went on to say that a good deal more money needed to be spent than our current budget provided in order to give a really satisfactory service.

At first glance this report was reassuring, but still it did not carry complete conviction. To begin with it emerged that this inspection had taken for granted that if a building or a piece of land was being maintained, then it was right that it should be. Secondly, much of the basic evidence of expenditure had to be taken on trust. By this I mean that where the work of a directly employed bricklayer was described as 'Maintenance at Army Camp ABC' it had been assumed that this meant exactly what it said: that the bricklayer was laying bricks and that these bricks needed to be laid.

When I came to question this I was not in any way doubting the propriety of the accounting work. I was quite sure that the bricklayer would be found to be working for the hours stated in the place described. What I wanted to know was *exactly* what he was doing and why; and on this the report did not really take us any further.

One afternoon in May 1967, in order to get some of the facts at first hand, I visited a depot[4] near my regional headquarters without warning. I asked to see the records which showed how the directly employed labour force was deployed on that particular afternoon, what they were doing, and where they were doing it. Leaving aside those who were absent for one reason or another, about seventy men were shown to be engaged in a variety of duties appropriate to a maintenance organization. A great many of the duties were described in terms which did nothing to resolve doubts. While a few men were shown as doing a specific job far too many others were engaged in duties described as 'general maintenance work' or 'routine maintenance duties'.

I decided to follow up this investigation by visiting a random sample of the jobs where the men were working. In almost every case the result was the same. Even the most useful work was of a kind which, in a commercial organization, would have to be charged to overheads – tidying stores, sweeping and whitewashing. The rest of the work, and this was most of it, was nothing more than filling in time. I should add that a number of the men involved were stokers and boiler men and since this was warm weather with the heating services switched off, the picture looked blacker than it would have done two or three months before. Nevertheless, it was typical of the situation which was going to exist for the rest of the summer, and in any case the stokers were not the only ones who were filling in time. At the end of the afternoon two conclusions seemed inescapable. In the first place, if this depot was typical, the amount of waste and overmanning was greater than anyone had suspected. Secondly, whatever the reasons might be and whoever was responsible for it, something would have to be done quickly to put this right.

The next stage of the fact-finding process was an investigation on lines similar to the one I carried out, but painstaking and thorough where mine had been superficial.

I was fortunate in being able to borrow for this purpose an M & E (mechanical and electrical) engineer with staff inspection experience, and an intense examination of the use of DEL at the depot I have just described was put in hand forthwith. It took about the same time as the earlier one carried out by the two

4. This depot was subsequently closed down completely.

professional officers, but there the resemblance ended. The whole effort was concentrated on one depot instead of covering samples spread over the region as a whole. The records of industrial staff time, the work done and the cost and value-for-money implications of these activities were for the first time dissected and analysed in a way which left nothing to guesswork.

The results were enlightening. The inspecting officer found considerable savings in the field in which he himself was expert, that is, on work involved in maintaining mechanical and electrical engineering plant, but found very little wrong on the bricks and mortar side of the depot's activities. The essence of his recommendations was that we could save about 15–20 per cent of the directly employed labour force if we carried out a programme of rationalization and cut out under-employment, and unemployment.

Leaving this report for the moment in cold storage I commissioned a second inspection on similar lines, in another part of the region, this time to be carried out by a professional on the building side. This time the findings were that there was not much wrong on the M & E engineering side but that there were many savings in the area in which the inspecting officer was expert. It seemed obvious, therefore, that to get the best of both worlds it was right to have a man from each discipline – an M & E engineer and a buildings man – and let them do a joint inspection. We could then expect on the basis of these two experimental reports to win savings of anything up to 30 per cent of the total expenditure, and this, in the event, is what we achieved.

In consultation with Alan Groves, the superintending civil engineer who was at this time the area officer, Abingdon, we set up a team consisting of Jack Holmes, a building and civil engineering technical officer; Harry Thompson, an M & E engineer; and Eric Turtle, an executive officer. The inclusion of the latter, a non-technical man, as a full member of the team was something of an afterthought but it worked very well. The use of knowledgeable non-specialists in these kinds of inquiries is always worth considering, providing they are additional to, not substitutes for, the technicians.

The team's brief was comparatively simple. They were to go

to a depot, spend as much time as was necessary to do their work thoroughly and examine every penny that was spent on maintenance by that organization. They were never to take either documents or statements on trust. They were in no circumstances to accept that because something had been done for years it was necessarily the right thing to do. They were not to accept documentary evidence that work was being done but were to see for themselves all that was being carried out.

There were two general propositions which they were to examine. Was the work essential in the sense that without it the customer department could not carry out its function? Secondly, if the work was essential, was it necessary to do it in the way in which it was being done, or could an acceptable result be achieved by spending less time or money?

As a result of the findings in the earlier surveys, the team was particularly enjoined, when looking at the standards of maintenance, to consider the speed of response of the maintenance service, because a fast service nearly always meant an expensive one. While for some purposes the fastest possible service (safety repairs, for instance) could be justified almost regardless of cost, there were plenty of others in which there was no great hurry. And lastly, as with the experimental surveys, the need to be thorough rather than quick was emphasized.

3   First Experiments

The establishment chosen for the first survey was the Royal Army Ordnance Depot, Bicester, Oxfordshire. An ordnance depot is a giant complex of store sheds, warehouses, offices, houses, roads and railways. In this case it extended over an area of twelve square miles or so. It was necessary to seek the agreement of the Army authorities before carrying out the work, but this was readily given by the representatives of what was then Southern Command, most notably by Colonel Alfred Taylor, who was the staff officer principally concerned with accommodation matters. In consultation with his Commander-in-Chief, he agreed that we could have a free rein to look at anything we thought needed to be examined and make recommendations on anything we thought desirable, providing only that before any action was taken we consulted fully with the military authorities. This undertaking we were glad to give, and the survey went ahead with the blessing of the Army.

At this stage also it was necessary to consult the trade unions. The joint management/trade-union structure and consultancy procedures in the department followed a pattern common to all government departments and were based on the Whitley principles which had been adopted by the Government half a century earlier. The first level of consultation was the depot Whitley Committee. This committee, under the chairmanship of the depot superintendent, had two parts – the trade-union side and the management side. The trade-union side had a number of members fixed by the constitution for that particular depot, which was in turn approved at national level, both by management and trade unions. In general, each of the major trade unions concerned with the depot had at least one member on the trade-union side of the depot Whitley Committee. These representatives were voluntary and unpaid, drawn from the ranks of the depot's work force.

The depot Whitley Committees met normally at least once a quarter but could meet more often if business warranted it, as it often did once a survey report was under consideration. In addition, the chairman and the secretary of the trade-union side would expect access to the depot superintendent or his senior officers whenever they thought that this was necessary (Figure 1).

This Whitley procedure for industrial labour at depot level had never been seriously tested before the maintenance surveys occurred. But in the event, I think everyone concerned agreed that it worked perfectly well.

The next level of consultation was the regional Whitley Committee, there being none at the area level. This committee, too, was divided into two parts – the management and the trade-union sides – and met quarterly under my chairmanship. At this level, all or nearly all of the trade-union representatives were full-time trade-union officials. The third and highest level was the departmental joint industrial committee, and on this committee the management side was made up of headquarters officers, and the trade-union side by representatives of the trade unions' national headquarters.

This was the consultative machinery which it was appropriate to use. So before the Bicester survey was begun I had two or three long sessions with the regional trade-union representatives. I put it to them that in the first place we were going to collect facts without bias or preconceived notions and to see to what extent these could be accepted as a basis for discussion. Secondly, if the agreed facts revealed that we were carrying passengers in large numbers in our directly employed labour force, it was in everybody's interests – trade unions and management alike – to do something to correct this.

In 1967, as in earlier years, there were plenty of critics of directly employed labour forces. Many people believed that they were expensive compared with contractors. The department itself was in the process of carrying out some kind of cost comparison between work done by DEL and work carried out by contractors. Parliament had approved a paper which made proposals to this end. Clearly the DEL force as a whole would be put at a disadvantage if they were carrying a lot of under-employed or non-essential men and were, therefore, made to appear more expensive than they need be. The effect of this would be to discredit, perhaps unnecessarily, not only the directly employed labour force involved, but the whole concept of DEL. Secondly, taking a wider approach, it was desirable from everybody's point of view that public money, which means taxpayers' money, should not be wasted.

Alongside these general propositions I put some further ones which I believed were justified in any case, and which, in addition, I hoped would make it easier for the trade unions to accept what was being proposed. First – and this was an entitlement under the Whitley procedure – in no circumstances would any action be taken as a result of the surveys without full consultation with the trade unions.

Secondly, I undertook that the reports which were produced by the survey teams would be made available in full, without any deletions or expurgations, to trade-union representatives. In this way they would have before them exactly the same information as management, and would be free to consult with anyone they chose about the facts and the recommendations.

Lastly, I said that although we might need to use compulsory redundancy if the evidence indicated that the directly employed labour force should be run down substantially, I believed that it would be possible to avoid this for the most part and that again nothing would be done without consultation.

The trade-union representatives to whom I was talking were all men of very considerable experience in this field. Many of them had spent a lifetime in the building industry, either as employees or as trade-union representatives, and I knew that much of what I was saying – and most especially the proposals for compulsory redundancy – would not make happy listening for them.

It is immensely to their credit that they looked beyond their short-term interests, whilst requiring naturally and rightly enough to be satisfied about the justice of our proposals. They accepted that there could be no justification for employing four men where three would do. They also accepted that the public interest and, in the long term, the interests of their members might very well require substantial reductions in staff. What they insisted on was that they should be satisfied beyond doubt, and by hard facts, that these reductions were wholly justified, and that economies could not be brought about in some other way, primarily by reducing the amount of work put out to contractors.

I was very willing to give this assurance, and on this basis the survey went ahead. If all senior management in the Civil Service had shown half as much understanding of the fundamental issues involved and half as much concern for the public interest as these trade-union officials, the story would have had a different ending.

At the stage when I was cheerfully urging the survey team to take whatever time it needed to do a thorough job and not to try to hurry the outcome, I had expected that, with three people working full-time, three or four weeks would see the survey completed. In fact the Bicester survey took nearly four months of hard work, and this proved to be the pattern for all the subsequent ones. The team was determined to show what it could do, and normal working hours went by the board. At the end of four months, exhausted but pleased with themselves, they presented their report.

They believed that immediate savings of approximately 30 per cent of the total maintenance budget and between 40 and 50 per cent of the directly employed labour force could be made. Further savings would be possible provided agreement could be reached on more far-reaching changes in the organization of the Bicester storage establishment, but these were of a kind not wholly within our control.

The economies proposed covered almost every aspect of the maintenance organization's activities. Less grass needed to be cut than was being cut, and what needed to be cut needed less painstaking cutting. Lawn standards were pointless for grass which stretched between store sheds and was criss-crossed by overhead pipes and cables. There was no useful purpose in heating gigantic stores the size of aircraft hangars to normal office temperatures when the contents would be quite safe at lower temperatures and the store's staff, on the occasions when they needed to go there, could be adequately clothed for the purpose.

There was no point in maintaining a depot railway system when roads could serve just as well or better at a fraction of the cost. And if the Ministry of Defence had to have the railway system, there was no sense in maintaining the permanent way to a standard suitable for inter-city expresses when the MOD trains ran at very low speeds. There was no need to conserve and maintain eighty or so cranes and lifting devices when experience over a long period showed that only half a dozen were needed, and that on the rare occasion when a special machine was required it could be hired at a fraction of the cost of permanent maintenance. And so it went on – the full report was a foolscap document, very nearly half an inch thick. The recommendations ran quite literally into the hundreds.

At this time the department's headquarters were beginning discussions with the trade unions at national level on a productivity agreement, and it was agreed that while negotiations were going on there would be no changes in the department's directly employed labour force until the details of the agreement had been settled. It was, therefore, impossible, for the time being, to do anything about that part of the Bicester report which involved DEL, but we went ahead with discussions with management in the region and with the military authorities on all the other recommendations.

It quickly became apparent that what the team was suggesting was practicable and desirable from every point of view They had not seriously miscalculated anywhere, either in their estimates of what needed to be done or of what was needed in order to accomplish it satisfactorily. I was satisfied then that the theory was right and the practice was within our competence, and two more teams were set up as soon as the right people could be found. The new teams were turned loose on other depots within the region.[1]

1. All the teams produced striking examples of waste and inefficiency which could be made into entertaining anecdotes. It was tempting to use some of them in this way, but I decided not to do so. Pumping millions of gallons of water daily round in circles, or to waste, at the taxpayers' expense, for example, is not funny. To make jokes of such examples obscures the seriousness of the waste involved.

Finding the right people for the teams was, in itself, quite a task. The critical, questioning approach to everything which was the most important quality required was not always to be found in those who had progressed steadily up the promotion ladder. This meant that although, within the team, each member enjoyed equal status, there were some odd mixtures of ages, grades, skills, backgrounds and experience. It may have been that the very oddness of the mixture was a source of strength. Every recommendation had to be unanimous. If the team members could not convince each other there was no hope of convincing others. So nothing appeared in print before being subjected to a critical crossfire.

Another problem arose from the physical demands made by survey work. The teams were normally away from home from Monday to Friday, and weekends were all too often used to catch up with the preceding week's paper work. If one man went sick the whole team was quickly brought to a standstill, so team members did not allow themselves the luxury of being ill! Ordinary leave was often not taken in full. No record was kept of what must, in aggregate, have amounted to tens of thousands of hours of overtime. There was no need. Everyone took it as quite natural that it would not be paid for. Despite this, we not only staffed our original teams with volunteers, but went on finding adequate replacements as changes were forced upon us.

4 Consultation Procedures

It was soon obvious that the new teams were going to match the type and scale of economies achieved at Bicester. This meant in turn that we would have to be very careful that all the appropriate interested parties were consulted, and that this was done at the right time. Sound recommendations for economies, supported by a wealth of convincing data, could be spoiled by a failure to observe all the niceties at this stage. Time-consuming (even exasperating) as it was, therefore, we found it best to follow a strict drill for consultation purposes.

We began always by serving notice on the various groups that would be concerned once the survey got under way. These included all the client departments whose accommodation and other services would be reviewed; the management of the depot and area concerned; the trade-union side of the depot Whitley Committee; and the secretary of the trade-union side of the regional Whitley Committee (Figures 1 and 2).

As a general rule we gave between four and six weeks' notice of our intentions to conduct the survey, but never less than two, so that at all times it was possible for those involved to have the time and the opportunity to make meaningful representations if they wished, although this happened very rarely. An explanatory statement was displayed well before work began on all notice boards available to the directly employed staff, and as soon as the survey was under way the teams let it be known that they were willing to hear representations from anybody about anything at any time.

The surveys lasted for four, five or even six months, depending on the size and the complexity of the depots' responsibilities. This included the time-consuming processes of preparing the reports and checking and double checking all the facts. It is very much to the teams' credit that there was not a single instance where a report was shown to have been inaccurate in a matter of any substance.

I usually managed to talk to each of the teams once or twice during the course of each survey, and immediately the report was finished I had a copy so that I could see how the work had gone. As the reports tended from the outset to be very bulky documents, and seemed to get even bulkier as time went by, we found it best to prepare separately summaries of the teams' recommendations and a financial evaluation of the savings which were expected. For this last purpose we worked on the basis that to reduce the staff by one saved £1500 per year in wages and overheads. I doubt whether this was ever quite adequate as a measure of the savings, and by 1970–71, when the bulk of the reports were being prepared and evaluated, we were almost certainly underestimating the cash value of manpower savings.

The next stage was to circulate the report and the recommendations to the regional, area, and depot management staffs concerned. This was to give an opportunity to our own people to point out any obvious snags or disadvantages in our proposals before we made them public. There never were such snags, and the next stage, which could in consequence follow very quickly, was to put our proposals to the client department. At this stage we tried to deal with those recommendations which would affect directly employed labour first. If there was nothing in dispute between us and the client departments on the DEL proposals, the next stage was to hold consultations with the unions.

Here we found it best to follow a very strict procedure. On an appointed day I went to the depot concerned and met the representatives of the trade-union side of the depot Whitley Committee, and sometimes full-time officials from the regional Whitley Committee. At that meeting I handed to them copies of the report and its recommendations in full, as they had been given to me. While I described very briefly what the recommendations were, especially insofar as they applied to directly employed labour, I explained that I was not asking for any kind of comment, let alone commitment or agreement, at that stage. The trade-union representatives were to take the reports away and study them for as long as they wished – usually about four to six weeks – and consult anyone they wished during that time, especially their own experts at trade-union headquarters.

At the same time we posted on the notice boards a summary of the findings affecting directly employed labour alongside a statement that these were proposals only, that they had not yet been discussed with the trade-union representatives and would not be for some weeks to come. The statement would go on to say that when the consultations with the trade-union side had been completed, the final version of the action agreed for the directly employed labour force would again be posted on the boards.

As soon as possible after that meeting but in any case *on the same day*, I would meet representatives of the local Press and again give them a brief summary of the proposed savings in money and staff. We found that even the shortest gap between publishing the results in the depot and briefing the Press could result in garbled and alarming reports appearing in the local newspapers which were difficult afterwards to unscramble. Subsequently a summary of the DEL proposals was given to the secretary of the trade-union side of the regional Whitley Committee, and a further copy was sent to the department's London headquarters for passing to the departmental Whitley Committee.

It was not often that the DEL proposals were amended very much at the meetings which followed this initial consultation. The Portland depot, where it was proposed that the labour force of 307 should be reduced by 125 (subsequently revised to 105), was the only place at which amendments of any consequence were made.

Once the staffing figures had been agreed, the next stage was to post them on the notice boards, on this occasion listing by name all the employees in the trades concerned, together with their seniority, so that everyone knew who was going to be affected by the reductions. Time was then allowed for this situation to be studied and digested and during that period, which usually lasted for several weeks, we did what we could to make it easy for people to leave if they were prepared to volunteer.

We tried to help in other ways as well, mainly by finding

alternative employment, sometimes with other government departments, more often in outside industry. The problem was eased in two other ways. First, in common with the rest of the department, we had retained men over sixty-five years old (the normal retiring age). Both management and trade unions knew that the time would come when we would have to terminate their employment, and that this would not constitute redundancy in the normal sense. This category of staff bore the brunt of the first reductions.

Secondly, once we had got the feel of the size of the direct labour reductions, we avoided recruiting for vacancies as far as possible, especially in the most vulnerable grades (stokers, for example[1]). In that sense, therefore, we started the reduction in the complement with something in hand. The running-down process was a slow one but eventually we achieved our objectives with a minimum of hardship. I believe that in the end the number of compulsory redundancies was less than 5 per cent of the total reductions.

It would have been possible, and strictly within the provisions of the department's redundancy agreement at that time, to attempt to reduce the labour force much faster. We could, in theory, have disregarded all the human problems involved, together with any question of the consideration owed by even a moderately good employer to his staff. We could have ignored the fact that management, not the industrial staff or their trade unions, was responsible for the overmanning. Notice of staff reductions could have been posted to take effect within a week or a month as was appropriate under the terms of the agreement.

I believe that if we had done so, every proposed reduction would have been fought every step of the way and we would have taken longer to achieve less satisfactory results than we did by using gentler methods. If ordinary standards of decent behaviour did not justify reasonable treatment of the work force then sheer economic and managerial expediency did.

Simultaneously with the talks with the trade unions on these proposals, other parts of management held discussions with the

1. In 1967 there were over 700 stokers in Southern Region. By 1973 there were fewer than fifty.

client departments. These, too, were more protracted than we had expected and it was not unusual for some parts of the reports still to be under discussion between regional management and the client department a year after the report was first presented. Where new building work or the provision of special machinery or equipment was involved, it could take longer still.

These protracted discussions with client departments meant that at any one time we could be dealing with ten or twelve completed reports. This created a formidable load of extra work for the regional headquarters' staff, ably led by Norman Wright, the regional administrative officer. Team members, too, often had to be involved in explaining their proposals so that they were obliged continually to leave their current surveys, on which progress therefore became slower and slower.

Nevertheless, unlikely though it seemed at times, we did eventually get to the end of the surveys and implemented all or nearly all these suggested economies.

For the results achieved by the surveys, I have drawn on a number of sources. As a consequence of the consultation procedures, the proposals for each depot were covered accurately in the local Press. There were also articles in periodicals with special interests in our field of operations. Furthermore, on 19 December 1976, the *Sunday Times* published an article for which they carried out extensive research. At intervals since then, national and local newspapers, magazines, television and radio stations have covered other aspects of the story. What follows is, for the most part, therefore, inevitably a summary of what has already appeared elsewhere, and, though adequate, is unavoidably less comprehensive than I would have wished. Acknowledgements of these sources are made in full at the end of the book.

Unused or under-used land was sold off, or where for some reason it was believed that it had to be retained, it was let for agriculture or afforestation. Most of the land with which we were concerned was maintained but not owned by us, and there was a limit to what we could do in the reduction of holdings. As a consequence, although we had our successes, the land disposed of was less than 5 per cent of the possible reduction. Nearly all the other 95 per cent is still there waiting for the time when the recommendations at the end of this book are implemented, especially those relating to the setting up of more effective audit controls.

Unneeded buildings were also disposed of, though again not on anything like the scale which should be possible. We had more success in getting rid of unneeded buildings when for some reason they could not be sold off. Since to leave them was to invite someone to find a use for them (in accordance with Parkinson's Law) we knocked them down. By the time we were about half-way round the region we had completely demolished seventy-nine, with another 307 agreed for, or in the process of, demolition, and a further 239 under discussion. For the delicate surgery of trimming surplus fat from government property holdings, nothing is as effective as a bulldozer.

People, stores and equipment were reaccommodated in appropriately sized purpose-built and purpose-sited places instead of in ramshackle makeshifts or in buildings which were sound enough in themselves but which were now far bigger than were needed. For a variety of reasons, mainly because the changes involved were outside our control, our recommendations and achievements in this field too were only a very small proportion of the total economies possible.

We reduced our holdings of plant and equipment – cranes, concrete-mixers and lorries, for instance. Most were used very rarely and it was much easier and cheaper to hire as and when items were needed. As always happens, when it was necessary to go out and hire instead of using something standing around the yard, even these occasional needs mostly disappeared. We made swingeing cuts in our own holdings, but these were trifling compared with the scope for reductions elsewhere.

The closure of uneconomic undertakings such as gravel pits (several hundreds of staff were involved in these) and the shedding of functions appropriate to local authorities and similar bodies are dealt with later.

Changes in the use of what is known as 'planned maintenance' produced very useful economies. Planned maintenance means doing repairs and servicing so as to stop things from going wrong, instead of waiting for a breakdown before putting them right.

The difficult part is balancing the risk of a breakdown (if you make the intervals too long) against spending a lot of money unnecessarily (if you make the intervals too short). On the one hand, a warning light at the end of an aircraft runway may need to be looked at every day, yet it may still be necessary to go out in the middle of the night to do emergency repairs. At the other extreme we found big store sheds with roofs forty to fifty feet high with light provided by banks of fluorescent tubes. Whenever a tube failed, a couple of electricians trundled a large mobile tower along to the spot and one of them climbed up and changed the tube. It took between thirty and forty minutes to change a tube and there were so many tubes that more than one pair of electricians was kept busy. As the amount of light was not critical and it was possible to operate with up to a quarter or even a third of the tubes out of action, the survey team concerned was able to establish an agreement for the batch replacement of all the tubes, the probable life of which could be estimated with astonishing accuracy. The saving was about 80 per cent on the original cost in this case, and there were scores if not hundreds of similar cases.

The lesson we learned – 'relearned' is perhaps more accurate – is that planned or preventive maintenance, if it is skilfully devised, and then reviewed regularly, can save a great deal of money, and yet provide a service tailored to meet the needs of the user. On the other hand, if it is not well planned initially, or is allowed to become out-of-date, potential savings are turned to waste. This is worth emphasizing, because government, local authorities and private-sector organizations all spend big sums annually on various forms of planned maintenance, and many opportunities for economy are being overlooked.

Savings were made right across the board. There was no appreciable difference between depots serving navy, army, RAF or civilian establishments. Many wasteful practices went back thirty years or more and all of them had survived several changes of management. The fact that the same sort of economies both in type and in scale were found everywhere we went ruled out any possibility that they were caused by failures by individuals.

The following analyses of the savings were made about half-way through the surveys, and I do not think the picture changed much thereafter. Fifteen per cent of the total savings was brought about by cutting out work altogether, and 85 per cent of the savings was made by economies whose results were still acceptable to those directly affected. No economies of any kind were forcibly imposed on anyone.

Acceptable reductions in expenditure can be subdivided in four ways. Fifteen per cent was saved by using different methods; and 15 per cent by using different standards; 10 per cent was saved by accepting a different speed of response and service; and 60 per cent was saved by a different use of DEL. These savings were made in the following types of work: building maintenance 35 per cent; grounds maintenance 20 per cent; mechanical and electrical engineering maintenance 45 per cent.

It was necessary to demonstrate that the reductions in the use of directly employed labour had not been achieved merely by switching work to contractors, and the following figures were produced in 1971–2:

Annual expenditure with maintenance contractors in the Southern Region rose from £4·9 million in 1966–7 to £6·1 million in 1971–2, an increase of just under 25 per cent. In that same period, however, the cost of building work according to the national index produced by the department had increased by 35–38 per cent. In real money terms, therefore, there had been a reduction in work done by contractors in the region.

The total savings in Southern Region achieved by this programme of surveys were as follows.

Overall expenditure was cut by about £3½ million per annum on an original budget of about £10 million per annum, both figures being based largely on prices and wages prevailing in the 1968–70 period.

In Southern Region, directly employed labour was reduced from around 4000 to under 2000. Nearly all these reductions had been implemented by the end of 1973.

By December 1976, according to the department's official spokesman, annual savings as a result of the Southern-Region-type surveys were running at about £12 million per annum.

5 Symptoms and Remedies: Three Case Studies

Although the reductions of maintenance expenditure were by far the biggest and most important of the economy measures taken in Southern Region, both in terms of staff effort and of the savings involved, a number of other measures were carried through during the period 1967–73, three of which I want to describe briefly in this chapter, since each serves to illustrate some of the general principles with which this part of the book is concerned.

The majority of civil servants needing to travel in order to carry out their business either use public transport or, especially outside London, drive their own cars. In both cases, of course, they are reimbursed for their expenses. Payment for the use of cars is based on a mileage rate agreed nationally and reviewed regularly. A much smaller number of civil servants, who either have no car or do not wish to use their own, use self-drive cars provided by the department.

In addition to these arrangements the Ministry of Public Building and Works operated for the whole of the Civil Service a Government Car Service which consisted of chauffeur-driven cars, organized in pools based in London and the regional centres. In London, where most of the cars were based, this chauffeur-driven car service was used almost exclusively by Ministers, visiting VIPs from overseas, and other distinguished people. I cannot recall a junior or middle-grade civil servant ever using the service in the 1940s. Even the most senior ones, in my recollection, usually took a taxi if they felt they could justify the cost and a bus if they could not.

I was, therefore, somewhat surprised to find during early 1970 that the car service in Southern Region appeared to be used very largely by junior staff in circumstances which led me to question the economics of the whole business. Quite obviously staff who needed to be driven, junior or otherwise, might need to have this or some equivalent service provided. The fact that many of the staff were junior was significant only because presumably if they could not or would not drive themselves, there must be plenty of others who could do the same job and who could drive. They would not, therefore, need to be provided with this very expensive service.

In order to get at the facts a thorough review of the use of the car service over a lengthy period was carried out, and this review was followed by an even more detailed one during a six-week period. For this sample we analysed every single journey made and all the costs involved. We found that nearly every journey had been made by junior staff, and of these about 80 per cent were by staff of the Department of Health and Social Security, the Department of the Environment (by then my own department), and Inland Revenue.

In the majority of cases the cars were booked by the day to make tours encompassing a number of stops. The mileages and the timings showed how uneconomically the cars were being used. A quite short run would be followed by a lengthy stop, during which time, of course, the driver sat in the car knitting or reading. At the end of the interview the passenger would emerge, step into the waiting limousine and be wafted to the next port of call. It was a very comfortable way of life for everybody except the taxpayers.

The facts revealed by this survey were discussed with all the other departments and it fairly soon emerged that there was no justification for continuing to use the car service in this way. In some cases the users could perfectly well drive themselves but preferred the added comfort and prestige of being a passenger in a chauffeur-driven car. In other cases, although there was some adequate reason why the passenger could not drive, it was obvious that there was no need for these particular individuals to be used for duties which involved such travelling.

It did not require management skills of a very high order to conclude that if the post required the holder to travel regularly and that this could best be done by car, then the first qualification needed by a person for such a post would be the ability and willingness to drive.

Although the car service outside London was under regional control for day-to-day management purposes, the responsibility for the overall policy and administration of this service rested with the supplies division, which was part of the department's headquarters. It was represented to those concerned in that division that in the light of this report things could not be allowed to continue as they were and that this was a case in which more than the reduction of the service was called for. The facts indicated that there was no justification for any car service. Accordingly, I proposed that the whole operation should be closed down forthwith.

This proposal was not well received. It was argued that the results of the survey could be open to question, if not for Southern Region then for London and the other regions. Moreover, closure of the service in one area might lead to difficulties elsewhere. Finally, it was said that the Government Car Service had always been a somewhat touchy and sensitive matter, and that it would be infinitely preferable if things could be left as they were for the time being, and that at some suitable opportunity at some unspecified time in the future steps should be taken to do something about the situation.

In the ensuing weeks it was pointed out again and again to the department's headquarters that the people who would be most affected by these arrangements, the client departments, had already agreed that changes could be made without any difficulty for them. Second, that if, as was expected, the chauffeur-driven cars could be replaced (for the most part) by people driving their own cars, savings would be approximately £30,000 a year at 1971 prices, without taking into account the full cost of the service and, therefore, of the savings accruing. These discussions went on for several months and at the end of that time the car service was shut down completely.

In the six months which followed we monitored very carefully the results of the closure. It was then quite apparent that the earlier judgements had been completely vindicated. No difficulties had been encountered by our own department or by the others, and only in a minute number of cases was it necessary to do anything other than to allow staff to drive their own cars. The estimated saving of £30,000+ a year was therefore fulfilled. These findings were passed to the department's headquarters but no other region made any changes in the car services operated by them, nor were changes made in the London car services.

A second project which was successfully carried through at about the same time related to the region's stores organization. Each of the region's thirty-two depots kept a store of materials and equipment for the maintenance works programme. Nearly all these stores required a full-time storekeeper. Some stores, at the Portland naval base, for example, had two or three store-keepers. It was as a result of the survey at Portland, in fact, that the prohibitively high cost of maintaining these stores, compared with the value of the goods being issued, had attracted our attention. At Portland it was calculated that it cost over £3 to store and issue even the simplest piece of equipment such as a tap washer. It was true that some of the items were much bigger and more expensive, but the great majority of the items issued by the stores were for the minor odds and ends used by the maintenance work force.

A thorough examination of the operation of the stores and their costs was carried out during 1970 by a regional team headed by E. T. V. Jones, who was also the regional establishments officer. This proved conclusively that small items could be bought locally quicker and more easily as and when they were wanted, and that larger items could be stored centrally and issued when required. In the end we decided to close all but three of the stores in the region, and after allowing for extra costs involving transport from central stores, the savings were of the order of 80 to 90 per cent of the earlier costs.

In the last of the examples of staff savings, the welfare service of the department, the money and staff numbers involved are so microscopic that at first glance it would seem foolish even to mention them. Yet small though it is, the way in which this service developed illustrates one of the most dangerous tendencies to be seen not only in central but in local government and many other big organizations besides.

Welfare services came into being in the Civil Service soon after the end of the war. It may very well have been that, at that time, with all the difficulties of finding accommodation, especially in London, staff did need help. But I was surprised to find that in the Southern Region in the 1960s there were two full-time welfare officers plus some part-time help. This organization was matched in the other regions in the United Kingdom.

Civil servants have their problems, domestic and otherwise, like everybody else. On the other hand with secure jobs, no threat of unemployment, favourable sick-benefit arrangements, good working conditions and an index-linked pension at the end of our careers, we are better insulated against the hazards of daily life than most. At first glance, therefore, it seems unlikely that we should need full-time welfare officers to look after us. On the other hand, as everyone in the advertising and public-relations world knows, it is no good sitting back and waiting for the public to realize that it needs something. The technique is to create the need and be ready to fill it.

This was certainly the case with our welfare services. The staff were reminded constantly that it was there; that it was there solely for the purpose of helping them; and that they were welcome to bring their problems along at any time. Inevitably there were plenty of people who took up this offer for one reason or another.

In addition, steps were taken to minister to the sick. Anyone who was on sick leave for any length of time, whether in hospital or at home, got a visit from a welfare officer. This sometimes involved round trips of up to 200 miles by the welfare staff and in these circumstances a quarter or half hour with the sick person could take a welfare officer most of a working day and involve substantial travelling costs. Clearly very few of those so visited were going to be so ungracious as to say that the visit was unwelcome or unnecessary. It was possible for the welfare staff to produce plenty of evidence that wherever they went they appeared to have been well received and were, therefore, doing a good job. I remember one sturdy citizen who did go so far as to question the need for a visit, indicating that he was well able to look after himself. But you can't win in the face of determined helpfulness. His irascible, even irrational, reaction was duly noted as evidence of how far gone he was!

These regional welfare officers were not left to struggle with their problems unaided. They produced reports and sent them to the department's headquarters, where a much higher-powered welfare officer would examine them, comment on them and consult with the other welfare officers on the issues and policies involved. But even these higher-powered officers did not function alone. They in turn reported to even higher-graded welfare officers in the Civil Service Department. These higher grades looked at reports, gave instructions, and sought further reports. Gradually a thriving welfare industry was built up. The welfare staff could not function single-handed administratively. They needed someone to type their reports, answer the telephone, and keep the files. At regular intervals they needed conferences with other welfare officers so that they could discuss problems and exchange ideas. In no time at all there was pressure to upgrade some of the posts not so much for the benefit of the individuals concerned, it must be understood, but rather in order to recognize the importance of the work being done, to give those concerned the status they needed so that they could do their jobs more effectively, and finally to provide a career structure.

At that point Welfare could truly be said to have arrived, and its supporters were looking round for fresh fields to conquer. In my last year the latest pressing problem needing attention was retirement. With retirement pensions for most civil servants based on 50 per cent of the best of the last three years' salaries, with a gratuity of up to eighteen months' pay and, above all, with pensions index-linked and cover provided for wives, most civil servants have retirement problems of a kind the rest of the world would be glad to share. Many of these benefits were a very marked improvement on retirement arrangements that had been running without any trouble for decades. So you might think that the retirement problem for the modern civil servant was a diminishing one. Not a bit of it. People who had been looking forward for years to their pension and a happy retirement discovered they were probably heading for a crisis. They started to get groomed for it with glossy booklets and helpful little chats well before retirement day. For the determined do-gooders of the welfare department this was not to be some last-minute superficial business. The educational and backbone-stiffening processes began a full three years before anyone was due to retire.

There is no doubt that most if not all of the welfare staff genuinely believed in the importance of what they were doing, and quite often cheerfully gave up their own spare time in order to deal with what they regarded as particularly time-consuming or difficult cases. But it is also true that if we had doubled, trebled or quadrupled their numbers there would always have been work for them, and I was not prepared to accept that for the most part what the welfare section was doing was essential.

This was illustrated very clearly when one of our depot staff was involved in what was no more than a minor domestic spat with his wife. The welfare section got itself involved. When a representative visited the house where the trouble was, he found that the wife was an employee of another government department and that that department's welfare officer had also arrived on the doorstep determined to help cure the trouble. Whilst the two of them were still trying to decide who should do what about which, a third welfare officer arrived – this time from the local authority – because a child of school age was involved. In the end the utter absurdity of the situation dawned on those concerned and the whole matter was allowed to drop and resolve itself without intervention – as it would have done in the first place.

In Southern Region at an early stage we closed down the senior welfare post (graded as higher executive officer in those days) and by 1970 we had reduced the welfare staff to one executive officer with a very small amount of part-time help. That post too would have gone but was retained because by that time the reductions in the directly employed labour force, and to a lesser extent in the non-industrial staff, as a result of the maintenance surveys, were beginning to mount up. With staff reductions running at the rate of several hundreds a year there was, for the first time, work for a welfare officer. But this was a situation which, especially insofar as it related to redundancy, was without parallel at any time in the past, and it was very unlikely to recur in the future. It had, therefore, already been announced that at the end of the staff run-down period we were not going to retain any welfare posts in my region.

In the case of the welfare industry, even some of my colleagues who had gone along with many of the other savings looked askance at cutting welfare activities. The only time that it looked as if I would have a difference of opinion with a visiting Minister (not one of those mentioned by name in this book) arose from the closure of the senior welfare post already referred to.

The curious belief that most things, if not everything, can be made better if you spend enough public money on them is illustrated by the operation of the welfare industry. People who are sick welcome visits from friends and colleagues. Apart from anything else they must be gratified that someone takes the time and trouble to see how they are faring. A visit from someone who does this on a full-time official basis for which he gets paid is totally different. It is about as meaningful as putting a penny in a slot machine so that you can listen to a recording by a stranger wishing you a happy Christmas.

There is a range of emotive words and phrases which seem to cause sensible people to lose their judgement and deplore anything that smacks of doing things on the cheap (or, as others might see it, with due regard for needs and value for money), and welfare is only one of these. Others include training, education, old age, youth, sickness, productivity and getting-to-understand-the-other-chaps'-problems. This last was the best all-seasons general-purpose cover for aimless wandering around, and I have known it used successfully to justify anything from trips to the next floor at tea-time to round-the-world tours. Even to contemplate saving money in this and many other related areas is to invoke real trouble.

6 The Wasting Sickness: General Diagnosis

This chapter deals with some general truths about the Civil Service which I have derived from my experience in Southern Region, and looks at their implications in terms of expenditure, especially wasteful expenditure.

First, it is clear that any organization in the public sector relieved of the disciplines of a profit-and-loss account, and relying for its income on taxes or rates, will find it very easy to conceal overmanning. This is rarely deliberate. The greater danger in the public sector is much more one of self-deception on the part of managers at all levels who, unless they go to a lot of trouble to get at the facts below the surface, will find comforting reassurances being supplied from all directions that all is well. And do not blame management alone for this. Almost every pressure on management in the Civil Service, and probably within the rest of the public sector, is a pressure to spend more and more money. The reason for this is that positive pressure to save can only come from those who would benefit from such savings, that is, the taxpayers, who have no organized voice. The pressures to spend or to avoid economies, on the other hand, fall directly and heavily on management. Suggestions that staff should be reduced, for example, will swiftly be opposed, on behalf of their constituents, by Members of Parliament, who a short time before were pressing for cuts in public spending. More senior levels of management will explain that while in principle cuts of this kind are admirable, there are several reasons why now is not the time for them (now never is the time, of course).

There will also be, reasonably enough in their cases, the defence by unions and staff associations of their members' interests. There may be also actual or potential opposition from those – client departments or members of the public – who feel that they may lose out if services are reduced. Any manager in the public sector bent on economies is likely to find that when the discussions end and the action begins, he has few friends.

This in turn leads to a 'play for safety' philosophy. A manager who presses on with economies despite the opposing forces, knows from the outset that if all goes well no one is likely to thank him. But what if something goes wrong? In any large organization this is a permanent hazard. People make errors of judgement, and occasional accidents will happen which are no one's fault. It is an unnerving thought for the would-be saver of public money that if anything goes wrong there will be many people willing to trace a connection, however tenuous, with those economies about which, as everyone knows, they, in their greater wisdom, expressed doubts at the time.

This form of disincentive does not only come into play in the context of something positively going wrong. What happens to a junior or middle-grade manager trying to do something about wasteful expenditure – one of Southern Region's depot technical staff seeking to reduce the acreage of ornamental gardens around a building, for example? He is likely to meet at first a gentle opposition voicing the theme that these grounds have been maintained for years (they probably have, too), and have been seen and quite rightly admired by all sorts of people from cabinet ministers downwards (also probably true). In the light of this, what makes Mr Z think that he knows so much better than everyone else, including his highly respected predecessors Messrs X and Y, both of whom left with promotion? In no time at all Mr Z, who started with the best of intentions, at least as far as the taxpayer was concerned, finds himself being regarded as a self-opinionated man of dubious judgement. Why should he take all the kicks when people who are being paid much higher salaries are content to leave things alone? Who can blame the well-intentioned Mr Zs (and potentially there are plenty of them in the public service) for deciding that the game is not worth the candle? What they need is not blame but help.

Another common cause of continually increasing expenditure is that most ordinary human beings have a not unreasonable wish to keep and if possible to improve what they already have.

Within the limits of the time and money available to them, for example, most private householders try to improve and embellish their property and guard it against attempts by others to take bits away. How much more tempting it is, therefore, for the controller of an organization, funded by the public, to fight off all attempts to reduce the size or scope of his establishment and to enlarge it wherever possible? It is not his time and not his money which brings about the 'improvements'. All that he has to do is to suggest them and argue for them and in the fullness of time they come about.

Time and time again the survey teams found that if they looked at the history of an establishment or a service over the years, there was a remorseless and apparently irresistible increase in the amount of money being spent, the standards being observed, the facilities being provided, and as a consequence an increase in the total cost to the taxpayer.

Yet another pressure to spend came from the need to uphold prestige. This argument was used endlessly to justify lavish accommodation, luxurious furniture, bigger cars, better-kept lawns and flower-beds and even higher staff gradings and salaries. Prestige in this context meant competing with other departments and also with the private sector, so that all the elements exist for a continuous series of leapfrogging claims.

These claims could be given a further fillip if by some stretch of the imagination justification could be found for involving visitors from overseas. It then became a matter of *national* prestige and pride that our establishments should be bigger and better, glossier and more expensive than had been the case heretofore. The underlying assumption was that the foreigners would go back to their own countries dazzled by the display of power and wealth which they had seen and would quite forget the drifting pound, the adverse balance of payments and our lagging growth in national productivity.

Closely allied to the prestige argument was the one related to recruitment. In the middle 1960s recruitment both into the armed services and into the Civil Service was not going very well. To attract recruits, my colleagues argued, it was necessary to show splendid surroundings and well-furnished buildings impeccably maintained. No one ever demonstrated that anyone was ever recruited for these reasons, but as an argument it enjoyed a boom for a number of years; and, of course, entirely incidentally, it helped to make life very pleasant for those already in.

Another very human characteristic which in the public sector can lead to continually increased spending and waste is the desire to do good. In the public sector the scope for doing good is endless, and the desire to do it, given that those who desire it are going to do it at the public expense, is equally unlimited. It is always possible to improve the staff rest-room or sports facilities, standards in the living quarters and the decorations in the hospitals and the churches. The list is as varied as it is long and there is something for every taste, so that each item has its own enthusiastic supporters and advocates and none is completely without merit.

Outside the public sector a system of choices has to operate. Either the money is spent for this purpose or for that. But all too often in the public sector only a moderate case for more expenditure is all that is necessary and there is no regard for the gradually increasing total cost. It is exasperating, even though inevitable, that although it is the taxpayers' money that is being spent those who advocate any such expenditure are regarded as warm-hearted, forward-looking and generous and those who oppose it are thought of and described as mean. Whether in the House of Commons or in the local Council Chambers, this phenomenon can be witnessed in most debates involving economies.

A popular and expensive illusion uncovered by the teams is what might be called the 'do-it-yourself' syndrome. This causes quite rational people to believe that if the organization does something itself it really isn't costing anything at all or certainly not very much. In the spirit of this philosophy we found in one small area around Aldershot alone civil servants operating a gravel pit, a saw mill, a sign-writing centre, a foundry, joinery and woodworking shops, a machinery maintenance workshop and a printing business. Elsewhere there were nurseries producing shrubs and trees, installations supplying domestic water, treating sewage, sweeping roads and similar activities. Civil servants have many good qualities but when it comes to running businesses they tend, albeit for reasons largely outside their control, to be disastrous failures. So it was with the gravel pits, saw mills, the nurseries and the rest. All these activities, having been costed, proved to be totally uneconomic. We could buy the same services or the same products for a fraction of the cost elsewhere, even without making allowance for the concealed capital investment which was nearly always involved. There was only one cure for this situation. The production operations were closed down completely and, except for a tiny minority of exceptional cases, services were transferred to the local authorities and other bodies (gas boards and water authorities, for example) who were specialists in the activity concerned.

One other matter which the teams were instructed to look at carefully and which deserves mention here was 'end-of-financial-year madness'. A great many people both in central and local government believe that, towards the end of a financial year, if there is money to spare it is spent quite commonly on unnecessary projects, and that at these times money will almost be deliberately wasted rather than left unspent.

It is true that in the situation where, for the reasons given in Chapter 2, next year's budget will be based upon this year's expenditure, there must always be a temptation to make sure that everything that should be spent, to say the least of it, is so spent. It is also true that if a budget is substantially underspent, it means, or can mean, either that the budget was overestimated in the first place as a result of errors of judgement or that the programme of work for which this budget was intended has not been carried out. In both cases management might feel that it had laid itself open to criticism. The teams found very little evidence that there was waste on this account and in general the problem is not nearly as serious as it is imagined to be. Nevertheless it is a risk which is inherent in all systems based on annual accounting and budgeting, and where money can be spent quickly and easily, for example by making grants or buying equipment, the temptations are that much greater.

One large-scale money-waster which was not turned up by the teams but which emerged frequently in the form of reactions to their proposals was the dislike that all big organizations seem to have for dealing with problems piece-meal. Almost everything we suggested as an economy seemed to have links with several other policies and practices, all of which might be affected by decisions taken elsewhere, and being affected might in their turn affect yet others. Even where nothing firm was involved we were assured there were matters under discussion or about to be discussed, and what was being proposed as an economy could perhaps (though it would be some time before a definite answer could be given) therefore be best dealt with by being associated with these other more general matters!

The problem was that there is much truth in this. Big organizations are complex, and the government service is the biggest organization of them all. On the other hand, if these arguments are accepted at face value then practically nothing would ever be changed. We found the most satisfactory answer to this dilemma, and I commend it warmly to others, was to put the equivalent of an administrative hobnailed boot into the middle of all these delicate considerations and negotiations and forge ahead with the desired economies. This action should always be linked with expressions of diffidence and regret beforehand, and deep remorse afterwards. It never fails.

There are three other general propositions illustrated by the maintenance surveys which are valid for the public sector as a whole. The first is that without any undesirable reduction in the standards of service, very substantial savings can be achieved fairly simply. For example, some savings in heating costs were made by the introduction of sophisticated engineering control equipment, but the amount of money saved by this kind of innovation was small compared with that which was saved by the much simpler expedients of not heating store sheds which were either empty or contained only barbed wire or horse-shoes. The teams did a first-class job but they would be the first to agree that the vast bulk of their proposals for economy were really no more than the most common commonsense. Much the hardest part of their task was not to find the savings but to produce evidence which would convince anyone either in management or in the trade unions that their proposals could not be gainsaid.

Although the economies achieved amounted to one third of the total budget, they were far from being all that were available and could almost be regarded as merely skimming off the cream. Further proposals for savings involving substantial capital expenditure or changes in operating methods which involved the client department went almost untouched.

Secondly, the full costs of fringe-type activities such as welfare and prestige expenditure are also largely under-estimated. They are higher than they appear because of all the services they consume; and this extra cost is not only high, it is mainly invisible. Clerical, typing, supervisory, accommodation and a host of other expenses are lost in the overall cost of the organization's public role and the snag is that it is possible to get to a point where the cost of the ancillary activities begins to overtake the cost of the main function without anyone being aware of it.

The third general proposition is that no one in any organization really believes that large economies are possible in their department. For example, each depot superintendent was convinced that when the team visited him it would meet its Waterloo. I found this, to my cost, after we had completed the first three or four surveys. I had assumed that it would be an easy matter to take the lessons learned from those surveys and ask depot superintendents throughout the region to apply them to their own spheres, and I called a conference for this purpose. The teams explained what they had found and how they had found it, and having laid all the evidence before the conference I invited the depot and area staffs to make their comments. They were all experienced and capable men but each in turn stood up and gave a wealth of reasons why the teams' findings could not apply to their particular responsibilities. It was soon apparent that there were to be no short cuts and that a detailed, time-consuming painstaking survey would have to be carried out at every depot in turn.

This was disappointing at the time but it turned out to be a blessing in disguise. We would not have had the success which we did have in consultations either with the client departments or with the trade unions if we had not been able for every single establishment to produce the exhaustive array of facts which the reports provided and which presented almost unanswerable arguments in favour of the proposed economies.

Whether it is regarded as a blessing or otherwise, however, it is inescapable that large-scale instant economies are just not practicable in the Civil Service, and all those interested in such economies need to come to terms with this disagreeable fact. 'Axing the Civil Service' and arbitrary percentage cuts in staff and money may sound impressive but they do not work in practice, and worse still they discredit the opportunities for genuine economies which can be uncovered by other means.

The examples I have given in these six chapters indicate the range and scale of the savings which can be made in a typical sector of public expenditure, without undue effort or much ingenuity, and without reducing standards of service below an acceptable level. They are not all that we did; still less do they cover all the opportunities that were available to us.

Part II deals with something more important and far-reaching in its implications than the actual savings involved. That is the way in which these ordinary manpower and money-saving activities were handled within the department from local level up to the top; by the Civil Service Department; by Exchequer and Audit Department; and finally by Parliament acting through the Public Accounts Committee.

Part II

Disease Resistance and the Failure of Old-Fashioned Remedies

7 Ministers and the Civil Service

The reaction of the trade unions at local, regional and national levels was, as I have described, constructive and forward-looking, both as far as their own members' interests, and also the interests of the public at large, were concerned. The reaction of the other major group directly concerned locally, namely the client departments of the Civil Service, was much more mixed.

From the armed services I was given, after a somewhat cautious start which did no more than reflect a healthy scepticism about cure-all labour- and money-saving schemes, a good deal of support. Once the services had had some experience of the teams' findings, we were also given some measure of freedom to comment on matters not strictly within our province provided these, in turn, could be shown to be practicable and could lead to savings in money. We discovered that it did not pay to push our luck with these extra-mural investigations. In consequence, not wanting to prejudice our primary interests, we did no more than brush the surface – just enough, in fact, to become aware of the enormous potential for economies here as everywhere else.

I was particularly helped by a series of generals commanding the South-East district of the Army and their senior staff officers. Nothing could be further from the widely accepted stereotype of army officers than the way in which they responded to our some-times disconcerting proposals for economies. At the end of this book I have tried to list at least some of these serving soldiers who helped me and my staff, but I fear that with the best will in the world there will be omissions.

By contrast with the helpful reactions from the services, the response from organizations and establishments managed by civil servants was much less gratifying, and the process of per-suasion was frequently tedious and laborious. By one means or another, however, objections were overcome in the end, and for both the services and the civil departments only a tiny minority of our proposals were abandoned. This degree of success reflected not so much our silver-tongued and winning ways as a deal of low cunning in deciding what was likely to be accepted and what was not. This was not simply a desire to avoid disputes. It derived from the knowledge that we could implement the easily agreed changes now and come back for the rest another day. While easy savings were available, we would be wasting time, and therefore other opportunities for improvement, if we allowed ourselves to be bogged down in slogging matches. These occurred most often in those cases where our proposals meant changes in the client's organization. However, even for some matters wholly within my control where feelings ran high prolonged objections could impede progress. Any proposals to reduce expenditure connected, however remotely, with safety, for example, were suspect, even though we never made them if safety was genuinely affected.

All in all, bearing in mind that we were breaking new ground and learning as we went, I had no cause to be other than quite well satisfied with the progress of events within the region.

But if, within the region, things were satisfactory, elsewhere the story was less happy. I had kept the department's headquarters informed of our activities and these had been received at first with a mixture of disbelief and amusement at the size of the projected savings; later, when it seemed that we might be achieving our estimates of the savings on direct labour and money, the reaction was one of alarm and hostility.

The department's discussions on DEL cost comparisons referred to, (p. 68) meant that as soon as the results of the early surveys were known a temporary standstill order was imposed by the department's headquarters on reductions in the directly employed labour force. By the summer of 1968 we had completed all the early experiments and were well on with the survey of the Bicester ordnance depot. The first three-man team was already showing the kind of savings which were later on to become commonplace but which, at that time, we ourselves could hardly believe.

I was fortunate at that particular juncture to be given great help and encouragement from Lord Winterbottom,[1] then the department's Parliamentary Secretary. Lord Winterbottom had no inhibitions whatsoever about trying to ensure that public money was not wasted or about telling everybody what he thought on this subject. He took a keen and close interest in the team's progress, in the Bicester report and in economy measures of all kinds which were then being proposed. He had had some first-hand experience of large-scale waste in his earlier job in the navy department and he welcomed the opportunity which these survey reports seemed to offer for a constructive attack on this problem in a new and wider area.

Somewhat half-heartedly, I counselled caution, but Lord Winterbottom was not to be discouraged. He took the view that the earlier, experimental surveys, taken in conjunction with the Bicester one, were evidence enough for anyone who was prepared to listen reasonably, and I had to agree that this was right.

As a consequence a memorandum was drafted and circulated very hastily to the other regional directors and to the department's headquarters officers setting out what had been done in the Southern Region and what, by implication, might be done in the others. At the September meeting of the regional directors with HQ staff (in those days we used to meet in London once a month) Lord Winterbottom left my colleagues in no doubt about the importance that he attached to this work of economy, assured them that he had no doubt about their capability to put forward similar programmes with all speed, and made it plain that he would be watching events closely.

Neither the memorandum nor Lord Winterbottom's address convinced most of my colleagues of the need for action. After he left the meeting it was clear that no one believed that economies on anything approaching the scale which I had described were available in other regions. The kindest reaction was that if my figures were right (and on that there had to be considerable reservations), and if the surveys so far effected were typical (on which there were further reservations), then it could only mean

1. Parliamentary Secretary, Ministry of Public Building and Works, 1967–8. Parliamentary Under-Secretary of State, RAF, MOD, 1968–70. Lord in Waiting (Government Whip), from 1974.

that I had inherited an extremely badly run region (I hadn't); or that there were some special characteristics of our client departments (unspecified) which made Southern Region different from the rest; or that it was something (also unspecified) to do with our geographical location. It was pointed out that we were nearer London than most, and while the precise significance of this went unexplained, it could not be disputed. (The same thing was to be said five years later about the car service economies.)

Nevertheless, in the light of the categoric instructions from the Parliamentary Secretary, the other regions began to do something along the lines that had been specified. Teams of a kind were set up and sent to Southern Region for instruction in our working methods. Over the next two or three months all the regions but one sent representatives to us to spend either a few hours or a few days seeing what had been done, the methods used and the results achieved. They then returned to their homelands, where, in theory at any rate, they began to put into practice what we had been able to show them.

Unfortunately theory and practice, as is so often the case, were a long way apart. In some regions teams were told that they must not in any circumstances investigate the directly employed labour arrangements, which had the effect of turning the temporary cost-comparison ban into a permanent prohibition. This not only cut off at a stroke a large percentage of the potential savings; it also made it difficult to look at many of the other areas of possible economies which, though not directly concerned with the industrial labour force, had some kind of connection with it. In two regions the three-man team concept was abandoned before it was ever begun and only one officer was used, in one case a member of the executive grades, that is, someone without any professional or technical training. Where, in our experience, three-man teams were finding it necessary to spend anything from four to six months to get below the surface and dig up the facts, some of the teams in the other regions were able to do the job to their satisfaction in a few days or a week or two. In another case the three-man team was appointed and made a very good first survey. Unfortunately there was a disagreement with the client department, the survey report was shelved and the team disbanded. It was hardly surprising that the results were nothing like those in Southern Region.

Soon after the September meeting Lord Winterbottom left the department to go back to the Ministry of Defence. This was a further blow, but before he left he kindly invited me to London and we spent a productive hour discussing what had been achieved and what the future might hold. I still believed at that time that the sheer weight of incontrovertible evidence which the teams were beginning to produce would mean that the economies would come about somehow and that commonsense would prevail. Lord Winterbottom, though expressing fervently the hope that I was right and making all sorts of encouraging noises, took a gloomier view. He said he thought that the vested interests of inertia would in the end prevail, for he had found that they were too powerfully entrenched throughout the public sector. In this he proved to be an accurate prophet.

Within Southern Region, however, the surveys were going ahead as planned. Not without a certain amount of difficulty the temporary ban on reducing the directly employed labour force was lifted. By the summer of 1969 we had completed three or four reports and the pattern was established – directly employed labour savings of about 50 per cent and overall reductions in the budget of 30–35 per cent. Events appeared, again, to be turning in our favour.

Mr John Silkin[2] had been appointed Minister to the department in April. On 11 July he visited my Reading headquarters and spent the whole of the day with us, not leaving, I remember, until well after six o'clock that evening, and only then because he had another ministerial duty to perform. He devoted the whole of that day to the economy surveys, and in addition to discussions with me and my staff, Mr Silkin had talks with the trade-union representatives. The Minister was not only concerned with the need for saving public money. Although it was clear that he

2. Rt Hon. John Silkin, PC, MP (Lab.) for Lewisham. Government Chief Whip, 1966–9. Minister of Public Building and Works, 1969–70. Minister for Planning and Local Government, DOE, 1974–6. Minister of Agriculture, from 1976.

attached considerable importance to this, there was another aspect.

Some time before, his predecessor, Mr Bob Mellish,[3] had told Parliament that he intended that the department should conduct a series of cost-comparison exercises to show the relative costs of work carried out by outside contractors on the one hand and the department's directly employed labour force on the other. This move had been received with a marked lack of enthusiasm, understandably enough, by the trade unions, but there had been no overt opposition to it, largely because, tacitly or otherwise, it was understood that whatever the outcome of the cost comparisons, there would be no question of widespread compulsory redundancy amongst the directly employed labour force.

By the summer of 1969 a number of tentative steps had been taken to make these cost comparisons. The argument that I put before Mr Silkin was one that I had used with the trade unions at the beginning of the surveys and with the department in the months following the parliamentary announcement. It was that since, as the survey teams were showing, we were employing far too much DEL for the work which was being done, it followed inevitably that if their costs were compared with outside contractors they would look extremely expensive. This, in turn, could discredit the use of DEL and, even without redundancy, would lead, in time, to a running down of that part of the department; and eventually, if the findings of these cost comparisons were implemented rigorously, to the complete disbandment of the direct labour force.

Yet the heavy overstaffing of the labour force was not the fault of labour or of unions. It was, quite clearly, the responsibility of management. It seemed to me a matter of common justice that before the costs of our labour force were compared with those of other people's the reductions should be implemented and the DEL given a chance to fight on equal terms. Besides, we might be making a disastrous and irreversible error. Once the directly employed labour force was run down we would never get it

3. Rt Hon. Robert Mellish, PC, MP (Lab.) for Southwark. Minister of Public Building and Works, 1967–9. Government Chief Whip, 1969–70 and 1974–6.

back. Our rates of pay were so poor that recruitment was bad and we already had an ageing labour force.

The Minister was completely persuaded by these arguments and said that he would go back to headquarters and give instructions at once that priority was to be given to these surveys; and, secondly, that wherever possible the surveys should precede cost comparisons in order to make those comparisons fair. He also agreed that where surveys could not for some reason precede cost comparisons the results of the latter would be studied in the light of the evidence of the surveys before any action was taken.

The Minister was as good as his word. He left me on Friday, 11 July, in the evening and by midday on Monday, 14 July, instructions to implement his wishes were being drafted by headquarters! What emerged, however, was something rather different from the Minister's expressed wishes. True, it was said that, wherever possible, the surveys should be carried out before cost comparisons were made, but the first part of the instruction, which was that the surveys were to be given priority, was not mentioned. I was assured that there was no particular significance in this omission. It was only that the implications of the Minister's directive and the consequences for staffing and allied matters would have to be worked out in consultation at headquarters before such a categoric and wide-ranging directive could sensibly be issued.

Whatever good intentions there may have been at headquarters, however, the fact remained that the further instructions were never issued. By early 1970 Mr Silkin had obviously become aware of this. This was probably as a result of comments made to him on the one hand by the trade unions who knew from his discussions with them in Southern Region what he intended, and on the other from their representatives in the other regions, that nothing appeared to be happening.

As a result Mr Silkin called a meeting with departmental headquarters officers in March and reminded them of his earlier directive. He and the new Parliamentary Secretary, Mr Charles Loughlin, refused to be put off by reports that it could take up to seventeen years to complete these surveys (this estimate, designed to be discouraging, was based on a region with thirty-four depots, using one team, with each depot taking six months to be surveyed). Mr Silkin said politely, but very firmly, that he was convinced about the rightness of the priority instruction for the economy surveys. He required that this policy be adopted nationally forthwith. Mr Loughlin was even briefer. He dismissed the seventeen-year estimate as 'nonsense'.

Two months later the instructions had still not been issued and there was a further meeting between headquarters officers and Mr Silkin. The Minister said again that he wanted it made clear to regional directors that he attached priority to these main-tenance economy surveys using the methods currently practised in Southern Region, and that if there really was a problem of staffing the teams – a line of defence which had been stressed in the absence of any other excuse – such cases should be referred to him personally.

For a few weeks it seemed that all would be well after all, especially as the Minister put it on record that he was going to call for regular reports of progress to be made to him. The opportunities for further postponement and delay seemed to be coming to an end. It was not to be, however. In June there was a General Election, a Conservative administration took office, and the next time I met Mr Silkin was at his farewell party.

. The General Election and a change of government notwith-standing, the Southern Region surveys were going full steam ahead. By the middle of 1970 the three teams which were now in operation were producing reports almost faster than my regional headquarters could cope with them. We no longer had worries that perhaps the earlier surveys had been non-typical. Every report that came in was producing results that matched or sur-passed those earlier ones. The teams' morale, always a matter of vital importance, was very high. They had behind them by now a body of solid achievement which no critic could dent. We had stopped being diffident and apologetic about what we were doing. It was quite clear that whatever happened, or did not happen, elsewhere, in Southern Region the work of the teams would lead to the saving literally of millions of pounds a year and of thou-sands of staff.

In October 1970 the Department of the Environment was

created and the Ministry of Public Building became a part of it.[4] Mr Paul Channon[5] was appointed Under-Secretary of State in the new department and in December of that year I was told that he wanted to come and see for himself what these economy surveys were all about.

His visit followed the usual pattern[6]: he met the teams, saw the figures, analysed and questioned them, and expressed great interest in and enthusiasm for all that we were doing. He asked several times why it was that these policies were not being applied elsewhere, and I think he must have thought that some of my answers were, if not evasive, then downright inadequate. What I could not tell him was that parliamentary secretaries and ministers alike from the preceding administration had given just such instructions and that they had not been implemented. It is accepted by Parliament that civil servants do not tell ministers of one administration about the instructions given by any of their predecessors of a different political colour. I am not quite sure what the authority for this is, although I expect it exists somewhere. While it may suit ministers in some ways, it certainly makes it easier for civil servants to forget about unwelcome orders. The rule is applied even where, as in this case, the different administrations were following identical policies and giving identical instructions. Puzzled or not, Mr Channon returned to London demanding that instructions for the adoption of these policies nationwide should be given forthwith and, like his predecessors, he said that he wanted to see progress reports.

4. In 1971 the Property Services Agency (PSA) was created by amalgamating the old MPBW with the Defence Lands Agency and given a separate identity within the DOE.

5. Paul Channon, MP (Cons.) for Southend West. Parliamentary Secretary, Ministry of Housing and Local Government, June–October 1970. Parliamentary Under-Secretary of State, DOE, 1970–72. Minister of State N. Ireland, March–Nov. 1972. Minister for Housing (DOE), 1972–4.

6. There was a 'usual pattern' because in the period 1968–72 twenty-eight senior officials visited my headquarters wholly or partly to discuss the economy surveys and their implications. Some of these visitors have since achieved still higher office. One such visit was followed by action – that of Sir Michael Carey (then Permanent Secretary) on 12 June 1969, which led to the meeting with overseas regional directors on 17 July 1969 (see p. 88).

The circular which followed the instructions given by Mr Channon was discussed with the department (which had now become the Property Services Agency) by the journalists from the *Sunday Times*. They were told that the circular required the setting up of two three-man teams on Southern Region lines in each region and made arrangements for regular progress reports. But during this interview, it was apparently admitted that there was no reference of any kind in the circular to any of Mr Channon's demands for urgency.

Nevertheless, it did seem at the time as if a step in the right direction had been taken, although London, the biggest area of all, was given permission to use only one team. This meant that it would have taken ten to fifteen years to complete one round of surveys. Sadly, Mr Channon himself saw only one of his progress reports. In 1971 he moved to another department.

In the meantime we were making a little progress in another direction. One of the most persistent criticisms of our surveys was that we were solving problems which were peculiar to Southern Region and that there was no scope for economies on this scale anywhere else in the United Kingdom or abroad. In order to try to resolve this problem, because clearly the belief was as strongly held by my critics as my own views were by me and my teams, I lent one of the teams to the South-East Region,[7] on the basis that they could go anywhere selected by that region's director. He could make his selection as tough as he liked.

The choice fell on some army establishments near Guildford, and during the course of that summer a standard Southern Region type survey was carried out. The proposed savings, nearly all of which, in the end, were implemented, amounted to £44,000 per annum,[8] approximately 50 per cent of the total budget. As the team (who had seen very little of their families while this survey was going on) said, 'It was hard work, but, by God, it was worth it to see their faces in South-East Region.' For myself, the outcome was a great relief. There had always been the remote possibility that freak conditions could have resulted in a report which found only small savings, and if that had happened I

7. Regional headquarters at Hastings.
8. Statement by PSA, December 1976.

doubt if the survey concept outside Southern Region would have lasted a week.

There was another cause for satisfaction. I knew that the trade unions felt that, although the teams' findings were fair, the labour force inevitably bore the brunt of reductions. At Guildford the team proved that quite a lot of money would be saved by terminating arrangements with contractors and taking on extra directly employed labour.

We continued this process of carrying the flag outside the Southern Region early in 1971 when Alan Grove, the area officer at Abingdon, who had from the beginning been a stalwart ally in these matters, was given a well-deserved promotion. He was appointed to the post of regional works officer (the senior professional post) in the Midland Region, based on Birmingham. He at once arranged to borrow one of my teams to make a full survey of the Royal Radar Establishment at Malvern and for them to take a shadow team of Midland Region staff to learn the techniques. The joint team found potential savings of nearly £180,000 a year, which was again more than 50 per cent of the total budget, and of these savings at least a half – that is, between 25 and 30 per cent of the original total budget – have already been implemented.[9]

But despite these small successes, the overall picture was still not very encouraging. At one time it looked as if the setting up of the Property Services Agency to take over and expand the functions of the old Ministry of Public Building and Works would itself make for progress and improvement; but the changes were in theory and on paper only. In practice nothing of importance changed whatsoever. Talking to a journalist from the *Sunday Times* in December 1976 one of the ex-regional directors said:

> If Southern could save a third of their budgets they must have been very inefficient to start with. I would send my chaps out hoping that they would find little or nothing.

This was a truthful and accurate description of the atmosphere

9. Statement by PSA, December 1976.

generally prevailing, not only in that region but in most of the others. Against this background it is hardly surprising that such teams as there were in the other regions continued to find economies on a much smaller scale than ours.

By the end of 1972 it was becoming increasingly apparent that these economies were not acceptable in the rest of the department and I was becoming convinced that things were unlikely now to change. A difference of opinion confined to the surveys would have been manageable, but the implications and consequences had for some time been spilling over into other spheres. At directing level some differences of opinion are to be expected and an organization which functions without them is suspect. This is not true of a difference which goes deep and wide and where there had been more than adequate opportunities for establishing the facts and resolving the dispute. It seemed to me that my choice lay between accepting the department's views or leaving the Civil Service. I had always had at the back of my mind the possibility of retiring in my mid-fifties and this had been made much easier by the new retirement arrangements which followed the Fulton Report. In early 1973 I asked for agreement to early retirement and, although this was refused to begin with, it was eventually conceded that I could go, and I actually retired on 1 January 1974.

But although I had concluded that I would be unable to bring about a change from within I was far from being ready to concede total defeat. On 18 December 1973, I wrote to Mr Wardale, the Director General of Organization and Establishments of the Department of the Environment (a post which is immediately below that of permanent secretary), giving a very full account of all these matters and enclosing a memorandum giving detailed documentation of the Ministers' directives and the failure to implement them, and ending:

I believe I owe it to the Service, and indeed to the tax-paying public (perhaps more obviously than ever in the current economic situation), to see that these matters and their implications are ventilated and action taken to see that there is no recurrence. Unless I am satisfied that this objective has been achieved by this letter I shall take further action whatever the cost to me, personally.

I sent a copy of this letter and the accompanying memorandum on 20 December to Sir William Armstrong,[10] then head of the Civil Service Department and head of the Civil Service.

The response from the Civil Service Department to these papers illustrates better than almost anything else in this book the essential nature of the problem which has to be faced. I was, after all, leaving a post which the Department of the Environment, itself one of the largest of government departments, described as 'one of the most senior management posts in the Department'. I had held the job for seven years and had spent thirty-five years in the Civil Service. I was complaining of massive waste of taxpayers' money and repeated failures to carry out instructions given by Ministers. A number of serious professional journals had in the preceding year or two produced articles examining the Southern Region work in detail and urging that similar things be undertaken elsewhere in the Civil Service and by the local authorities. Nearly all this was evidenced and documented in great detail in the memorandum, and the rest could have been checked for the price of a local telephone call to the DOE. The considered reply to this statement came in a letter which I received early in January 1974 from one of Sir William Armstrong's staff. It says:

> I write to acknowledge your letter and enclosures of 20th December to Sir William Armstrong. These have been read with interest. Yours sincerely.

This was the measure of the Civil Service Department's interest in such matters and was the last I ever heard from the Civil Service Department.

The response from Mr Wardale, the Director General, was friendly but amounted to saying that he would want more time to consider what I had said, though he did not promise to do anything thereafter. Three months later, by which time nothing had happened as far as I was concerned, I let it be known to Mr Wardale's office that I had not forgotten the matters which I

10. William Armstrong, PC, KCB, GCB (created Armstrong of Sanderstead, 1975). Permanent Secretary, Civil Service Department, and Official Head of Home Civil Service, 1968–74. Chairman, Midland Bank, from 1975.

had raised and that he should not expect that as time went by I would let things drop. If I did not receive a reply from the department within a few weeks I proposed to raise these matters in other ways, beginning but by no means ending with my Member of Parliament. Shortly afterwards I was told that a high-level inquiry was being made into my letter and that I would be hearing the results as soon as possible.

I duly received a reply on 23 May 1974. Mr Wardale states in this letter that a very searching inquiry was carried out by senior officers as a result of my allegations, and official papers were examined and numbers of people interviewed. He rejected my allegations and went on to say:

> Your view was that priority should be given to maintenance economy reviews on the lines you had instituted in your Region. What is apparent is that you did not succeed in convincing your colleagues that this was necessarily the most productive approach.

No comment of any kind was made in reply to my detailed and documented assertions that the Minister had given instructions which had been ignored. Can it really be doubted that, if it had been possible to refute this assertion, this would have been done in this letter? Can it really be doubted that, notwithstanding instructions given by Ministers, senior civil servants decided to act – or rather not to act – as they saw fit?

While I was still thinking about the best step to take next I had word that Exchequer and Audit Department (E and AD) were again beginning to take an interest in the maintenance economy surveys. Exchequer and Audit Department is a Civil Service Department but its head is the Comptroller and Auditor General (the C and AG). His salary is paid by Parliament so that he should not be subject to civil service pressures, and to underline the fact that his sole duty is to Parliament. E and AD auditors are usually provided with accommodation alongside the departments which they are auditing, often stay with the departments for a number of years and have the right of access to all official papers. I was well aware of their interest in the Southern Region economies because in the early 1970s audit staff had spent some time in my region interviewing me and my staff at various levels and going through the books to assess the results we had so far achieved. They had professed to be very interested but very disturbed by what they had found, and I knew that they had also paid brief visits to other regions.

If, after making inquiries of this kind, Exchequer and Audit Department are not satisfied that all is well, and believe that there is a case for the department to answer, their next step is to send what is called an audit reference sheet to the headquarters of the department concerned. A reference sheet of this kind was duly served on the department in August 1974. Amongst other things the audit reference sheet asked why £6·4 million a year was being saved by 1973 in the PSA as a whole. Nearly half of this had come from Southern Region, 17 per cent from the Midland Region; and less than 2 per cent from London, the South-East and the North-West, with the other regions somewhere in between. Departments are given two months as a matter of routine, and longer if they want it, to answer questions of this kind. Only if, when the answer is received, the auditors feel that it does not dispose of their doubts satisfactorily is the next step taken, and then only after top-level consultations within the Exchequer and Audit Department. This next step is to raise the matter in the Comptroller and Auditor General's formal published report to Parliament on the Appropriation Accounts (see Chapter 15) for the financial year concerned. That was done in this case (reproduced in full as Appendix 1) and it was the prelude to an inquiry by the Public Accounts Committee. This took place in April 1975.

8 The Public Accounts Committee:
Case Study I

The Public Accounts Committee is a Select Committee of the House of Commons. It has been in existence for a long time and is generally regarded as the most powerful of the Select Committees. Much of the strength of the PAC derives from the services it is given by E and AD, who do the groundwork which MPs could not do for themselves and provide them with the material for their inquiries. The PAC also works closely with the Treasury, and is generally much in sympathy with it insofar as economies in the public service are concerned. This partnership has worked well in the past, with the Treasury following behind the PAC to make sure that its strictures, wishes and observations were put into effect by the departments concerned and anyone else to whom they could be relevant.

Given that Parliament, in the view of nearly everyone who is familiar with this subject, is becoming increasingly incapable of playing any useful or effective part in the control of public expenditure, the role of the Public Accounts Committee has become more important in recent years than ever before. Newspapers are fond of referring to the PAC as 'Parliament's watchdog on public expenditure'. Certainly if at present the taxpayer has any hope of his interests being protected it is with this body that this hope should rest.

This chapter analyses how well these procedures worked and in order to do this realistically and effectively it is necessary to examine in minute detail what was said and who said it. All the constitutional means for control exist on paper, but I am concerned here to look at the actual working of the civil service and Parliamentary machinery for financial control.

After the publication of the Comptroller and Auditor General's report representatives of the Property Services Agency were called before the Public Accounts Committee on 14 April 1975. The proceedings and the PAC's subsequent findings were published in due course and are reproduced in full as Appendixes 2 and 3 at the end of this book. The PAC hearings take place in a House of Commons committee room, and the committee itself is normally made up of nine members, four from each of the two main parties and a chairman drawn from the Opposition. The chairmen are frequently people of note on the Parliamentary scene. Sir Harold Wilson had been chairman of the PAC before he became the leader of his party; in 1975, Mr du Cann, chairman of the Conservative Party Organization, was in the chair.[1]

The proceedings are quiet and informal, with the chairman taking the lead on questions and other members of the committee coming in as they wish. The department's representative is nearly always the accounting officer, that is the Permanent Secretary, and he is usually accompanied by his principal finance officer, normally an under-secretary. Two other departments are represented at the hearings – the Treasury and Exchequer and Audit Department. The Treasury witness is quite often invited to make comments on general questions arising from particular ones, but it is unusual for anything to be said by Exchequer and Audit Department representatives, either publicly or by way of prompting to the committee chairman or members.

In addition to his principal finance officer the accounting officer will normally have with him a document known as the PAC brief, which is similar to the brief which a Minister has when he is answering questions in the House. The different range and pace of events in the PAC means that the brief for the accounting officer is a much more complex and detailed document. It gives the accounting officer an opportunity to answer almost any kind of supplementary question regardless of

1. Col. Rt Hon. Edward du Cann, PC, MP (Cons.) for Taunton. Economic Secretary to the Treasury, 1962–3, Department of Trade, 1963–4. Chairman, Conservative Party Organization, 1965–7. Chairman, 1922 Committee, from 1972. Chairman, Liaison Committee of Select Committee Chairmen, from 1974. Founder Chairman, Select Committee on Public Expenditure, 1971–2, Public Accounts Committee, from 1974.

the way the discussion develops. Time is allowed for the accounting officer to leaf through his brief and find figures, either in order to give factual information in answer to a question, or to help him defend his department if this should be necessary.

The preparation of this document involves much research and documentation and consultation between the interested groups in the department; quite commonly it takes several months to prepare. Of necessity, it tends to set out the 'Departmental View' (a phrase which will be examined later[2]) and to provide the answers to criticisms of it, whether these are based directly on the contents of the C and AG's reports or on the department's own guesses about the PAC's line of questioning. After the brief is prepared the accounting officer has several weeks to go through it, familiarize himself with the arguments and problems, and prepare what he believes is the right way of answering the implied criticisms of the C and AG's report and the committee's likely questions. For this purpose there may be extended consultations between the accounting officer and his senior staff. Indeed, in my young days one accounting officer used to take the brief and go into retreat in the country for several weeks. There he was visited by relays of senior staff who supplemented the papers where necessary, acted as Devil's Advocate and rehearsed the whole act. Although this was somewhat unusual (and the subject of a good deal of irreverent comment within the department at the time), accounting officers always did take seriously the prospect of an appearance before the PAC and I believe that this is still true. For Mr W. R. (later Sir Robert) Cox,[3] therefore, by now the chief executive officer of the PSA and ex-officio its accounting officer, who had been in the department for hardly a year and who had therefore no personal responsibility if anything had gone wrong in the past, the prospect of being examined on the subject of the Agency's maintenance programme must have been mildly daunting, particularly as this was the kind of subject which lent itself to an infinite number of supplementary questions.

2. pp. 132–3.
3. William Robert Cox, KCB, Deputy Executive III, Property Services Agency, DOE, 1974. Chief Executive (Second Permanent Secretary), PSA, DOE, from 1974.

However, on this occasion proceedings started off slowly and quietly. The C and AG's report paragraphs contained some background statistics about the size and scope of the department's maintenance responsibilities and, being invited by the chairman to do so, Mr Cox filled out this skeleton with an impressive barrage of figures. It was all good background material but it wasn't taking very much further forward the question of economies. Neither, for that matter, was the next part, which was a discussion of the basis on which the department decided to use its own staff or those of contractors for any given piece of maintenance work. This, again, was good basic data for a beginner's guide to the department's general activities and way of working, but it was not really relevant to the question of maintenance economies. And finally, two-and-a-half columns of close print later in the official proceedings, the chairman turned to the subject of economies. He said that one matter that had surprised him, at any rate, was the differences that there seemed to be between regions in their enthusiasm for economy reviews and he asked why that should be.

Mr Cox replied that it was not simply a matter of enthusiasm; it was a matter of opportunities and timing, and he said that there were two or three main reasons for that. First, the Southern Region had started earlier, before other types of savings were made which were 'registered in different ways'. Secondly, there had been greater opportunity. One of the most effective ways of achieving maintenance economy, he said, was to reduce the number of buildings and 'the areas to be covered'. Southern Region covered, among other things, the Aldershot area, and as a result of a substantial redeployment of military resources, many staff had moved north. There were, therefore, opportunities in the Aldershot area and in the Southern Region generally for proposing to the Army that there should be economies in the use of buildings. Other regions, Mr Cox said, did not have the same possibilities because the same redeployments had not taken place.

This, as far as the PAC was concerned, answered the question why Southern Region had been doing things and finding savings and why other regions had not. It effectively disposed of any implied criticism which might have been read into the C and AG's report. The PAC abandoned that line of inquiry at this point and never once returned to it.

Of course, Mr Cox's integrity is not in any sense in question here or elsewhere in the book, but it is useful to stop here and examine this exchange of questions and answers in more detail. First, there is the proposition that an important reason why Southern Region had found substantial economies was that the Army in the Aldershot area had been substantially reduced and that economies, therefore, were readily available. Superficially it looks like a devastating answer to anyone who was suggesting that things were unsatisfactory in the PSA maintenance organization. In reality, it could have been pursued by searching supplementary questions.

Exchequer and Audit Department, on its own showing, had spent a great deal of time looking at the results achieved by the maintenance economy surveys in Southern Region and looking at action – or inaction – in other regions. This process had started as far back as 1972–3. During that time they examined all the basic documents, including the teams' reports, correspondence with all the client departments, the Army amongst them, and all the exchanges inside and outside the PSA about what had been found amiss, why, and what was to be done.

This had been followed by a very lengthy series of questions to the PSA through audit reference sheets, followed no doubt by a good deal of further work within Exchequer and Audit Department while those answers were examined and digested.

Straightaway, therefore, a number of questions suggest themselves. First, since the answer was, quite simply, that a lot of soldiers had been moved out of the area, why was it that the Exchequer and Audit Department did not find this out for itself? It had every possible opportunity to do so and, whatever the deficiencies in the rest of the Civil Service, E and AD staff know their business in matters of this kind. Secondly, if it did not find out for itself, why did the PSA not give Exchequer and Audit Department this answer when it was replying to the audit reference sheets? It would seem the obvious, logical and sensible thing to do, and indeed, if such an explanation was available, the Agency had an obligation to give it at this stage. If, on the other hand, the Agency did give this answer and Exchequer and Audit Department nevertheless proceeded to go ahead with all that was involved in making a formal and public special report to Parliament, thereby bringing into train all the procedural machinery of which this PAC hearing was the climax, does it not follow that Exchequer and Audit Department, who had seen all the papers and had all the facts, had not been satisfied with this answer? Alternatively, if Exchequer and Audit Department should have been satisfied with this answer, were they not gravely at fault in causing these questions to be published in the first place and wasting a great deal of time and money on the part of Parliament and many others as well? These questions were not asked.

Another series of questions might have run on these lines. If in fact it was the redeployment of Army resources, notably from the Aldershot area, which played such an important part in making economies practicable, why was it that the same order of savings was found in Army establishments far removed from Aldershot; that in some of those establishments there had been not staff reductions but increases; and that there were exactly similar, very substantial economies at Royal Air Force bases throughout the region; at the naval base in the region; at civilian establishments throughout the region; at Army barracks in Guildford, outside Southern Region, to the south; and for that matter at a civilian research establishment outside Southern Region to the north?

Supplementary questions might similarly have been directed at the second main reason why Mr Cox thought that Southern Region had been able to achieve savings where others could not, namely that Southern Region started its surveys before a number of other and different management initiatives took hold. The Public Accounts Committee has obligingly listed these other measures in its report (Appendix 3). They were, first, changes intended to secure better planning and control of the directly employed labour force; second, the productivity agreement; and, third and fourth, a new system of planned maintenance of mechanical equipment and sophisticated fuel-saving methods. Again, at first glance, these look like a formidable array of activities designed to save money which any energetic and forward-looking organization might well be proud of. They all have, unfortunately, one major drawback as an alternative to the form of maintenance economy surveys practised in the Southern Region. None of them begins to do anything about the most fundamental problem: the maintenance of things which, for one reason or another, do not need to be maintained. On a static maintenance programme these measures, listed by Mr Cox, would all contribute to making the best use of resources. However, only the Southern Region economy surveys began from first principles by examining the work-load as a whole and reducing it as necessary. As Mr Cox said himself, and as I have quoted above, one of the most effective ways of achieving maintenance economy is to reduce the number of buildings and 'the areas to be covered'. The measures which he listed did nothing towards that end.

Finally, as is obvious to any reader, the fuel-saving methods, both the sophisticated kind and the more ordinary, but even more effective ones, such as not heating empty buildings, had been an essential part of the Southern Region surveys from the outset.

Further evidence that 'sophisticated management initiatives' were not a satisfactory alternative to the surveys, and an up-to-date insight into the size and kind of savings still available, was provided in early 1977, two years after Mr Cox gave his evidence. According to newspaper reports[4] based on an account given in the PSA's own house magazine, Mr T. Carberry, a member of the PSA staff working at RAF Honington, was awarded £1,000 for a money-saving suggestion. Mr Carberry was at the time a chargehand electrician – an industrial grade. His suggestion, which related to just one part of the PSA's activities in only one part of the RAF establishment, will save £40,000 per annum. And how is that saving to be made? Nothing very sophisticated. Nothing very revolutionary. The gas cookers in the mess kitchens are in future to be turned off when not in use!

In later questions and answers, the report quotes the chairman as saying that he was surprised that the department had claimed that it was unable, because of lack of resources at its head-

4. *Sunday Express*, 16 January 1977; *Daily Telegraph*, 17 February 1977.

quarters, to disseminate information on uneconomic practices. I doubt very much if the chairman was the only one who was surprised. I would have thought that very large numbers of people would have been astounded. In the six or seven years during which this unfortunate shortage of resources existed the department must have issued literally thousands of circulars on a very wide range of subjects. Many of these dealt with matters which, though official, were not of the first importance. And there were others which might be described as peripheral to the activities of any big organization: appeals for money for a variety of causes; how to start getting ready for retirement; and the availability of courses on beekeeping offered by the Civil Service Further Education Organization. On the other hand, of course, it may have been just because there was such pressure on resources from these enormously worthwhile activities that it proved impossible to disseminate information on economies running into millions of pounds and thousands of staff. And who is to say, in these circumstances, which shall have priority? Not the taxpayer, to be sure.

In his next inquiry the chairman asked what the position was in London. I have described how in 1971, after Mr Channon's intervention, the regions had been instructed to set up teams and go ahead with the surveys, albeit in a way that did not reflect any great urgency. London had opted out, for the reason that it had chronic staff shortages. Bearing in mind that the number of staff needed for one team was precisely three, it would have been interesting to know exactly how many staff there were during this period in the London Region, and how many in the department's London headquarters. Although there are no published figures showing detailed numbers of staff and their locations, the PSA as a whole had, according to its published estimates, about 20,000 non-industrial staff, of whom around a half were in London. It would have been interesting to know how many, during this period, of those thousands of staff had been given leave, paid or otherwise, to attend a wide variety of official and extra-official activities; background courses; attendance at staff meetings; attendance at sports days; participation in sports and social events, local, departmental and all-service; annual leave and exchanges with other organizations; and visits abroad. It would be interesting to know how much time was spent on private telephone calls. According to a report in the *Daily Telegraph* a check on telephone calls in 1976 made for quite different purposes showed that in three or four days over 5000 telephone calls to get cricket match scores had been made from just one of the DOE headquarters buildings, in official time and at public expense.

It would be interesting, too, to find out how many people, because of the pressure of work, were refused leave. It is well known that all leave in the Civil Service is subject to the exigencies of the Service and may only be asked for and granted if the work situation permits. Taking a staff of only 1000 and an average annual leave entitlement of five weeks (which is probably an underestimation for the grades concerned) there is the equivalent of 100 staff always on leave – enough for thirty-three teams.

Perhaps some of this was at the back of Mr Cox's mind when he said that: 'The situation in London is that we are not satisfied.'

Although Mr Cox himself had arrived only recently, the department as a whole must have been struggling bravely with its dissatisfied feelings ever since 1968.

There is one last puzzling feature about these proceedings which the PAC could not have known about. After Mr Wardale, the Director General of Organization and Establishments, had completed what he himself described as a very exhaustive inquiry into these matters, he said in his letter to me (p. 76), that the reason why things had been done differently in other regions was that I had not succeeded in persuading my colleagues that my methods should be adopted, and Mr Cox gave his evidence also on the basis of a thorough-going review which led up to the preparation of his brief. And yet, Mr Wardale's answer and Mr Cox's answer seem to be different.

When the PAC published its findings (Appendix 3) they appeared to have been persuaded about the reasons for the difference between Southern Region and the remainder of the country. They make no comment on that. On the other hand, they did not accept the explanations put forward to some of the other questions. They say that they think the resources should have been found at headquarters to disseminate information on uneconomic practices to all regions. They noted that the PSA itself was not satisfied with progress in the London Region and they said that they trusted that the Agency would pursue this work energetically. And they went on to say that they looked to the Agency to take steps to satisfy themselves that uneconomic practices were persistently sought out and eliminated.

The PAC returned to this subject during the hearing on 12 May 1976 (Appendix 7). Mr Cox reported that one survey team had begun work in London, two in Germany, and that action would be taken in Gibraltar. In London the team had completed surveys on six districts out of twenty-nine and savings were already '£600,000 per annum' with 'more to come'. In Germany a survey had been completed on the Düsseldorf depot and part of the Bielefeld depot. Savings were already running into six figures and would in the end be 'up into the millions'.

Mr du Cann said that the Committee was very pleased with this report. He was right to be pleased that action was being taken at last, and if Mr Cox was responsible for this, he deserved to be commended. But what of the past? The story begins in 1968, not in 1975. Using the evidence given in 1975 and 1976, it is possible to go beyond the superficial level of the PAC's inquiries.

First, the London results show that if six districts produce savings of £600,000 and more, it is reasonable to suppose that the total for the London area is going to be about £3 million per annum. The only reason put forward for failing to start to do this in 1968 was a shortage of staff – that is, three staff needed for one team. This has produced a loss to the taxpayer of £3 million per annum for seven years, which is £21 million.

Earlier in this chapter I suggested further questions about the PSA's reasons why large economies were found in Southern Region and not in other regions. The first was that there had been an exodus of soldiers from Aldershot. This could not have explained the London savings – the Army accounted for only a small part of the cost of London services. And if their numbers had diminished at all, this was more than offset by increases in numbers of civil servants in the London area. The second was that other management initiatives had by then pre-empted most of the savings which might otherwise have been found by the survey teams. By 1975–6, these management initiatives must have been in full swing in London, and yet the survey teams there have produced savings measured in millions. This raises further doubts about the validity of the PSA's explanations.

The results from the overseas regions also warrant a closer look. I met all the overseas regional directors in London on 17 July 1969 and explained exactly how we were doing the surveys and what the results were. Even without this, however, management throughout the department knew what was being done, and there is no reason why the survey work overseas should not have started in 1968. What has been the cost of delay? In Germany, since savings are going to be 'up into the millions', the lowest annual figure qualifying for this description is two millions. This indicates that the cost of the seven-year delay in this one region is at least £14 million.

The reason for the failure to begin the surveys overseas is given in the C and AG's report (Para. 34, Appendix 1). The PSA had decided earlier that the pressures on budgets automatically ensured that there was no waste. The change of mind in 1975 which led to the surveys in Germany was clearly correct. Equally clearly, the results demonstrate that the earlier decision was wrong. What evidence is there that the decision was not equally wrong in the case of the other overseas regions? There seems to be none. By 1975 Mr Cox was telling the PAC (Q. 1331, Appendix 2) that it was too late to start surveys in Singapore and Malta (where withdrawal was planned for in 1976 and 1979 respectively), and that it was not suitable to deal with Cyprus at that time. Although this explanation is accurate and reasonable in 1975, it had no validity in 1968. Can it be doubted that if action had been taken then in these other regions, further millions would have been saved?

It is unnecessary to pursue these speculations. It is enough for our present purposes that on the basis of evidence produced for London and Germany alone, a minimum of £35 million of taxpayers' money has been lost. The final figure will probably be much higher.

9 The Public Accounts Committee: Case Study II

The superficiality and ineffectuality of the PAC's examinations is further illustrated by the handling of its questions about the Government Car Service, which, as I have described, was abolished in Southern Region and maintained without reductions in the other regions. The remainder of the story is contained in the Comptroller and Auditor General's report[1] on the Appropriation Accounts (1974–5), Paras. 145 to 150 (Appendix 4), and the sixth Report from the Committee of Public Accounts, Session 1975–6 (Appendixes 5 and 6). The Report paragraphs led, as they had done in the case of the maintenance expenditure, to the appearance of the PSA before the PAC (10 May 1976).

The proceedings began with the chairman referring to the relevant paragraphs of the C and AG's report which made it clear that substantial savings were made by withdrawing the Government Car Service in the Southern Region from 1972 onwards. There was, said the chairman, a proved economy, and, that being the case, why was it that the PSA did not insist at that time on similar reductions, or at any rate planning similar action, in other regions? In reply Mr Cox made two points. He said first, that it was necessary for the PSA to satisfy themselves that the economies made in the Southern Region were genuine in the sense that there clearly was a saving for the PSA, and also

1. For the record, the C and AG's report is wrong in one respect: Para. 146 begins by saying that the examination of the car service was carried out by the department's Directorate of Management Services. It wasn't. The survey was carried out by a team of three, two of them my staff and one man borrowed from the Directorate of Management Services because they were short of work. All the subsequent work was done by Southern Region staff headed by the regional administrative officer, Norman Wright.

to make sure that the additional expenses incurred by other departments did not exceed the saving to the PSA. Secondly, that the PSA had to be quite clear that the conditions in other regions were sufficiently similar to those in the Southern Region to justify similar steps being taken elsewhere. In answer to a further question Mr Cox said a report had been obtained from Southern Region 'last June' (that is June 1975) as a result of which they (the PSA) became convinced that it was possible, and safely possible, to make the savings. In November (1975) all the regional directors were asked to make proposals for cutting down the numbers of cars. As a result, reductions from 172 cars to 87 were agreed for the car pools outside London. Asked if he did not think that the time between the Southern Region action and the proposed moves in the rest of the country (timed to be completed in 1978) was very long, Mr Cox said that he agreed. He explained the delay by saying that at the first inquiry the regional controllers (he meant, I think, regional directors) were not in favour of complete abolition. Secondly, there was a certain amount of administrative difficulty because the PSA had recently been set up and there was a good deal of reorganization going on. The supplies division of the Agency, which was responsible for the car service, was being turned over to a system of accountable management and it was not clear to people at that stage just how the financial arrangements would work. Mr Cox ended by saying that he did accept that it could and should have been possible to have followed up the Southern Region experiment more quickly than was the case.

But this time the chairman was not going to let up too quickly. If the withdrawal of the car service was made in the Southern Region in 1972, he said, it must have been done for a good reason. Someone must have been very clear that this was going to result in a substantial saving. (He might also have said, but unfortunately did not, that the C and AG's report had already covered this aspect very adequately in its references to the Southern Region action.) In these circumstances, said the chairman, and there is no way of telling whether he had his tongue in his cheek when he said it, it seemed to him particularly surprising that it took so long to deal with the other regions. Mr Cox replied, yes, it was true that the Southern Region action was taken as a result of a thorough management survey. He repeated that it was necessary to be certain that the costs were not being inflicted upon another department, and went on to say that unlike the Southern Region, which was fairly close to London, the remaining regions would always need a Government Car Service to look after Ministers and senior civil servants visiting the regions in the course of their duties.

I shall come back to other parts of the evidence later on in this chapter but that covers what Mr Cox and the chairman had to say, and for the moment we will jump ahead to the findings of the PAC (Appendix 6). The relevant paragraph (number 69) reads:

Your Committee consider that the time between the abolition of the Southern Region car service in 1972 and the agreements to halve the car fleets in other Regions by 1978 was excessive. We think that the Department and Regional Directors should have realised from the outset that substantial economies were possible. The Agency informed us that most Regions need a car service for visiting Ministers and senior officers. We accept this, but we look to the Agency to press ahead quickly with the reductions now decided upon and to make sure that no further opportunities are lost to make all justifiable economies.

In the next paragraph, dealing with the setting up of an inter-departmental committee to review the arrangements for the use and operation of transport services, the committee says:

We expect the inter-departmental study to be quickly concluded and all possible economies to be promptly implemented.

And in the final paragraph the PAC tries to make sure that wider lessons are learned. The paragraph reads:

While the car service is not a major function of the Property Services Agency it involved sizeable expenditure and it has been shown that useful economies can be made. There may also be activities in other Departments which may escape proper economy reviews because they are not central to the Department's main functions and Your Committee stress the need for all Departments to seek out and effect economies over the whole range of their activities.

This was a very proper sentiment on which to close the proceedings. The ordinary reader can be forgiven for thinking that the taxpayer's interests had been served, that justice had been done and that there was a good chance that all would be well in the future.

But now, looking in more detail at the questions and answers (Appendix 5), it is possible to see how inadequately they covered the situation. It was claimed, first, that, at the beginning, other regional directors were not in favour of complete abolition. Of what significance is this defence? The choice was never between complete abolition on the one hand and total inactivity on the other. What was there to stop then the action now agreed to be possible, that is, an immediate fifty-per-cent reduction?

Next, take the explanation that it was necessary to be satisfied that the economies that had been made in the Southern Region were genuine in the sense that there would be savings to the PSA; and that any additional expense incurred by other departments would not have the effect of nullifying these economies. This was a sensible course of action. Indeed it was more than sensible – it was an absolute prerequisite for any action at all, and it was never questioned at any time by anybody. The report of the Southern Region survey made it abundantly clear that if every car which had been supplied from the Government Car Service had to be replaced by a hired car or taxi there would still have been a small but useful saving of between £5000 and £9000 a year at 1971 prices. This was the very least satisfactory result that could have been achieved in these improbable circumstances. The probable results – a much reduced use of *all* cars on official business – provided far greater savings.

All such inquiries had been made, and all doubts resolved before the Southern Region's action was taken. The discussions with the other departments also made it perfectly clear that the reductions did not in any sense affect the way those departments did their job, still less make it impossible for them to do it. It is, therefore, difficult to see the relevance of this defence. All the figures were available and all these doubts could have been similarly resolved in the other regions, as the C and AG's report makes obvious, in 1972.

As to Mr Cox's second point that the PSA had to be clear that the conditions in other regions were similar to those in London, he says they were now (1976) satisfied that this was so. But what stopped them from being so satisfied in 1972? The proposition that Reading is close to London and could, therefore, undertake a total abolition of its car service, where the other regions, being further removed, would always have to keep some cars for visiting Ministers and senior officers is fair. But the Southern Region survey showed that the bulk of the use of the car service was not accounted for by these senior people, but by junior staff, and that over 80 per cent of the total usage was by junior staff of just three departments. The Comptroller and Auditor General's report stated that his examination of requisitions and log sheets for regions outside London had shown a pattern of car usage in 1974–5 (which was when he carried out his survey) similar to that which had led to the abolition of the service in the Southern Region. It follows inevitably from this that had the other regions carried out this survey then they would have found that notwithstanding the need for cars in those regions for visiting VIPs, at least 80 per cent of the journeys could have been subjected to the kind of reduction made in the Southern Region. As a reason for delay, therefore, this answer too seems to be irrelevant.

Next, Mr Cox said that reports were obtained in June 1975 which resolved all their misgivings and doubts and uncertainties and made it possible for them to go ahead. What caused this action to be taken in June 1975, at least three years after it could have been taken? This, essentially, is a matter for speculation. It may be that after all the troubles and uncertainties of departmental reorganization this was the first opportunity that the PSA had had, and that in no time at all (five months anyway) the report of June 1975 was followed by instructions to the other regions to make economies. That is one possibility. The alternative explanation is that by June 1975 it must have been apparent to the PSA that Exchequer and Audit Department was taking a close interest in the car service and that they, the PSA, were, to say the least, going to be presented with some very awkward questions to answer.

Another reason for delay given was that the PSA had been

recently set up and that there was a good deal of reorganization going on. I suppose it depends on what you mean by 'recently'. In fact, the PSA had been set up four years before, in 1971. While it was true that many changes in the structure of the department's headquarters were taking place (though not to any great purpose as far as the taxpayer was concerned), why could not changes in the car service be a part of that great reorganization? It involved very little work, no dislocation of other services, and it could be put through just about as painlessly as any kind of reduction could be. This had already been demonstrated in Southern Region and it is always easier to follow once such action has been shown to be practicable elsewhere.

Lastly, it was claimed that the accounting system was going to be altered and it was, therefore, not clear just how these financial arrangements would work. Now this is really very intriguing. What kind of accounting system was being envisaged, we wonder, which could cope with 172 cars but not with 87? Or rather, could cope with a reduction from 172 to 87 in 1978, but not in 1972? The government service has dreamed up some startling accounting arrangements over the years, but this one must have been one quite new to human experience.

The chairman, questioning the need even for the reduced fleets of 87 cars, said he could not believe that all those Ministers travelled at the same time. The answer from Mr Cox was: 'Eighty-seven was the figure that we got down to, and that covered six regional offices in Scotland and Wales.'[2] There are no regional offices in Scotland or Wales. Each of those two countries has just one headquarters office, and I can only think that what Mr Cox meant was that this figure covered the fleets based outside London, other than those in Scotland and Wales (and Reading).[3]

On that assumption, the reduced car service now provides something like fourteen or fifteen cars for each region on a full-time all-the-year-round basis. It is well over three years since I left

2. Q. 2384, Appendix 5.
3. If Mr Cox's evidence should have read that the revised figure of 87 cars related to the six regions *and* Scotland and Wales, the argument is substantially the same, except that this figure would then amount to about eleven cars per pool.

the department and much can change in that time, and in any case I never had the occasion to study the use of the car service in regions other than my own. Nevertheless, sitting here without any information or facts other than those published by the Comptroller and Auditor General I can say categorically that the car service proposed under this new reduced scheme is still wasteful and extravagant. My estimate of need would be between two and four cars per region.

There was a further question which was not asked, although a good many harassed taxpayers would no doubt have liked it to have been. Although the wasteful use of the car service was brought to an end in 1972 in Southern Region and perhaps will be, to a limited extent, by 1978 in the other regions, the waste did not suddenly start in 1972. It had been going on for years. Would it not have been relevant to ask for how many years, and why? And whatever the answer to that, relying for the moment only on Mr Cox's own statement that the Southern Region experiment should have been followed up more quickly than was the case, was it not appropriate to ask who exactly was responsible for the delay?

According to the C and A G the cost of the car service at 1974–5 prices, which will obviously have increased considerably since then, was £1·7 million per annum. Rather less than half the fleet was based in London and the remainder outside. So it looks as if something like £850,000 a year or a little more was the cost of the service outside London. This service is now being halved, so that the annual saving on this calculation is of the order of £450,000 a year. On the PSA's own calculations, therefore, we are talking about £450,000 a year for six years being wasted because action was not taken earlier. That is to say, admitted and avoidable losses of between £2½ and £3 million. As with the millions lost in connection with the maintenance economies is it not reasonable for the taxpayers to ask for a more precise explanation of who, if anyone, was responsible, and what action, if any, was taken against those concerned?

Leaving the PSA for a moment and turning to the Treasury, the proceedings show that they were represented at this hearing by Mr Kemp, an Assistant Secretary. Seeking some reassurance about the way in which the Treasury operates to help avoid waste and having been told that at the time of the preparation of Annual Estimates the Treasury divisions should look at these things with the departments, the chairman wondered if the committee (that is the PAC) had the feeling that that examination was always made effectively.

This is the chairman of the parliamentary body most concerned with public expenditure talking to the representative of the Treasury, which most people would regard as the lynch-pin of the business of the control of government expenditure. In effect, the chairman was asking for a statement on a crucial function which should be performed at a critical stage in the preparation of the Estimates for Parliament upon which expenditure is based. The Treasury representative's answer was:

I am saying that it should happen, certainly. As I say, there is an opportunity for it to happen, and I hope that it happens.

This is a completely accurate and truthful appraisal of the situation. But does this give the impression of an enormously powerful Treasury department which, hard though it may be on the spending departments, and disagreeable its financial disciplines, is at least looking after the taxpayer's interests?

Finally, in answer to Mr Costain,[4] who asked whether consideration had been given to getting estimates from hire firms, Mr Cox replied:

Yes, we have done this. This, indeed, was part of the southern region examination. This was clearly shown to be more expensive than using the Government car service.

In actual fact the Comptroller and Auditor General's report had made it clear that the Southern Region survey indicated that the use of a hire service would be cheaper, and it was this report which was the basis of the PAC hearing. Mr Cox corrected his evidence by a note subsequently given in writing to the PAC. In this he said:

4. A. P. Costain, MP (Cons.) for Folkestone and Hythe. Private Secretary to Sec. of State for the Environment, 1972-4. Member: Committee of Public Accounts 1961-4, from 1974-.

. . . on an hourly basis during the normal working day the Government car service tends to be cheaper than private hire, though overall costs may be higher because of the need to provide a continuous service.

The use of hire firms overcomes the need for a continuous service: cars are hired only when they are required. This, in turn, was what the original Southern Region survey and the C and AG's report was all about. Obviously we failed to make the point clear.

The reduced numbers of cars proposed for the regions is still extravagant. Similarly, the car and driver strength in London could and should be reduced by 60–70 per cent. I hope that this service will continue to be critically scrutinized on behalf of the taxpayer either by the official machinery or – more probably, I fear – by the Press. It will be interesting to see whose estimates are right.

Part III

The New Remedies and Parts for Treatment

10   The Civil Service

Making fun of the Civil Service in this country has long been part of our national heritage.

Civil servants have been the target for fairly good-humoured jokes certainly since mid-Victorian days along with seaside landladies, slightly dotty earls and absentminded professors. In the attitude towards the Civil Service there were, I think, always two conflicting strands. One was that those who were responsible for operating the machinery of government should not be allowed to get delusions of grandeur, either as a result of the functions which they performed or because they had won their appointment in the face of fierce competition. But, second, alongside this, there was also some considerable degree of complacency, if not pride, in the way in which the Civil Service was believed to carry out its day-to-day functions.

For the first forty years of the twentieth century most of the public had fairly vague ideas about the functions of the Civil Service, knowing only that it was an essential part of the government machine which administered a quarter of the earth's population. The Civil Service tended to share by association the claim of the British Empire itself to be the biggest and the best that the world had ever seen. Such few serious critics as there were of the Civil Service would frequently conclude by saying that, with all its faults, we had in this country the best Civil Service in the world, and this seemed generally to be accepted.

The first scratches on this polished image occurred during the last war, ironically enough for reasons which were not the fault of civil servants. Wartime brought in its train an enormous increase in civil-service functions and many of them were of a kind which involved an unsatisfactory relationship between the Service and the public. These included rationing, the direction of labour and many controls and regulations. Together with the increase in functions there went a vastly increased staff, which meant a great dilution of the pre-war Civil Service. As a consequence of this everyone had stories to tell, many of which were well founded, of incompetence and mismanagement in the public sector from the local offices upwards. Whether, given all the circumstances, these shortcomings were avoidable, or whether, on the whole, the country was reasonably well served by its Civil Service during the war years is a matter of opinion. Rightly or wrongly, by the end of the war the reputation of the Civil Service in this country was probably lower than it had ever been. Many of the unpopular wartime measures were continued for the first five or six years after the war and the reputation of the Service stayed low. After that, although it never quite recovered its pre-war image and reputation, in the twenty years between 1950 and 1970 the Civil Service made some progress towards rehabilitating itself in the public esteem. But in the last four or five years the tide has turned against it again. Heavy taxation, cuts in services to the public and the recession in the private sector have given a bitter edge to jokes about overstaffing and waste in the public service. Managers of all grades from private industry, some of them sacked and many more feeling far from secure about their future, look with envy at the job security enjoyed by their counterparts in the Civil Service and elsewhere in the public sector.

Nor has the new spate of critical questioning been limited to the old and well-tried favourites. There has been a great deal of comment and appraisal, both within government and outside, of the problems of the relationship between government and the Civil Service, and the extent to which the Civil Service adequately and satisfactorily performs its function of carrying out government policies. I am concerned in this chapter, as well as in later ones, with only a small part of this large problem, and that is the contribution that it makes to the waste of public money.

It is convenient to begin by looking at the Civil Service as a whole. In 1854 at the time of the Northcote-Trevelyan reports, which created the Service in a form which remained largely unchanged for more than a century, there were 16,000 civil servants, including Post Office employees. In the year 1975–6 the total number of civil servants reached a figure not far short of three quarters of a million excluding PO employees, having grown by 50,000 in just one year. In the period 1966 to 1976 the growth was from about 660,000 to just under 750,000, and this was probably more truly the measure of growth than the figure for 1975–6 suggests. The Conservative administration had held down civil-service numbers whilst they were in office and by 1974–5, therefore, a Labour government searching for ways of reducing unemployment was presented with a tempting opportunity. By any calculation, however, the rate of growth must be regarded as alarming.

The defenders of the Civil Service, and many of its critics who are really aiming at governments, especially Labour governments, always point out at this stage that this is not the fault of the Civil Service. If governments will demand new services or extensions to old ones from the public services, they must, these people argue, with what appears to be irresistible logic, expect that the numbers of staff needed to provide these new or more extended services will increase.

This defence overlooks the fact that it is only one half of the story. Certainly, if there are new or increased functions extra staff are required. But at the same time there are some functions which are dwindling, and other functions which, for one reason or another, can be carried out with fewer staff. Changes in the size of the Civil Service ought, in theory, to reflect both the ups and the downs. But, in practice, it seems to reflect only the ups.

The reason for this is not very hard to seek. Extra civil-service functions, whether by way of extensions to existing ones or by the addition of completely new duties, tend to come from well-publicized government decisions, frequently in the form of legislation. The demands such government decisions make in terms of both money and staff are immediate and usually yield to a precise evaluation. The need for staff for new services is advocated by management and staff associations alike and it is improbable that Ministers would need persuading on this point.

Potential savings, on the other hand, tend to develop gradually with the erosion of demands for a particular service or by the slow development of changes which make it possible to perform the same service more economically. But there are no advocates for reductions of staff. Those who should know best will run their empires as they have always done, accepting unquestioningly the unchanging order with which they are familiar. Many, especially in the higher reaches of departments, will be unaware of the opportunities for economy.

The concept that staff economies in the Civil Service can stem only from new, planned major reductions in civil-service responsibilities has been repeated so often in recent years that nearly everyone has come to believe it. At a House of Commons inquiry into the Civil Service[1] Sir Douglas Allen, head of the Civil Service,[2] claimed, as his department's considered opinion, that to save about £140 million a year on staff costs would involve a staff cut of about 35,000. He went on to say that this could be achieved, in turn, only by a major change in functions for the Civil Service.

There are several aspects of this evaluation on which it is appropriate to comment. Sir Douglas Allen was telling Parliament what he believed to be the truth of the situation and giving the best advice that he could. He will have arrived at his conclusions as a result of reports made by his own and other departments. Those reports, in turn, will have been based on others still. Information will be at third, fourth or fifth hand. The maintenance survey teams had first-hand knowledge of what happens in the spending departments, and leaving aside for the moment the economies which we ourselves made, the most commonly used expression by the teams about wasted resources of money and manpower which they saw elsewhere was 'heartbreaking'. I think Sir Douglas Allen is wrong. A reduction of 35,000 staff could be made in the home Civil Service not only without difficulty but without most people except obviously those directly concerned being aware that it had happened. According to the C and AG's report on the maintenance surveys

1. These examples and the other references in this chapter to the proceedings before the Committee are based on a report in the *Sunday Times*, 9 January 1977.

2. Sir Douglas Allen, GCB, KCB, CB. Head of the Home Civil Service and Permanent Secretary, Civil Service Department, 1974–7.

(Appendix 1) the PSA's directly employed staff (industrial) had been reduced from 31,000 in 1968 to 22,000 in 1973, a total of 9000 staff or a quarter of the numbers about which Sir Douglas Allen was speaking. How many people could claim to have been adversely affected by this reduction or even to be aware that it had been made? The answer to these questions is very, very few.

One of the most interesting aspects of the evidence given by the Civil Service Department was the choice of examples of what staff cuts of 35,000 could entail. It illustrates a defence mechanism, probably an unconscious one, which automatically comes into play the moment anyone talks of reducing public expenditure.

To go back for a moment to the responsibilities of the Ministry of Works, there were times when some cuts or decreases in the rate of expenditure had to be accepted. It was well-known throughout the department that such cuts found their way into the maintenance budget and from there to the money provided for painting and decorating. This provided a quick and easy solution and, more importantly, one where the results could be seen by those who imposed the cuts and those who suffered them alike. The wicked injustice of the cuts, the desirability of replacing them as quickly as possible, the unwisdom of those who imposed the cuts and the long-suffering patience of those who received them were all demonstrated in one convenient package. No one thought it necessary to go and have a look at the empty buildings which were being kept warm, the money spent maintaining land we did not need and all the rest. No one thought to try to make the kind of savings which, as the PAC itself said, one would have expected all the time. This happens over and over again whenever cuts are proposed. Take £1 million off the annual budget for the Health Service and does anyone look at waste and extravagance? Of course not. They refrain from paying a justified increase to underpaid, overworked hospital doctors, or they reduce the number of hospital beds.

So it is with the Civil Service. Sir Douglas Allen, warning on the dangers of staff cuts of 35,000, explained that if Inland Revenue staff was cut the Revenue would suffer; and that if the staff at the Department of Health and Social Security was cut there would be a lot of hardship to the public. Both were examples calculated to strike a chill into the hearts of the Members of Parliament who were conducting the inquiry. But why choose to make cuts in those two cases?

Some instances of economies already made or pending in the public sector were given to this committee. The impression produced by these examples was that while they were admittedly small, they did seem to show that everybody was honestly trying to do their best to find a few odd pence to save wherever they could. Official library stocks were being weeded out, saving half a million pounds a year in accommodation services. Whitehall was going to use less paper: it had cut back by about £4 million, and although it was creeping up again it would be carefully monitored. Economies in the Government Car Service would save £600,000 a year.

It all sounds very impressive – rather like a band of devoted men fighting a desperate rear-guard action against encroaching higher costs. Does it perhaps look a shade less convincing when, as you know, all these examples together do not add up to the £12 million a year which the PSA concedes is now being saved from Southern Region-type maintenance economy surveys? These were savings which the PAC said were of a kind that management should have been putting into effect all the time and about which more disquieting things might have emerged had the committee had the opportunity to probe deeper and further (such as the £35m lost through delays). It is even less convincing knowing the story behind that saving of £600,000 per annum in the Government Car Service.

The first step to be taken along the hard road to a more cost-conscious Civil Service is to change the climate which has allowed the development of this nothing-can-be-done frame of mind; and this change is one which must involve all levels in the Service. Whatever popular legend suggests, most civil servants – which means in turn most of the people in the lower and middle levels – are neither lazy nor inefficient. On the other hand, neither are they always selfless, dedicated public servants. They are, as you would expect in an organization of this size, merely a rough cross-section of the community as a whole.

Most civil servants, like the majority of people elsewhere, spend their lives doing more or less what they are told to do, more or less in the way they are told to do it. Doing what they are told in this sense does not mean only the execution of specific instructions; it means the continuing conduct of business in a manner which reflects the prevailing climate of opinion in the Civil Service, which, in turn, is created by senior management. In an ideal world, if a junior officer of the Civil Service found that a job was not needed he would say so to his department even if it affected him personally and directly. But this is asking a lot in any circumstances and it is asking too much when such a junior officer knows full well that in nine cases out of ten his proposals will not be well received and may be derided. It is in order to help those in that situation that I make my first suggestion for action by the Government.

It needs to be restated with all the authority of the Prime Minister and the Government that the function of civil servants is to carry out the duties given to them with a proper regard for the interests of the taxpayer. Similarly, it needs to be re-established that economizing in all ways is something that all public servants should be doing all the time as a matter of course in the public interest. Civil servants should be required to sign a declaration that they have understood this directive and will conduct themselves accordingly.

The phrase 'the public interest' used to crop up continually in discussions two or three decades ago when decisions were being taken. It comes up very rarely nowadays, and often in a slightly apologetic manner. I believe that there is a need, therefore, to restate the fundamental duties, responsibilities and objectives of public servants and, in the process, put into the hands of those who would like to make economies a potent weapon which can be used against those who try to stand in the way.

By itself such an instruction from the Government would achieve nothing. What it would do would be to provide a back-cloth against which other actions can be taken and give a crumb of much-needed spiritual comfort to those who would like to do something about saving money.

The reasons why civil servants protect their little empires are enormously varied and change from time to time. In recent years one of the most popular and superficially defensible arguments against cutting staff has been that when there are already so many unemployed such a staff reduction would only add to their numbers and consequently to expenditure by the Government in social security and unemployment benefits. This argument, like all the others, needs to be set aside by an instruction couched in the most explicit and emphatic terms. The function of management inside and outside the public sector is to manage efficiently. If the Government decides that the public interest is best served by retaining unneeded staff it makes a political decision open to challenge. But it is not for civil servants to make covert assumptions about what is needed, and to fail to discharge their management obligations.

The management skills involved in initiating and directing the maintenance economy surveys were no more than average. The skills used by the teams (and I am sure they will forgive me for saying so) were, for the most part, also fairly low-powered. The use of a balanced survey team of technical staff coupled with an administrator was merely a small local variation of an old principle which happened to suit our particular circumstances and needed neither great skill nor ingenuity to be put into effect. The economies are there for the finding, and there are plenty of people in the Civil Service now who, given half a chance, would do something about them.

Next, having done something to improve the general climate, some more positive incentives are needed for individuals. At the present time promotion for civil servants, certainly in the junior and middle grades, is based on annual reports by superiors within the division, and these are put together and monitored in the department's establishment headquarters. The reports are made under several specific headings not one of which relates to proposals for saving money or staff or achievements in the reduction of public expenditure. This could be put right very easily. Every annual report could have an extra section overprinted to cover this particular aspect of an officer's career and it could quickly become the practice that the absence of anything positive in this category would at least put a tentative question-mark against the suitability of such civil servants for promotion.

A change of this kind would help, also, to offset another feature of the annual reports, and the people affected by them, by diminishing the emphasis that is currently placed in all the annual reports with which I was familiar on the ability of a civil servant to get on with other people. Currently, where relations with other members of the staff are concerned, the worst thing that can be said about someone is that 'his relationships with other people are rather difficult', and the best is that 'he gets on extremely well with everyone'. Nobody in a big organization wants a bad relationship for its own sake, but I do not believe that a good manager, pushing through reductions of staff and expenditure, with all the implications this has for those around him, is going to 'get on well with everyone' unless he has saintly qualities which qualify him for a quite different career. A manager who is pressing ahead with economy measures of this kind might very well have awkward relationships with a few of his colleagues, and more power to his elbow!

Next, in order to underline the importance attached to measures designed to save public money, there should be more publicity given, not just within the departments but elsewhere, to achievements in this field. Nor should this merely be a matter of reporting. People who achieve substantial savings in the future should have this recognized in the same way that good service has been recognized in the past. Instead of routine honours for all senior staff and routine honours for a few selected junior staff, there could be a period of years when no honours or awards were given for long, loyal and uneventful service, but were bestowed, rather, on people, no matter how junior in grade or short in service (or how badly they got on with their colleagues), who had come up with ideas to save staff and costs.

Coupled with the need to do more about rewarding initiative is, I think, a need to make lack of initiative less rewarding. In the Civil Service everyone who is on a salary scale, which means nearly all junior and middle grades and many of the higher ones, has annual increments paid (sometimes over quite long periods) up to the maximum for that particular grade. These increments are paid automatically unless someone takes positive and difficult steps to prevent them. The practice of not awarding annual salary increments unless those concerned are positively recommended should be adopted forthwith. I am fairly sure that this was common not all that long ago. Civil servants should, in other words, only be paid more when there is some good reason for it. This proposal will be fiercely opposed by the Civil Service staff associations, but I am not so sure that it would be so unwelcome to the staff. There is quite often a considerable difference between what trade-union leaders want and what their membership believe in their hearts to be right. I believe that many people would like to think that they have been awarded their increments as a result of service which has been valued rather than because everybody gets it automatically.

Next, there needs to be a re-examination of the arrangements for dealing with staff reported as inefficient. Over the years the position of such people has become increasingly safeguarded. When I left at the end of 1973, it was extremely difficult and very time-consuming to dispose of an incompetent member of the staff. Indeed, it had reached the point where I was giving instructions that we were not to try to deal with more than three or four cases at one time. Whatever the theory may suggest, in practice it takes between two and three years to remove an inefficient civil servant, except in the most extreme cases.[3] The same is true of people who are physically unfit. It is right that people should not be penalized because they cannot get on with their boss, or because their face does not suit in some way; and it is even more right that the Service should deal compassionately with those who become sick. But I believe that the majority of people in management would now feel that the pendulum has swung too far and that the arrangements for both categories are such that the efficiency of the Service is being substantially impaired.

The rules, and the difficulties in applying them, are not only a problem for management; they apply equally to the managers themselves. The need for swifter and simpler measures is far greater for management grades. The loss caused by an inefficient clerk is bearable; the waste caused by an inefficient manager is much greater.

None of these proposals will, by itself, do more than remove a

3. I understand that this is equally true in the nationalized industries and local government.

few obvious obstacles in the way of sensible management and create the kind of climate in which there is a slightly better opportunity for management to function efficiently than is the case at the moment. Large economies either in staff or money cannot often be expected to come from junior grades. It is to the higher echelons of management that we must turn for this kind of action. It is the responsibility of management to initiate it and to see it through, and management must, therefore, bear the blame when these things do not function properly. The next chapters, accordingly, deal with the central direction and administration of the Civil Service and the role of individual managers within it. A convenient starting point for both is the Fulton Committee Report of 1968.

11 Civil Service Management

In June 1968 the Fulton Committee published the results of two years of examination of the structure, recruitment and management, including training, of the home Civil Service. The committee's recommendations covered a wide field and, by any test, ought to have had considerable influence on the workings of the Service for many years to come. Unfortunately (and this is no criticism of the Committee, whose function was purely advisory), the recommendations could not be presented as a package deal, nor could a timetable for their adoption be set down. Consequently, the Civil Service was able to seize with enthusiasm the recommendations which it liked and ignore those it did not. As well as improvements in pension arrangements and allied matters, which were selected for swift implementation, the favoured recommendations included those which created extra staffs and more top jobs. Diligent students of recent reorganizations in local government may have noticed odd traces of the same phenomenon there. The committee listed five proposals which involved extra staff.

(a) The establishment of planning units.

(b) The creation of a Civil Service college and the expansion of the training programme.

(c) Greater attention to personnel management and career development.

(d) The expansion of departmental management services.

(e) The creation of the new Civil Service Department.

All these were implemented within two years.

The processes by which only acceptable changes were implemented were assisted by the fact that the Civil Service was itself largely responsible for dispensing and administering its own medicine. Moreover, within the Service, the direction of these matters was in the hands of the administrative class, whose deficiencies will be examined in Chapter 13. Finally, the Fulton Committee did not do much by way of specifying a timetable of priorities. It gave emphasis only to improved training and to the setting up of the Civil Service Department. Within the Fulton Report relative importance (as opposed to urgency) is also hard to judge. Three pages were devoted to accountable and efficient management, which was the principal area where reform was badly needed, and nearly two pages to the management of new entrants, which, though deserving attention, was hardly in the same category. The proposed creation of the Civil Service Department with all the opportunities for new senior posts was a most acceptable change, and the priority urged by the committee was not needed to ensure its speedy implementation. Much less popular was the supervisory and management role of the Civil Service Department as envisaged by the committee.

It was acceptable to encourage the new Civil Service Department to do more about boosting training in the departments (more jobs), more specialized training (more courses, more leave on full pay) and more highly specialized training involving a staff college for civil servants. This meant not only more senior jobs but a country house with magnificent grounds. It was also right to give the new department the old recruitment functions of the Civil Service Commission and the pay functions of the Treasury. It was likely that both transfers of function would result in more staff being needed for the same work. It was quite unacceptable, and therefore still not implemented to any extent, that part of the new Department's duties (which was the committee's fundamental reason for establishing it) should include the central management of the Civil Service and the supervision of departmental organization.

On the contrary, such changes as have taken place have been in the opposite direction. The big departments tend more and more to say that they are supposed to manage their own affairs. Where the pre-Fulton Treasury could bring pressures on departments through controls on expenditure, the Civil Service Department seems to be largely powerless. Its basic philosophy seems to consist of a vague well-meaning desire to do good, by consent and by stealth. To appear to interfere with other departments seems to be the worst crime. This is an absurd situation. The essential feature of all kinds of efficiency checks, staff inspections and other audit functions is precisely that of interference with management. Experience has shown that management, not only in the public sector (though more obviously and urgently there), needs such outside checks and that they should as a matter of course be imposed, not used by consent. The question of consent, and the division of responsibility between managers and inspectors arises after the facts and recommendations produced by an inspection have been established. At that stage it is a management function to decide what to do, since it cannot be held responsible and accountable if others have taken decisions for it. If it fails subsequently to justify its decision and can be shown to have ignored sound recommendations, management must accept the consequences. The least of these would then be the imposition of recommended changes without more ado.

While it is true that large-scale organizational changes cannot usually be agreed and implemented overnight, it is equally true that in the nine years since the Fulton Report the Civil Service Department has had more than enough time to develop its role of central management. In practice, its pitifully small and weak staff inspectorate operating a policy of non-interference has had little or no impact on the problem of the efficient and economical staffing of departments, nor is there any evidence that effective strategic control has been exercised through supervision by the Civil Service Department's own inspectorate machinery. Whatever else it may do, the contribution of the Civil Service Department to expenditure controls of these kinds may be ignored.

The Fulton Committee quite rightly did not limit its proposals for improving management to changes in the central control and direction of the Civil Service. It also looked at the structure within departments and the changes needed at those levels in order to increase efficiency. Not surprisingly, the committee put first the need for accountable management, and for those not familiar with the jargon the committee's own definition of this is as good as any.

Accountable management means holding individuals and units responsible for performance measured as objectively as possible. Its achievement depends upon identifying or establishing accountable units within Government Departments – units where output can be measured against costs or other criteria, and where individuals can be held personally responsible for their performance.

The three essentials for creating accountable management are:

1. To define a task or series of tasks in precise terms so that those concerned know what it is they are supposed to be doing.

2. To provide as nearly as possible *all* the resources needed to meet the objective.

3. To measure, assess or evaluate the results achieved and where desirable do something about those results whether good or bad.

These general propositions can be applied in detail to the Civil Service.

It is useless to try to make management accountable if responsibilities are not clearly defined, since otherwise it is impossible to decide whether tasks have been performed in the way required and, if not, who is responsible. This is as important to the manager who is trying to do the job as it is to those to whom he is responsible. What managers need more than anything else, and indeed what they *must* have, is a fighting chance to manage effectively. In the Civil Service this opportunity is too often not available. In very large areas no one man below the grade of permanent secretary is wholly responsible for anything and even there, as we shall see, doubts can be caused to arise.

For some people, accountability has very considerable disadvantages. If responsibilities are clear, responsibilities cannot be avoided and errors of judgement, waste of money and all the other ills we have been looking at in this book can be brought home to one individual. On the other hand, if you create a management structure where responsibilities are divided and where for anything that needs to be decided there is a committee, and perhaps more than one committee, involved, you are well on the way to creating an organization where no one can ever be blamed for anything. Soon, in this situation, decisions are never taken or, when they are, because they have been so long delayed, events have pre-empted them. Management by drift allows waste and incompetence to flourish.

If, in the case of the Government Car Service, the regional directors had been accountable managers they would have borne the complete and sole responsibility for a substantial waste of money in their organizations. But not having that clearly defined liability they were able to advise that there was very little value in a detailed investigation, quite possibly influenced by the departmental headquarters view of the economics of the car service. Thereafter, until the PAC presented its report, they were out of the act. In the meantime when the views of the regional directors were received in the PSA's headquarters those responsible there allowed matters to drift, safe in the knowledge that a majority of those in daily contact with the problem had recommended that no one should waste their time looking at the facts. The smoke-screen provided by diffused responsibilities would ensure that no one was ever blamed.

Just how well this worked in practice is demonstrated by the findings of the PAC (Appendix 6). The relevant sentence reads:

We think that the Department and Regional Directors should have realised from the outset that substantial economies were possible.

Although for convenience we all use expressions like 'the Department should have realised', the fact is that a department cannot realize anything; only individuals within it can do that. By naming the regional directors as being responsible at one level and referring only to 'the Department' thereafter the PAC comment reflected the impossibility of laying blame on any individual or group once matters reached the department's headquarters.

Nor does this apply only in connection with small-scale operations. If we go back to the role of the Civil Service Department we find Mr Michael English, MP, of the Expenditure Committee on the Civil Service, trying to find out who exactly was responsible for staffing. He said:

What we are talking about is this. What Department of State is responsible for determining the efficiency of other Departments of State?

And he asked a similar question about who was responsible within a department for determining its efficiency and whether it could be improved. The answers which he was given illustrate the old saying that everybody's business is nobody's business. A Treasury spokesman attributed the prime responsibility to each department. The Civil Service Department said that in the last analysis the responsibility lay with them. Somebody else believed that it was 'a collaborative effort'.[1] In practice, departments regard themselves as responsible, if only because the Civil Service Department, to a large extent, and the Treasury, to a lesser extent, have shown themselves in recent years to be ineffectual in trying to exercise control. But it is equally true that under pressure the spending departments try to shuffle off some of the responsibility – and the blame – to these other two departments and, where the opportunity offers, on to each other. A clarification of roles at all levels is an essential first step towards making responsibilities clear and management accountable.

To achieve this reform it would not be necessary to create new posts and more jobs in order to make a more widespread use of the accountable manager concept, nor would it be necessary to reshuffle staffs or departments. Often it would be a matter of re-defining the roles of individuals in existing posts. On the other hand, as accountable management became established it would become apparent that quite large numbers of senior staff, who hitherto have merely been helping to pass the papers round and round without playing any useful part, were no longer required.

One of the objections put forward to this kind of change is that it might be difficult to find the kind of men and women that would be required. I do not believe that this is so. There is plenty of good management potential in the Civil Service – at least as much within it as there is outside. All that people need is the chance to do some managing. Moreover, those people, and there are many of them in the higher reaches of the Civil Service, who have made

1. Extracted from 'The biggest official secret – how to cut the Civil Service' by Michael Jones, *Sunday Times*, 9 January 1977.

a very pleasant career for themselves without ever taking a single decision do not lack, whatever else they may be deficient in, a strong instinct for self-preservation. They would either shy away from the accountable management post and its responsibilities or, being in one, would get out of it again at the first opportunity. Either way, the path would be open to those who have both the inclination and the ability to take on this kind of job.

Much of the advantage of this reform would be lost if, after appointing these managers with their clearly defined responsibilities, they were not given equally clear powers and resources. In a surprisingly large area this would involve no change. As a regional director, for example, I had no complaints about my powers in connection with finance, administration or contracts. It was quite true that there were enormously detailed codes of rules and practice for all these purposes, but I think that the Civil Service, whatever people may believe, has always accepted that rules are intended to cover only the majority of cases. Breaking the rules, or, more accurately, deciding that the rules were not appropriate in a particular case, was something that happened all the time and I cannot remember a single instance of someone getting into trouble for doing something against the rules if it was the sensible thing to do.

The one field in which this was not true relates to matters involving staff, where, under present arrangements, managers are hamstrung. I have already referred to the difficulty of dealing with staff who are either inefficient or sick, but that is not the whole of the problem. If retribution for failure is inadequate so is reward for merit. Over the years the Civil Service has developed a neurosis about the risks of favouritism leading to undeserved advancement. Consequently, coupled with the protection of the undeserving, a system is taking shape where everyone gets the same – the same salary, the same increments, the same promotion prospects and the same steady progress towards retirement.

In these matters at least, the staff associations reflect the opinions of the majority of their members. Since the majority of any group are not high flyers, pressure on and from those associations tends towards the protection and advancement of the mediocre at the expense of the outstanding. I am not in favour of giving unlimited powers in personnel matters to managers, but they need more than they have at the moment. One possibility would be to let them make special pay awards for specially meritorious service – some kind of bonus, in other words. The size and duration of these rewards could be limited, and the Civil Service Department could soon work up two or three pages of instructions and advice. That would not matter, providing the essential quality of the award is retained, namely, that it should be wholly within the gift of the accountable manager.

The problem of providing adequate resources is closely linked with that of defining clearly the responsibilities of the individuals concerned. It is not much good telling someone that he is wholly responsible for something and then withholding from him the control of resources he needs. On the other hand, no one inside or outside the public sector has anything like full control of an organization. Even the biggest firms are subject to government and trade-union interventions, economic and social pressures. The objective should be to set up accountable management units which can be reasonably self-contained and then provide the opportunity to use other resources in a way which does as little damage as possible to the full accountability concept.

Much more could be done in the Civil Service than has been the case so far, and the difficulties said to exist in large and complex departments have been greatly exaggerated. The division of a department's main function into smaller units, usually geographically based, is now commonplace. The regional organization of the PSA is just one instance of this trend. The process can be taken further in two ways. Where it makes for greater efficiency, including economic efficiency, to keep some work centralized – the computerized payment of accounts, for example – the bill-paying function can itself be a unit of accountability. Other functions such as Organization and Methods work, training, staff inspection and central administration may need a different approach. Those functions which can be treated as a tool of management by accountable operational units should be hired

by them in the same way as they would buy outside consultants'
services. O and M surveys and staff inspection work lend themselves readily to this treatment. The higher levels in the department's headquarters will also need to impose some checks on
management from time to time and similarly to test its judgements in this direction against the results achieved. The cost of
these servicing organizations would be justified, first, by the
extent to which the lower levels were prepared to be held accountable for the cost of their use in improving their own organization,
and, second, by their value to the upper levels of management.

When all that can be done in this way has been done there
would almost certainly be a large residue of activities which
would not be accountable. This residue would include the
central administrative and policy-planning activities. Although
the Fulton Committee recommends very strongly that these
functions, too, should be made accountable wherever possible, I
do not believe that it would be worth struggling very hard to
achieve this. Frequently it will be enough merely to isolate these
staffs from their 'productive' colleagues, so that their full cost can
be determined and set against the end-product of their labours
instead of being lost in the sheer weight and volume of the department's routine operational functions. The upper reaches of the
administration of the Civil Service would thus be exposed for the
first time to effective critical scrutiny.

None of this thinking is new. Most of it was covered by the
Fulton Committee recommendations and some of it is pre-
Fulton. Some departments have already implemented some of the
recommendations, and they and others, no doubt, plan to do
some more at some time. What is so unsatisfactory, then, about
the current situation as to justify the charge that the Civil Service
has implemented only those parts of the Fulton Committee
Report which were acceptable? It is not only that progress has
been too slow. It is also that setting up accountable units is only
part of the process of creating accountable management. In fact,
it covers only the first two of the three essentials for a reformed
Civil Service listed earlier. It is as if, having used great skill and
energy in diagnosing a malady, nothing is done by way of treatment. It is vital, thirdly, to do something about the results pro-

duced by examining the performance of these units. To fail at this stage makes the whole business worse than useless. It is bad enough to be unaware of inefficiency or at least to be lacking conclusive proof of its existence. It is far worse to bring the facts into the open and still do nothing about them. This is tantamount to saying, not only that inefficiency exists, but also that it does not matter enough to justify doing anything about it, which amounts to condoning it by implication. It is therefore essential that managers should not only become *potentially* accountable by virtue of the changes in organization and accounting already discussed but, in reality, should be called to book personally for their performance.

Quite simply, managers in the Civil Service should be treated like their counterparts anywhere else: that is to say, if on the whole their performance is creditable and effective they should be regarded and rewarded as successful managers. The opposite should be equally true. If civil servants consistently fail to produce results they should be, within civil-service procedures, dealt with as inefficient. This means the use of demotion, sideways transfer to a job with less pressures and no prospects, or, in more extreme cases, premature retirement. No new principle is involved in this. There is already provision for early compulsory retirement. All that needs to be done is for a greater use to be made of the existing procedures. It ought to be accepted that this is a bigger occupational risk for higher grade staffs than for lower ones.

In other words, as the Fulton Committee said:

... the Service should have wider powers to retire on pension those who have ceased to earn their keep, and should use them with more determination. Where culpable inefficiency is in question, the present powers seem adequate, though we suspect that they are not always used as fully as they should be.

In a report which was notable in its efforts to be fair to the Civil Service and, like most committees of this kind, very restrained in its language that last sentence must stand as the most notable understatement of all.

Evidence of the extent to which the Committee's views have

been acted upon should not be difficult to provide. On page 43 of the Report details are given of numbers of civil servants of executive officer grade and above – that is, from minor management grades and upwards – who were compulsorily retired or dismissed on grounds of inefficiency or misconduct in the years 1963 to 1967. The Committee said that they found it 'hard to believe that these figures should not have been higher'. What is now needed is publication of the figures of premature retirements and dismissals (excluding those cases resolved by agreement) in the years since the Report was published. I doubt very much if anyone outside the Civil Service will believe that these numbers, when published, will match even that tiny minority of cases of inefficiency and maladministration which somehow slip past the Official Secrets Act and become public knowledge. There is everything to be said for this information being published in detail in the future.

The effective application of accountability and the measures for dealing with inadequate management would produce a permanent increase in the turnover of staff in these posts, and for the first few years while management was being shaken up this increase would be considerable. It would be wrong, however, to assume that the findings would be all one way. It is just as important for the well-being of the Service that if inefficiency is to be penalized, efficiency should be rewarded. The opportunity to get on and do the job effectively, in an atmosphere where the effectiveness is welcomed and praised, is more important to good management than increases in salaries or bigger cars. This is not optimistic guesswork. Men in those few jobs in my old department which had some limited resemblance to accountable units often refused promotion which would cause them to revert to central administrative posts. Higher pay and better long-term prospects were no match for job satisfaction.

To say that pay and promotion are not the only, or even the most, important incentives is not to say that they do not matter at all. Given a substantial increase in the numbers of posts of this kind there should be more opportunities for able people to stay in accountable posts and still climb the promotion ladder. This process will also be helped by the way in which accountability should begin to bite in the higher levels. Nothing is more likely to cause senior management to ensure that able men are chosen than the knowledge that failure lower down is going to come home to roost with those who do the choosing. Urbane, articulate and largely useless organization men will find their ability to keep paper moving round in circles being valued less highly.

This change in thinking would follow fairly quickly as accountability spread, but it would still need to be supplemented by one other measure. Civil servants who have brought about economies of staff and money would be likely for a little while yet to be regarded as dangerous or disloyal. Provision would need to be made for civil servants who believed that they had brought about economies, or who had tried to and been frustrated by their departments, to appeal against non-promotion or any other unfair discrimination. Such appeals should be heard by a board or tribunal on which there should be at least one nominee from professional bodies closely concerned with management and efficiency, and the results of such appeals should be published in general terms while preserving the anonymity of individuals. There should be provision also for identifying cases where the non-civil-service member or members disagreed with the others.

Finally, improved opportunities for promotion as a reward for efficiency could be achieved by using a more flexible approach to the grading of posts. It is rarely good, either for the organization or for the individual concerned, to be moved as soon as efficiency is improved: yet that is what nearly always happens at present on promotion. With greater emphasis on the recognition of good work the level of staff turbulence (already high enough to be a hindrance to the efficient dispatch of public business, noted the Fulton Committee) is likely to rise higher still. One way of reducing the problem would be to give promotion but leave the individual in the same post. This is not completely new to the Civil Service. The Treasury used to do this for their own staff when they were responsible for civil-service staffing matters, but they never allowed anyone else to do so – I think on the assumption that sharp tools were best kept out of the reach of children! I found it very helpful to use a similar if unorthodox variation on this theme for some of the members of the Southern Region maintenance survey teams.

Another variation, which has the advantage of avoiding difficulties about staff complements and costs, is to give promotion without pay, so that the individual concerned can, without more ado, move into the higher grade when it suits everyone, possibly two or three years later.

These measures would go some way towards meeting two criticisms levelled by the Fulton Committee:

[1.] Nor is there enough encouragement and reward for individual initiative and objectively measured performance: for many Civil Servants, especially in the lower grades, promotion depends too much on seniority . . . [and]

[2.] One of the main troubles of the Service has been that, in achieving immunity from political intervention, a system was evolved which until recently was virtually immune from outside pressures for change. Since it was not immune from inside resistance to change, inertia was perhaps predictable.

How very true!

12 Permanent Secretaries and Accounting Officers

I have already referred briefly to the role of the accounting officers in the control of public expenditure. At present, the accounting officer is always the head of the department concerned. He is either the permanent secretary in the ordinary departments of State or, as in the case of the Property Services Agency, its chief executive. There are now (June 1977) forty-four of these jobs in a Service numbering 750,000, which means, first, that they have to be fairly capable to get there in the face of competition of that size: not supermen, but not mediocre. It means, second, that there is not the remotest prospect, even if they were supermen, of controlling £40,000 million a year of public spending in the way that their title and theoretical duties suggest.

It used to be the practice, and I think still is, that when these people were appointed they were given a letter by the Treasury appointing them specifically as accounting officers, rather than letting them acquire this responsibility on an ex-officio basis. This was done in order to underline the very special and serious responsibilities that went with this part of their job. It was also made clear that the liability for financial error in their department was a personal one, and an almost mystical significance was attached to this particular constitutional device. Indeed, some poor chap in the very early 1920s did contrive to get himself into a position where the Public Accounts Committee of the day decided that he would have to pay £100 or so for some culpable error. As the ultimate deterrent against inefficiency on the grand scale, in departments with budgets running into thousands of millions of pounds, this does seem to lack something, especially when you bear in mind that even in those days it could cost you forty shillings to spit in a tram and £5 to pull the communication cord on the railway.

It is a long time since those powers were last used and I cannot see them being used again in the future. Even if they were, I think it could only be in the somewhat curious circumstances of an impropriety or an illegality in the accounts akin to the situation that gives rise to members of local councils being surcharged by the District Auditors. As a factor therefore in the safeguards for controlling public expenditure, this theoretical personal financial liability can be disregarded.

Nevertheless, the role of the accounting officer is still a vital one in present circumstances. He is still the one man who is charged with the responsibility for financial matters in his department, and with occasional exceptions he is the man who appears before the Public Accounts Committee and answers for what has happened.

In Victorian times all this probably worked very well. The scale of events was far smaller and the pace far slower. Accounting officers had time to write in their own copperplate hand chatty little memoranda on a wide range of subjects. The idea that the accounting officer could and should know what was going on in his department and be responsible for it was one which was completely credible. This is no longer true and the change has been twofold. Not only has the scale of expenditure increased enormously, but the range of activities which it encompasses is far more complex.

There is a further difficulty which today's accounting officers have to contend with which their predecessors did not: like many other people inside and outside the Service they are now always on the move. Between 1967, when I began the surveys, and 1975, when Mr Cox was talking to the PAC about them, there were five changes of accounting officers. To this we must add two more facts, again not peculiar to the PSA. First, in 1967 we were just getting over a major reorganization, and in 1970 and 1972 we had two more. Second, all the five accounting officers were completely new to the department when they took up their appointments, and one was new to the Civil Service. In these circumstances, to say that any one man should have a real personal responsibility for the range of activities of a modern department is to state something which, from the outset, is manifestly absurd. The whole procedure then becomes a charade.

It is not, unfortunately, a harmless charade. The Public Accounts Committee knows the facts of life as well as anyone else and knows that it cannot expect to hold responsible, in any meaningful way, the accounting officers who appear before it. On the other hand, there is no one else that they can turn to, so that, in a sense, they are partly disarmed before they begin. No doubt this accounts for the very mild, almost diffident manner in which their comments are made. The PAC knows that the men appearing before it have a technical, almost fictional responsibility, not a real one.

At least part of the answer lies in recognizing the change in the scale of operations and in appointing more people with the responsibilities now given to the accounting officers as they are at present constituted. A change of this kind would fit in admirably with the extension of accountable management.

The size of one of these mini-accounting officer's realms, measured in money, would vary considerably. An accounting officer responsible for an organization which disbursed authorized sums of money, for example, statutory benefits, would be able to control effectively a very much larger flow of cash than someone responsible for an establishment dealing with research and development. The demarcation of these posts should have regard only for the creation of units of manageable size and complexity, and arrangements would vary considerably from one department to another.

Taking the Civil Service as a whole, a tenfold increase in the number of accounting officers would be the very least that would be desirable. This would not involve any increase in the number of senior posts. As with the creation of the accountable management posts, it would be a matter of changing the terms of reference of people already there.

It may be objected that these arrangements would create difficult problems in that one of the new mini-accounting officers might disagree with the head of the department, the permanent secretary. Naturally this is possible, at least in theory.

In these circumstances the decision of the permanent secretary would prevail, for it would be quite wrong to undermine his authority. It would only be necessary to have a very brief exchange of memoranda, making it clear that it was his decision which was prevailing and who, therefore, was responsible. There are precedents for this. There are already arrangements to cover the situation where a permanent secretary-cum-accounting officer disagrees with a Minister. In practice this hardly ever arises, nor would it, I believe, between the permanent secretary and his subordinate accounting officers.

Once appointed, the new-style accounting officers would be the ones who appeared before the PAC and in every other way, too, assumed full responsibility for their own decisions and those of their subordinates. They would be responsible for the efficient running of their establishments, for taking steps against overstaffing and ensuring that there was no waste of money in other directions. All this having been done, they would be responsible also for ensuring that, within the limits of policies defined by others, what they were providing was good value for money for the taxpayer.

13 The Higher Civil Service

In the preceding chapters I have argued that the majority of civil servants in the lower and middle grades are neither better nor worse than their counterparts outside the Service; and that the men at the very top, the permanent secretaries, are prevented from being fully effective in the control of expenditure only by the overwhelming size of their tasks, rather than by any lack of competence. This chapter discusses the powerful group between the middle and the topmost grades, which is made up of four levels – principal, assistant secretary, under secretary and deputy secretary, and especially the central two levels – and others of equivalent grades wearing a variety of different labels, including regional directors, controllers, chiefs of this and that (the titles vary). As a very rough guide, there are between 150 and 200 in the deputy secretary or equivalent grades, and between 700 and 800 in the under secretary and equivalent grades.[1]

This block which, in the pre-Fulton era, was largely made up of the administrative class is responsible for information and opinions going upwards to Permanent Secretaries and Ministers and for direction and management going downwards to the remainder of the Civil Service. Between them they control nearly all the day-to-day conduct of affairs and a large part of such influence on policy as is had by the Civil Service. When the media and the politicians foam at the mouth with baffled rage and fury over the incompetence of civil servants or their obstruction of policies, these are normally the people they are talking about. If there are to be changes in the Civil Service, more particularly of a kind which will increase efficiency and reduce waste, this is the place where the changes need to be made first.

Ex-Ministers of both parties, who might be expected to know

1. Staff gradings and numbers are shown more fully in Figure 1 (p. 19).

the problem better than most, are in significant agreement about the need for such change and there is an embarrassment of raw material available on the subject. From it I have chosen two examples. In 1973, at the time of my retirement, Mr Nicholas Ridley, MP,[2] wrote a pamphlet which was so apposite that I quoted from it in my letter to Mr Wardale (pp. 74-6). He said:

The British Civil Service is sometimes compared to a flywheel; to slow it down or speed it up immense effort is necessary; it has a vast inbuilt momentum of its own. Rather, I think, it is like an enormous steel spring; it can be pulled out of its natural position by great exertion but it eventually pulls you back by its sheer persistence. Thus, towards the middle and end years of each government some of the same policies begin to appear whatever the reforming, even crusading nature of the incoming government. Undermined by the system, exhausted by the workload, battered by events, they relax their pull upon the spring and are pulled back, themselves, to the position the Civil Service always wanted.

He went on to describe how, in his view, a Conservative government's efforts to reduce expenditure by cutting staff at the Atomic Energy Authority, for example, had been blocked by civil-service opposition, and he produced some evidence (there has been much more lately) that the supporters of Labour governments feel the same about the frustration of their policies.

On 11 June 1977, while I was writing this chapter, there was a BBC programme entitled *Talking Politics* which sought the views of a number of people on this and allied topics. In the course of it Mrs Barbara Castle[3] spoke of the 'entrenched lethargy' of senior civil servants and of obstruction to Ministers' wishes being 'manifested in incomprehension and disbelief – hostile disbelief'. Whether or not you like Mrs Castle and her politics, the fact is that she was a powerful and senior Minister with great experience when she met this kind of reaction from civil servants.

2. Hon. Nicholas Ridley, MP (Cons.) for Cirencester and Tewkesbury. Parliamentary Secretary, Ministry of Technology, June–Oct. 1970. Parliamentary Under-Secretary of State, DTI, 1970–72.
3. Rt Hon. Barbara Castle, PC, MP (Lab.) for Blackburn. First Secretary of State and Secretary of State for Employment and Productivity, 1968–70. Secretary of State for Social Services, 1974–6.

In the same programme there was an interview with Mr William Whitelaw.[4] His experience was that civil servants operated in this field by postponement and delay, hoping that their Ministers would forget. He said that he had found it necessary to extract promises from these civil servants about dates by which action would be taken and then make a note in his diary in order that he could keep checking to make sure that things were done as promised. Whether or not you like Mr Whitelaw or his politics, he, too, was a senior and experienced Minister at that time.

There is a common thread running through these comments, although for me Mrs Castle's diagnosis of 'entrenched lethargy' is the one which takes the prize for accuracy and penetration. Do not the events described in earlier chapters provide evidence of precisely this failing? Is there not evidence of Ministers having to call for reports on progress in order to try to ensure that their instructions were being followed – and still not succeeding?

The comments made by these ex-Ministers related to the difficulties in putting over new policies, that is to say, matters on which the Ministers would expect to be well-informed and up-to-date, perhaps operating on a mandate from the Cabinet or implementing a party strategy which had already been developed to some extent. They would be in a position to take a close and continuing interest in progress. If they meet the kind of opposition they have described in this field, what hope is there for an effective performance in the field of continuing expenditure, where their sanctions and approvals are not needed and about which, for the most part, they can know nothing? And if they are badly placed inside the departments, how much worse is it for the Public Accounts Committee operating from outside?

I do not believe that there is within the Civil Service a left-wing Socialist philosophy which tries to frustrate Conservative Party politics or a right-wing Conservative philosophy whose exponents set out to frustrate Socialist ones. It would probably be easier to cure the troubles if this were so. The problem is that this powerful group of civil servants resents and opposes change of

4. Rt Hon. William Whitelaw, PC, CH, MC, MP (Cons.) for Penrith. Secretary of State for N. Ireland, 1972–3. Secretary of State for Employment, 1973–4. Deputy Leader Opposition, from 1975.

any kind. As with the Fulton Report it will only implement acceptable proposals.

This resistance is not active: civil servants do not meet in order to pass resolutions in favour of defending the status quo. It all comes about quite naturally. If there is a proposal for saving money, questions arise about the validity of the proposition. If those questions can be answered, then the next stage is to raise doubts about their applicability and, therefore, their importance outside a very limited field. If that fails, the timing can be queried – is it right to do this just at this time? From there it is possible to find all sorts of other reasons for delay: for instance there are no staff available to do what is necessary to show that there are too many staff!

Why should this be? What are the circumstances which make it possible? First there is an absence of reasons why it should *not* be. There is no profit-and-loss account and no competition. Failure to respond to change is not peculiar to the Civil Service, but outside the public sector even the household names in industry and commerce suddenly find themselves bankrupt or taken over if they do not compete and perform satisfactorily.

Second, there is the already-noted absence of accountability for everyone, either individuals or organizations. Individuals are protected by the absence of clearly defined responsibilities. Departments are protected by the Official Secrets Act, their enormous size and the virtual impotence of those who are supposed to have some responsibility, however limited, for investigating them.

Third, there is the immunity from personal consequences which almost complete job security guarantees even in the unlikely contingency of the failure of the first two lines of defence. From this stems the kind of civil-service inertia about which the Ministers complain with, I believe, every justification.

Another facet of this inertia is the established consensus of traditional opinion on any given subject within a department which someone has christened 'the Departmental View'. It is essential that a Departmental View should not be obviously wrong – indeed it may be right or it may have been right in the past but in any case it must be defensible, at least against any superficial questioning. Once enshrined as the official line it becomes a painfully slow business to make changes. To quote Mr Ridley again:

> This feeling that it is the repository of ultimate wisdom causes the Civil Service to be very slow to alter major policies. To overthrow conventional Civil Service wisdom requires a political determination which British Governments rarely possess . . . The case for change has to be proved beyond peradventure before it can be contemplated.

Ministers and Permanent Secretaries tend to get fed on an exclusive diet of Departmental Views and it is not easy to see how it could be otherwise. They do not have the time or the opportunity to go back to first principles and re-examine everything the departments do. Departmental Views are accepted for a good portion of the time.

In its most malignant form 'the Departmental View', or civil-service inertia, or 'Entrenched Lethargy' – take your pick, they are really all the same thing – causes civil servants to refuse even to make an examination of facts which might result in proving the need for change. (Was there not some evidence of this in the response to maintenance surveys and proposals for reductions in the car service?) It is these responses which produce the kind of civil servant who has an administrative and managerial Maginot Line mentality. In turn such civil servants prop up and defend the system which provides the protected environment within which they can flourish. This does not apply to the whole of the higher Civil Service. Many are hard-working and, within the limits imposed by the system, effective in their jobs. There is, however, a substantial proportion, concentrated particularly in the assistant and under secretary grades, who are a dead weight on the Service and on their colleagues above, below and alongside them. These are the men who are able to turn out a well-written memorandum or make a well-phrased contribution to a discussion, both so shot through with provisions and hedged about with reservations that they can never be wrong. They are great people for committees and in this business they excel. Whenever anything new is proposed they see the possibility of complications and find it necessary to consult numbers of other people of their own kind. Their attitude to all things, especially to proposals for change, and, most of all, to proposals for increasing efficiency, is one of mildly amused unconcern. Enthusiasm is vulgar. Certainty about anything is probably irresponsible. They are the products of a system which was designed in the middle of the nineteenth century, and they have no relevance to the conduct of public business today. The salaries they draw are a waste of taxpayers' money and by blocking changes and improvements they cause the waste of immensely greater sums.

I have devoted a good deal of space to this group not only because this is the source of much of the troubles of the Civil Service but more especially because this is where diagnosis can be followed by a fair measure of cure. Some of the proposals in earlier chapters will help to get rid of diffused responsibilities and sharpen up accountability. The essential additional requirement is an instrument for breaking down the stone-wall defences, the skilful blocking, the smooth blend – as someone recently called it – of partly persuasive and partly evasive explanations.

14 The Treasury

In this chapter on the Treasury most, if not all, of the argument relates only to the restricted field of the control of public expenditure and the avoidance of waste in executing policies already settled. This is an important reservation in discussing the Treasury because it has functions other than the control of public expenditure and, even on that subject, has responsibilities and powers which go far wider, and in some ways are more important, than the areas with which we are concerned here.

For a long time the Treasury has enjoyed a considerable reputation both inside and outside the Civil Service as one of the most effective barriers against waste and extravagance. If there were criticisms of the way in which it conducted its business they were directed more towards its meanness or penny-pinching – criticisms which one supposes the Treasury would welcome as an indication that it was discharging its duties properly – than otherwise. How well does the Treasury continue to protect the public purse?

In answer to questions by the Public Accounts Committee about the role of the Treasury, the Treasury representative, quoted in Chapter 9, said there was an annual opportunity for the Treasury divisions to examine spending proposals at the time when Estimates were being approved. The department's Estimates which covered the Government Car Service had certainly been put to the Treasury every year for twenty-five or thirty years. The Estimates for maintenance work probably dated back for as long as there had been government building and, in their current form, certainly for forty or fifty years. The first fact to emerge, therefore, is that, leaving aside all questions of praise or blame, the Treasury, having had, at least in theory, repeated opportunities to take the kind of action or to ask the kind of questions that might have led to economies in these two fields, did not do so.

Is it right to regard this as a failure on the part of the Treasury? The Treasury representative said:

As a general proposition we come up against the difficulty that departments and their accounting officers are there to handle things and there is a limit to what the Treasury, as such, can do by way of getting involved in detailed management.

The chairman took this even further. He said, and was obviously restating commonly accepted practice: 'I agree, of course, that the Treasury does not want to get into the area of management'. That view is consistent with what the Treasury and the Public Accounts Committee have been saying for years and is consistent also with the role of the accounting officers.

To accept this is to rule out the Treasury as an effective contributor in this area of expenditure controls. Management, for which the Treasury disclaims responsibility, is what is at issue. There are no questions of policy in this, save the general, over-riding policy of all governments at all times that public money shall not be wasted, and that is not in dispute by anybody, any-where. There is no difficulty about enunciating the policy of wise spending, avoiding waste, and getting value for money. It is executing the policy – the management of it – which gives rise to the problems. The kind of waste involved in both the mainten-ance work and the Government Car Service was precisely of the kind that comes from a lack of proper detailed management.

The Treasury representative did record the hope that the Treasury might say or do something at Estimates time, but not with any great conviction or certainty. And nothing was brought out in the evidence to suggest that there had been anything unusual or any unfortunate temporary lapse in the procedures or anything of that kind.

But is there any reason to suppose that Treasury intervention ever could and should be effective even in this limited way given the current range and scale of public spending? Critical scrutinies of this kind can only be made on the basis of fact-finding, and even if the Treasury had the inclination to make detailed investigations inside departments, and departments had the inclination to let them (and neither is true) they lack the means. They do not have the staff capacity to conduct such fundamental investigations. We have already seen how professionally qualified men could spend weeks looking at maintenance problems and still be unable to unearth possibilities of economy. What hope then for a Treasury representative with no qualification or skills in this field and infinitely less time at his disposal?

Very occasionally luck or circumstances drop the kind of information into the hands of the Treasury which can be effectively used. Had there been some other organization running a car service to which the Treasury had access, it might have been possible to set up a series of comparisons, always a favourite ploy of the Treasury's, and this might conceivably have helped them along the way. But even this is unlikely to have done what was needed. The most probable result of such an examination would have been a comparison of mileage costs. It is very unlikely that it would have revealed that most of the mileage, whatever it cost, was being wasted because it was being used on carting junior staff around and that this was all quite unnecessary. That, again, could be got at only by the detailed examination of the facts on the ground.

The Treasury can, of course, and does from time to time pick up the weaknesses and waste revealed by Exchequer and Audit Department and subsequently dealt with by the Public Accounts Committee. But, in doing this, it is really acting as little more than a spokesman for effective action taken by others. For the most part, therefore, it seems that the Treasury role in this field has become so limited as to be almost non-existent.

This would probably have happened anyway as a result of the rapidly rising tide of government functions and expenditure, but any slender prospects that there might have been for the Treasury to keep up some semblance of its traditional duties were slaughtered by the Fulton Committee. Once the Treasury had been emasculated by the removal of its control over staffing and allied matters to the Civil Service Department it ceased to have any opportunities whatsoever to act effectively in this area.

In the late 1940s or early 50s Sir Edward (later Lord) Bridges, then head of the Civil Service, delivered a public lecture during which he said that the Treasury role was changing in relation to the spending departments, whose financial activities could no longer be monitored as closely as had been the case in the past. This worried the PAC, which called Sir Edward before it to explain what he had said and implied. In the exchanges which followed, interest centred particularly on one phrase which Sir Edward had used, 'withdrawing the legions from the frontiers'. He was referring to the Treasury legions manning the financial defences at the frontiers against the spending department barbarians. (It was rather daring, then as now, for a senior man to draw financial and managerial parallels from a period as recent as the fall of Rome. Early and middle Greek history provided a more usual source.) The PAC was eventually persuaded that these words should not be taken too literally or seriously and that there was nothing to worry about. But I suspect that Sir Edward was right the first time, and that he had noted the beginning of a process which has been going on ever since, as the public sector grows in size and complexity and the Treasury task grows steadily less manageable. At the risk of doing the metaphor to death, if, in 1950, the legions were being withdrawn, in 1977 the barbarians are rioting and carousing through the city centre.

15 Exchequer and Audit Department and the Public Accounts Committee

Government departments get their spending money from Parliament, which gives it to them in the form of a series of Votes. The Votes are divided into categories or classes and numbered. Each Vote – and a spending department may have one or many – has a defined and limited purpose for which the money can be used. This is called 'the ambit' of the Vote. Generally the money voted is subdivided into a number of categories called subheads, each relating to a separate and specific purpose.

To take an example at random from the accounts for 1974–5, class 11 covers Health and Personal Social Services and contains four separate Votes. Vote 1 deals with Health and Personal Services in England, Votes 2 and 3 relate to Scotland, Vote 4 to Wales, and there are separate subheads and groups of subheads within the Votes. Current advances to health authorities are kept separate from capital advances; dental services from ophthalmic ones; expenditure on vaccines and drugs from grants to training colleges. There are a good many rules which control the ways in which money can – or more often cannot – be switched from one subhead to another.

Each Vote relates only to the current financial year, which runs from 1 April to 31 March, and the Votes show the allocation of money in this way. On the other hand, a great deal of expenditure involves continuing commitments, and the division of the supply of money into one-year blocks is largely artificial if not totally meaningless.

At the end of each financial year every department produces its annual account, the Appropriation Account. Using as a framework the same Votes and the same subdivisions of Votes described above, each department records how it has spent the money allocated to it under those headings. The Appropriation Accounts differ from those of a commercial company because, with a very few exceptions, they deal entirely with cash. That is, they record only the money received and the money disbursed during the course of the year without any regard to capital investment or money owed to others or money owed to them by others. There is no balance sheet and no profit-and-loss account.

In order to ensure as far as possible that the Appropriation Accounts tell Parliament what it needs to know about the way the money voted has been spent, there has accumulated over the years a rich variety of rules governing the presentation of these accounts and of the explanatory notes that go with them. Most of these derive from particular cases, many of them in the distant past, which have caused the Public Accounts Committee to decide that in future it needs to keep a sharp eye on this particular type of transaction. Any kind of loss of money, for example, has to be treated specially and so do things like thefts and fires. There is yet another category, called 'constructive' losses, where the public service receives something less than full value for money spent. But that general proposition, too, is hedged around with many provisions. The civil servant who wrote the rules on that particular subject, clearly having no illusions about the world he lived in, hastily added that it would not, of course, be practicable to record all such cases; an obvious example of impracticability being those instances where because an officer was inefficient the public service got less than full value from his salary!

In the bad old days when monarchs had a free hand, skulduggery with public money and the false accounting for it were commonplace. As a result, the chief function of Exchequer and Audit Department when it was created was to take care of the propriety of the accounts work of all departments. This is still a primary responsibility. All through the year Exchequer and Audit staff are keeping tabs on the way accounts records are being made up, noting those items which appear to require special treatment in the Appropriation Accounts and generally putting themselves into a position where they can say that the department has properly accounted for the monies for which it is responsible. In order to discharge these responsibilities effectively

Exchequer and Audit staff are attached to departments and have access to all official papers.

In the twentieth century this book-keeping audit is largely a waste of skilled staff time in E and AD. Whatever other faults it may have, the modern Civil Service does not go in for fiddling the petty cash. In any case, modern accounting techniques mean that too many people would have to be involved. Departments could well be left to keep their own accounts, no doubt making occasional unimportant mistakes in the process. What is more important is that E and AD staff would be freed for constructive work.

The Vote for Health and Personal Social Services, England, 1974–5, already used as an example, will serve also to illustrate the futility of much of this detailed accounting work. This one vote deals with gross expenditure of nearly £3400 million per annum and receipts of nearly £235 million, which, even by government standards, is fairly big money. Against that background, consider some of the items in this account.

Subhead A6 shows that £10 was voted by Parliament for bank charges and was not spent. £2010 was voted for grants for Civil Defence to local authorities. Subhead F6 deals with 'enquiries, tribunals, committees', which seems comprehensive until we come to subhead F7, which deals with 'other enquiries'. The difference between 'enquiries' and 'other enquiries' is unfortunately not defined, but the expenditure was stated – all £1479 of it!

Many of the explanatory notes are also good value for the discerning reader. On subhead E3 £9000 was provided for the Malaria Reference Laboratory, but only £3321 was spent. A special footnote to the account explains this in the following terms: 'E3. Expenditure was less than expected.' We must hope that not too much overtime was used in thinking up this ingenious and informative explanation.

Another sizeable chunk of the account is taken up with notes on losses. Of the twenty groups listed, seventeen are under £10,000 each, and most of these deal with individual items of a few pounds each. It all wastes time, and, worse still, by swamping the accounts with useless information obscures the information which does matter.

There is no reason why all this clutter of useless detail should not be scrapped. Exchequer and Audit Department could be kept informed by departments and use their discretion to decide when, if at all, items should be published. The pressure on Parliament is such and government expenditure is so great that there is probably a good case for not recording separately, save in exceptional circumstances, any item of expenditure of less than £100,000.

In any case, it is not usually this book-keeping role which produces the kind of inquiry which can end up before the PAC. Exchequer and Audit staff also monitor a wide range of other activities directly related to the spending of money. They might, for example, inquire into an apparent breach of rules requiring competitive tendering for a contract or a decision being taken to spend money by someone who, in the light of the department's own rules, had no authority to take it. Certainly they could have inquired into any of the forms of waste which were discovered by the maintenance economy teams. Is Exchequer and Audit Department, then, the effective defence against waste for which we have been searching?

The answer is that it is to a very limited extent, and could be to a very much greater extent. And the reasons for the limitations are fairly simple. The first and most obvious is that E and A staff are too few. A hundred years ago the department had a staff of about 120. Today they have just over 500. In that same period government expenditure has grown from just under £40 million to £37,000 million a year. Even allowing for inflation this is a hopeless situation, more especially when you bear in mind how much of the available staff time is absorbed in the purely routine book-keeping duties referred to earlier. The amount of staff capacity left for the more constructive forms of criticism, for investigations in depth and the fact-finding which is needed to overcome the neglect of years and the departments' defences is negligible.

More and more, auditors have had to rely on leads supplied from other sources, including activities within the departments themselves, as in the case with the maintenance economy surveys and with the car service. There is nothing wrong with picking up that kind of lead and it is still a vitally necessary function which, in the circumstances, no one other than E and AD can perform. There is, however, a need as great or greater for the initiation of inquiries by E and AD. At the current staffing levels this is often out of the question. It is doubtful whether E and AD staff allocated to the PSA or the Ministry of Public Building and Works could have sustained for one year just one of the teams involved in the surveys.

Nor is this the only limiting factor placed on E and AD functions. Whether from some uncertainty about its powers in relation to the spending departments, or whether it has become reluctant to antagonize those departments, the fact is that Exchequer and Audit Department approaches its role in a markedly diffident manner. It is not that its staff can be bullied or frightened off, or that they lack persistence when they believe that they are on the right track in any inquiry. But if, for example, E and AD staff find money being wasted on heating an empty building and they feel that this should be pursued, they are likely to address an audit reference sheet to the spending department in terms rather as follows:

'In the course of a visit to establishment ABC it was observed that five buildings once used for storage purposes were still being heated. As a result of inquiry it was ascertained that these buildings had been empty since 1923 and have been heated continuously throughout that period until the present time. Will you please confirm that this is in accordance with the Department's policies?'

This way of working is not without its advantages, because, as they are merely asking a question, it cannot be objected that E and AD are telling a department that it is at fault and making judgements by implication. There are circumstances in which there is a reasonable explanation to what appears at first sight an unjustifiable state of affairs. By asking a question instead of making an assertion the auditors are saved from making a mistake and losing face. But when this approach is coupled with the kind of timetable involved in E and AD operations the whole process begins to take on the atmosphere of a stately minuet rather than an exercise in chivvying management to make sure that taxpayers' money is not being wasted.

The reason for that is that if the audit reference sheet reveals that the building in our imaginary example should not have been heated for the last half-century, and if further inquiries by the auditors reveal more instances of this and, therefore, some weaknesses in the department's arrangements, although the department may voluntarily bestir itself, Exchequer and Audit Department can do nothing for the time being. Only after the Appropriation Accounts have been prepared at the end of the financial year can the Comptroller and Auditor General (C and AG), using the evidence provided by the reference sheets (some of them perhaps going back to earlier years) and the department's answers to them, produce the kind of report paragraph which we have referred to in earlier chapters and which are reproduced in Appendixes 1 and 4.

If we go back to the example of the Government Car Service, the C and AG published his report on the basis of expenditure incurred in the financial year 1974–5. As a result of the time needed first to prepare and then to publish the Appropriation Accounts and his comments on them, and to put in train the proceedings of the PAC, it was not until May 1976 that PSA representatives could appear before the committee. It was getting on towards the end of that year before the account of the proceedings could be published together with the comments of the PAC. While it may just not be possible to work faster than this, given the current methods of working by E and AD, this timetable suggests a lack of urgency which does nothing to help the drive for economy.

If Exchequer and Audit Department have their difficulties, those of the Public Accounts Committee must be regarded as even greater. The fact that it is composed of Members of Parliament means that, even before they start on their PAC duties, they have a frighteningly heavy load of responsibilities. The problem of finding the time to attend the committee even without doing any homework must, for many of them, be formidable. And attending the committee hearings is the least demanding aspect of their duties.

Accounting officers are able, as I have described, to prepare for their appearances before the PAC. The accounting officers normally deal only with one or two subjects relating to their own department. The PAC members, on the other hand, cannot spend months preparing. They have no great fund of information about each department available to them, nor a detailed brief on the particular subject before them. Not for them either the luxury of being able to concentrate on one subject or one department.

On 10 May 1976, the day that the PAC examined the PSA in connection with the car service, it also examined witnesses from the Ministry of Defence and the Civil Service Department in connection with the implementation of new computer projects. Next it examined witnesses from the Department of the Environment and the Ministry of Defence in connection with delays in revising rents for accommodation occupied by sponsored organizations in Germany, an inquiry which ranged over a wide area including problems arising from monetary rates of exchange. This, in turn, was followed by yet another inquiry, this time into the construction of low-speed wind tunnels for the Royal Aircraft Establishment in Farnborough, which involved some complicated technical problems.

To these disabilities must be added the fact that the membership of the group of MPs from whom the committee was nominated was constantly changing. Of the fourteen Members of Parliament nominated for the committee on 18 December 1974, eight had been replaced within twelve months and one, who was only appointed on the 24 January, was off again on 1 May. The rapid turnover amongst accounting officers which we have already noted is matched amongst those to whom they are accountable.

In Chapters 8 and 9, which deal with the course of the proceedings before the PAC relating to the maintenance economy surveys and the Government Car Service, there are listed the kinds of questions which could have been asked and which would have made the examination far more effective. Considering the difficulties under which the PAC and E and AD operate, the wonder is, not that the machinery works as badly as it does, but that it works at all. The most pressing prerequisite for a less wasteful and more cost-conscious public service must be the replacement of this part of the governmental procedural machinery.

16 The New Audit Department

In the public sector there are no balance sheets and no profit-and-loss accounts, no bankruptcy proceedings for the totally inefficient, nor the shake-up of boards of directors, nor take-overs by other companies. The products of government departments are, for the most part, services which cannot be priced out of the market and for which there is no alternative source of supply. Whatever changes are made, therefore, in management structure, there remains in the public sector the need to replace the checks and balances, the spurs and the penalties of the private sector with some kind of alternative.

This alternative discipline must be imposed on spending departments from outside; for our purpose self-discipline is likely to become ineffectual or to amount to no discipline at all. It is very probable and very understandable that departments will not like this kind of intervention, which they may regard as interference. The public interest urgently requires that such objections, if made, should be over-ridden by Parliament.

Understandably, too, criticism from outside and the exposure of weaknesses and shortcomings will not be liked by those who are the subject of these investigations. Nevertheless, while understanding the objections, it must also be understood that widespread waste of public money and the community's resources will continue until there are more effective means, first, of revealing and then, subsequently, of curing inefficiency and waste. This chapter deals with the kinds of changes which would help to bring about an improvement.

Limited though the activities of Exchequer and Audit Department have been as a result of the inadequacies listed in the preceding chapter, they have achieved a certain amount of success in the fields in which we are interested and have traditions and techniques of the kind which are required. E and A D would, therefore, provide the best foundation on which to build the kind of organization that is necessary, providing that it can be modified to meet the challenge and the needs of the present day.

To begin with, its terms of reference need to be changed or clarified. It must cease to be a detached, uninvolved recorder of facts, careful to avoid all suggestions of criticism, praise or blame in its observations of the activities of the departments. It must be seen not only to be entitled to inquire closely into all aspects of management, but to be operating under a clear obligation to do so. Departments must come to terms with a situation in which a newly formed E and A Department (which, in order to avoid confusion will be referred to henceforth as the New Audit Department or the NAD) would, as a matter of course, inquire into management decisions, or lack of them, and the consequences of both.

It may be argued that this would place managements in an intolerable position and that the net result would be damaging to the efficiency of the public sector rather than an improvement. There is no reason why this should be so. For a long time government departments have been liable to questions in Parliament or correspondence direct from MPs seeking information about what they have done and why they have done it. This has presented no difficulties in practice, though it does impose a moderate extra work-load on departments.

The New Audit Department, on the other hand, would use its direct access to papers within each department to make its own inquiries and do all its own researches. Any extra burden on departments arising from their activities should not therefore be as great as it would at first seem. None the less, if there is an extra work burden, and it does cost time and money to meet the new demands, then the extra time and money must be found in the reasonable certainty that, before long, handsome dividends will be paid on this investment.

In 1969–70 we calculated that the once-for-all cost of each Southern Region survey was repaid between twenty and fifty times on implementation of the economies, and at the same rate for every year thereafter.

Next, the use of the formal procedures involving audit reference sheets in the way already described (which at present is almost the only form of contact between E and AD and spending departments), though being retained for special purposes, should cease to be the normal way of conducting business. At all levels business between the NAD and the departments it audits should be conducted both in writing and orally as it would be between two spending departments. The NAD should be ready to offer criticisms and pass opinions and make assertions and the spending department should have the same rights. Communication between the two departments should much more nearly approach an ordinary dialogue than is the case at present. Spending departments should cease to be touchy about their rights and, indeed, they would no longer have any right to object. NAD staff should be less cautious in their approach, ready on occasions to stick out individual or collective necks and be wrong.

Next, using these much freer exchanges between the two sides, the NAD should be able to conclude agreements with the spending departments about the fact of waste, its extent where appropriate, and the measures taken to reduce it. It would not be necessary and, indeed, would normally be wrong under these arrangements to wait for the end of the financial year for the preparation of the Appropriation Accounts and the drafting and publication of a Report paragraph, in order to settle what is wrong and what needs to be done. Nor should it be necessary in the majority of cases to refer the facts to the PAC, with all that this involves. The whole process of investigation, discussion and correction should be much more informal and very much faster.

One problem which the new organization would have to face would be that there would come a point where their investigations and criticisms began to impinge, not only on the conduct and execution of policy, but on policy itself. For this purpose, the NAD would have to deal with all its activities in two parts. First, where the execution of policy is involved, that is to say, management in the sense that we have been using it in this book, there should be no restrictions or inhibitions. In many areas, this would be all that the spending department and the NAD needed to discuss and settle. Second, policies themselves can become outdated or other changes take place which call into question the rightness of original decisions. Since spending departments themselves cannot be relied on to take the initiative to bring about corresponding modifications of policies and practices, valuable opportunities for large-scale savings would be lost if the NAD were completely prohibited from entering this arena. Against this, it would lead immediately to overwhelming difficulties of all kinds if civil servants had a function which involved the public or private criticism of government policies. Most of the advantages could be retained and all the disadvantages avoided in this state of affairs if, when meeting a policy issue of this kind, the NAD reverted to its factual reporting role and merely stated, without comment, the financial implications of policy.

The extended role of the NAD would require a substantial addition of staff and I make no apology for suggesting that the increase needs to be of the order of three- or fourfold. Such a suggestion obviously invites the criticism that measures proposed for dealing with waste and swollen staff are themselves prefaced by an almost unprecedented increase in the size of a government department. The answer to this is that, although this is a very large percentage increase, the increase in terms of actual numbers of staff would be between 1000 and 2000. The reductions in staff numbers which I believe could be brought about over a period of years by the intervention of effective checks on management would be of the order of 40,000–50,000.

Almost any critical appraisal of the way in which management, especially in the Civil Service, is conducting its affairs must, from the beginning, involve consideration of staff numbers. In addition to its other staff reinforcements, therefore, the NAD should have added to it the staff inspection groups from the Civil Service Department together with all that department's responsibilities in the field of staffing levels in the Civil Service.

The next change in the role of Exchequer and Audit Department would be that it should be encouraged to emerge from the mists of anonymity in which it has, for the most part, operated hitherto. The public face of E and AD has, until now, been the coldly impersonal and formal C and AG's Report on the Appropriation Account. It would be desirable for the New

Audit Department to have discussions and negotiations with the spending departments and where possible to agree with them on changes in the department's way of proceeding. These agreements should not be in any way private and confidential. On the contrary, steps should be taken to give them wide publicity. For this purpose, an Annual Report should be published describing precisely which questions had been raised and the answers which were agreed. Where no agreement was concluded and further action seemed to be appropriate, the failure to reach agreement should also be recorded.

There are several reasons why publicity in these circumstances is desirable. First, it encourages those who are conducting the investigations and pushing through the initiatives which will yield savings to the public purse to find that, instead of labouring unseen for all the days of their official life, their work is not only being recognized but acclaimed. Saving taxpayers' money is news, and personal recognition for those who have served the public well should be given as a matter of course. Reports of potential economies uncovered and agreements to implement them made with spending departments should, therefore, carry with them the names of those principally responsible. It is the easiest thing in the world to call this a publicity stunt and poke fun at it, but there is not very much in the public sector that management can do to reward individual enterprise and initiative, and in my experience a measure of public recognition goes a very long way indeed. The obverse is also true: departments will be helped to improve their ideas on management if they find that, repeatedly, they are appearing in the Comptroller and Auditor General's annual report for wastage exposed by the NAD. Certainly publicity would cause ruffled feelings and hurt pride. So much the better. The remedy is in the hands of the spending departments. Let them look around and put their houses in order with all speed without waiting for the NAD to arrive and do it publicly. There is, also, a certain amount of educational value in disseminating information on the way in which economies have been secured.

It will probably be a great comfort to those who have doubts about the wisdom and practicability of all these suggestions to learn that, like everything else in this book, there is nothing new

in them. The General Accounting Office of the United States
under the Auditor General proceeds much in the way described
above and appears to have met and overcome all the different
kinds of difficulties which might be envisaged.

Consider, on the one hand, the lengthy ritual involved in the
inquiries on the Government Car Service, ending with an
HMSO publication of the PAC findings. Compare this with a
report taken at random from the General Accounting Office's
annual Report for 1974:

Cancellation of back orders. The Military Services could save more
than $100 million annually in transportation and handling costs and
in material purchases by more frequently and effectively invalidating
unfilled orders and removing past demands associated with invalid
orders from requirements computation. Unnecessary transportation
and handling costs of about $15·6 million were identified in a quarterly
invalidation. These costs were incurred because invalid orders were not
detected or were detected too late to stop shipment. Also $22 million of
material was purchased unnecessarily because invalid orders identified
during the quarterly examinations were not eliminated from past
demand histories used in requirements computations. The Department
of Defense agreed with our findings and have taken or plan corrective
actions which, if properly carried out, should bring about needed
improvements . . .

Despite all the regrettable officialese and gobbledygook the
message comes through quite clearly. Something was found to
be wrong; it was discussed with the department; and subsequently was put right. The savings are there for everyone to
see and so are the methods involved. And this forthright approach
is repeated endlessly throughout the Report. There are innumerable paragraphs beginning with headings such as 'Improvements
needed in use of formal advertising for Government procurement', 'Airmail improvement objectives unrealized', or 'Improvements needed in the overall management . . .' All in all, it is a
considerable advance on the Sixth Report from the Committee of
Public Accounts Session 1975–6.

One of the first tasks for the NAD which would have considerable value in its own right and would also provide a number of
useful investigatory leads into waste and unnecessary expenditure

would be the revamping of the annual Appropriation Accounts. Parliament has always attached a great deal of importance to the sanctity of the ambit of Votes, ensuring that nothing be spent and charged to a particular Vote which is not strictly appropriate to that Vote. For example, if a department had two Votes for a particular type of expenditure, one at home and the other overseas, and the expenditure appropriate to one was charged to the other, it would be regarded as a serious breach of the ambit of the Vote concerned and there would be much huffing and puffing in consequence, even though the money was spent quite properly in the public interest. To many this would be a book-keeping error of no great significance.

On the other hand, nowadays the ambit of the Votes seems to be sufficiently elastic, by everybody's consent, to allow with propriety expenditure which seems to bear no relationship at all to the ambit of the Vote concerned. Money voted for a particular purpose, for example a programme of scientific research, can be used not only for that purpose but for the other activities needed in order to enable it to function – the provision of the necessary office accommodation and furniture and the like. It can be stretched a little further to cover the lawns round the buildings, for these days staff need reasonable amenities and, as a good employer, the Government should play its part. But how far can this tolerance go on being stretched? Can it be extended to cover the maintenance of large, formal gardens which happened to be there when the organization took over its accommodation? Is it all right to spend a small fortune on rehabilitating an amusing architectural folly in the bottom left-hand corner of those acres of formal garden? There is a very wide range of expenditure of this kind and it accounts for a surprisingly large proportion of day-to-day routine costs. In consultation with the departments concerned, therefore, the NAD might begin by separating all such fringe expenditure from the department's main activities and showing this separately with suitable comments in the Appropriation Accounts.

Information of this kind, which both Parliament and the public might find instructive, and the publication of which the departments might find something of a deterrent, could well replace the existing notes on the Appropriation Account, which we observed earlier on in this chapter, and which deal, for the most part, with trivia. They do nothing to illuminate the dark corners of the areas with which we are concerned.

The NAD should be charged with one other vitally important task. While it should be accepted that it is not for civil servants, as we have already said, to comment on or criticize policy there can be no objections to the factual reporting of the financial consequences of a policy, at least in some areas, so that Parliament can make judgements on the value for money which such policy decisions achieve. Exchequer and Audit Department already do some very limited work of this kind but it is more commonly the sort of project which is undertaken at times by newspapers or crusading Members of Parliament. The NAD would do this as a matter of course over a wide range of government activities. At best it would lead to the ending of activities where the public was receiving poor value for money. At worst, it could at least assist Parliament, the Government and the Civil Service to be more cost-conscious and more aware of the financial implications of their decisions.

It goes almost without saying that the prospects for success of the NAD would depend almost certainly in the first few years upon the energies, abilities and standing of the head of the organization. As a general rule I am not in favour of bringing in people from outside to run civil-service departments. They are rarely a success. For the first five or six years of the life of the NAD, however, there would be benefits in having at its head someone of national status drawn, not from commerce or industry, but from the government field outside the Civil Service.

It would probably be as well at this stage to make it clear that this function of the NAD in stating costs, especially unit costs, will not only avoid infringing the policy-making functions of Government; it will also not overlap (though it might become complementary to) a similar function performed by the Treasury. In 1970 a very old technique for long-term thinking about expenditure was brushed up here and there, given one or two adjustments in the way it was used, and, most important, a new label, and was presented to the admiring world as Programme Analysis and Review (PAR).

These comments are not unfair. It is almost impossible to invent something new in this business. Too many good men here and abroad, in government, the Civil Service and industry, have trodden over the ground for anything much to have been missed. Mostly it is a matter of making small adjustments to existing techniques and then using them with renewed vigour. Anyway, new or old, P A R got off to a good start. The Prime Minister continually boosted it publicly, many top civil servants were doubtful about it, and the rest of us did not know what it was all about but were determined not to admit it, so its future in the short term, at least, was assured! P A R was always handled in a very secretive sort of way but the general idea was that all spending departments' programmes would, over a period, be analysed and costed. This would enable Ministers to make rational choices in policy decisions based on facts and, I suppose, this was the new element in the situation which attracted so much interest!

By 1973–4 P A R had lost a lot of its shine. This may have been due to the fact that in a good many instances there was some uncertainty about what could be done with the results of analysis. Whether the cost of educating a primary-school child turned out to be £200 a year or £10,000 a year, the one certain thing is that children are going to go on being educated just as they were before. However, whether P A R has faded away for this or some other reason, or whether it is still playing a vital if less publicized role, does not matter for the purposes of this chapter.

It is enough that the N A D function would be quite separate and distinct from P A R, though what is proposed for it could be regarded as complementary to P A R or its successors. P A R took as its starting point costs as they were, with a view to changes in those costs being made, if at all, by changes of policy. Doubts about costs and value for money and efficiency would be based on doubts about strategy. Change in strategy would come slowly if at all because the use made of the facts would involve opinions, which, even within parties, would often be mixed.

The N A D, however, and the P A C would work the other way around: they would accept the strategic policies as they are, but seek to ensure that they are carried out as efficiently and economically as possible. If, having done that, a statement of costs led on to consideration elsewhere of policy changes, all well and good, but this would be a gratifying bonus rather than the main function. There would also be a difference of scale. The NAD would steer clear of subjects which would involve prolonged or inconclusive debate. I cannot think, for example, that it would ever be right for it to start costing school places; the subject is too big and the prospect of progress too remote. On the other hand, it might well take a look at the cost per place of a student at the Civil Service staff college (an expensive white elephant from the day it began) or the Royal Military College of Science at Shrivenham. In each case the facts can be established and comparisons made, either with other parts of the public sector, or with the public services of other countries, or, where appropriate and practicable, with private industry. This having been done, Ministers would have alternative choices before them of a real and meaningful kind and could give a decision which would finalize things one way or another very quickly.

17   The New Public Accounts Committee

The establishment of the New Audit Department would need to be matched by comprehensive changes in the duties and powers of the Public Accounts Committee. The inability of the committee to pursue its questions, or to explore effectively below the immediate surface of the implied criticisms put before it by Exchequer and Audit Department, was demonstrated in Chapters 8 and 9. Committee members come and go and therefore frequently have too little experience to make an effective contribution. Indeed, knowing themselves that they are birds of passage, they may lack the inclination to become too deeply involved. Even if they are so minded, they usually cannot find the time which is needed to equip themselves adequately to question official witnesses or to reach satisfactory conclusions. It is not likely that, under present arrangements, this will change. The range of activities which is the proper subject for scrutiny by the Public Accounts Committee is far too large for any one man, even if he were working full-time and with undivided energies and enthusiasm for the committee, to go far beyond superficial inquiry.

This is not a view based on the admittedly small sample covered in this book. The evidence here is intended only to illustrate in more detail an assessment which now seems to be generally accepted, namely that the PAC is no longer effective in controlling public expenditure or, more particularly, as an effective barrier against waste and extravagance.

No one is more aware of this nor better placed to make a judgement than the Chairman of the Public Accounts Committee, Mr Edward du Cann, MP. On 21 December 1976, within a few months of the PAC proceedings described in this book, he made a speech in the House of Commons in which he warned

MPs that Parliament itself was failing in its duties. For some parts of this overall failure, notably the scrutiny of estimates, the Public Accounts Committee has no responsibility. But in the conduct of financial affairs after supply has been voted the PAC is the Commons' chief instrument. Mr du Cann's speech bears directly on many of the arguments of the book. He said:

I am a proponent of two things. The first is that in the British Parliament we should have effective systems of control. We do not have such systems. Secondly, I am a proponent of obtaining value for money. Alas, again Parliament in my judgement, does not sufficiently insist on this . . . We do not adequately scrutinise supply and we have not developed in Parliament the right institutions to monitor public spending . . . No wonder there is such cynicism about the way in which we conduct our activities in this House. Indeed *The Times* put it well the other day when it said that we had a Rolls-Royce of a machine but drive it like drunken drivers . . . What I complain about is the fact that the need remains as is obvious, yet still nothing continues to be done . . . I hope that you will agree that for the House to attempt to get better value for money is much the wiser course than our clumsy cuts in expenditure.

This House is failing in its duty and is failing the nation . . . what is the reality? It is that all the pressures are always continuously the other way, namely towards increasing expenditure. I reflect how little we parliamentarians truly understand the priorities of the parliamentary game. We must never forget that we are trustees for the taxpayer and we must see to it that his or her hard-earned money is properly spent.

This was not a point of view confined to the Opposition. Mr John Cronin, MP for Loughborough, replied:

I think that all Hon. Members would agree that there is room for more efficiency in public expenditure for some type of control to ensure that there is more frugality and prudence such as a housewife uses. It is certainly not used in every Government Department.

Mr Cronin had put his finger on precisely the kind of saving which this book has been about.

The first step, then, must be to reduce the size of the task facing any one MP or group of MPs on the PAC. This can be done by keeping the PAC very much in its present form while increasing its numbers and subdividing it into committees, each with its own special field of responsibility for inquiries. There is an almost infinite number of ways in which public expenditure can be divided up and the new responsibilities allocated, and it is unnecessary to specify subdivisions and allocations at this stage. The aim should be to make sensible groups of subjects of a size which are more nearly manageable than in the present hopeless situation. For this purpose a division into about five to ten groups would give the kind of structure for which we are seeking. The PAC sub-committees would want to decide this for themselves and could be changed in the light of the experience of the new way of working.

The load can usefully be lessened in another way. There are some superficial resemblances between the proceedings before the committee and other kinds of courts of inquiry, but uniquely the members of the PAC have to be prosecuting attorneys, sometimes defence counsel, frequently the jury and always the judge. It is a mixture of roles which does not serve the public interest well.

There will be those who will protest that even to think in terms of defence and prosecution for illustrative purposes is to misunderstand the functions of the PAC, and the position of those who appear before it. This must remain very largely a matter of opinion. If, however, even a small part of the case put forward in earlier chapters is accepted, then the size and the complications of the operations being examined by the PAC dictate that members need help in framing and following up questions. This is true when civil-service witnesses are anxious to help and even more true if they are defensive.

There is, therefore, an urgent need to assist the PAC through the maze and, where it is necessary, to fracture this defensive screen that surrounds the spending departments. The most effective way of doing that would be to separate the PAC quasi-judicial function from its investigatory ones.

The conduct of questioning must be taken over from PAC members by committee assistants, probably lawyers and sometimes accountants or management consultants, professions which need to be used far more in the Civil Service. They would put to the civil-service witnesses the kinds of questions needed to establish the whole truth of the case being examined. The committee assistant should come armed with an adequate brief provided by the NAD. He would have had adequate time to study it, obtain and digest all the facts, ask supplementary questions and in general put himself in a position where he could be an effective inquisitor. Once again there is nothing new in this way of proceeding and there is no reason why it should be regarded with repugnance by anyone. There is a vast range of subjects in the public sector of a good deal less moment than the kind of waste and extravagance with which we are concerned and which are dealt with in precisely this way. It is true that generally the civil-service witnesses would have a very much rougher ride than has been the case in the past, and for some the proceedings may be very disagreeable indeed. Nevertheless, if any real impact is going to be made on this problem of penetrating civil-service defences or of unravelling the facts of complex cases, this is the kind of assistance that the PAC *must* have.

Relieved of the necessity to take an active role in the questioning and with the questioning itself expertly directed to the nub of the matters giving concern, the members of the committee could act more effectively in what should after all be their real role: that is, to listen to the evidence and to decide whether any action needs to be taken and if so, what that should be.

Members of the committee would be as free as they are now to intervene as they wish, and to ask their own questions at any time. They need not feel that their powers and authorities in this field of investigation were being in any way usurped. Similarly, the proceedings should be sufficiently informal to enable civil-service witnesses to make statements on their own initiative. They might feel, for example, that the questions had not covered the points they would like to raise or that in some other way the line taken by the examining assistants was not revealing the whole truth as they saw it. Equally if they chose to make such a statement it would be open to the examiner to re-examine them on the points raised.

As is already the case, the principal witness from the Civil Service would be the accounting officer, except that he would now be the mini-accounting officer described in Chapter 12. Also, as at present, it would be open to the accounting officer to bring with him witnesses from his own department, either to give him supplementary briefing as the questioning proceeded or to appear as witnesses in their own right. It should be open to the examiner to confer with NAD representatives if he thought that it would help to get at the facts, and to take evidence from NAD witnesses before the PAC.

Despite the difficulties, the balance of advantage would lie in making public all proceedings before the PAC. The obvious objection to this, of course, is that there would be some lines of inquiry which could not be pursued publicly because of security considerations. There would also be other problems arising from what might be termed commercial security – matters like prices and special arrangements with commercial undertakings. But it should be possible to manage without any difficulty by holding that part of the hearing *in camera*. The problem is not very great. Very little of the proceedings before the PAC is omitted from the published evidence.

There would be considerable advantages in holding such public hearings especially if on suitable occasions the PAC decided that those proceedings could be televised. The public would be interested in what is being done to safeguard their position – and this is something about which taxpayers need reassurance. It is also very likely that the members of the PAC would themselves be more interested and effective, and more likely to strive for continuity of experience, if their contribution could be appraised by those whom they represent.

The subjects dealt with in this way by the PAC would fall into two groups. First, those matters referred to it by the NAD, and those in turn could be put to the PAC, for two reasons. There would be the important cases or those cases which illustrate a more general problem. Here the NAD might consider that the issues involved could best be dealt with by the PAC with all the authority of Parliament behind it. Then, there would be those cases where the auditors had had discussions with the spending department, had failed to reach agreement for some reason, but believed that the issues involved were not ones on which they were prepared to give way. In those circumstances, the PAC, after expert examination of witnesses, would in effect be acting as a court of appeal.

A safeguard against the over-use of this part of the PAC machinery would be the desire of both the spending department and the NAD to avoid going before the committee and taking the risk of having judgement found against them. There would, therefore, be a continuing incentive for both sides to reach reasonable agreements without recourse to appeal.

Secondly, the PAC should not be limited to the consideration of cases put to it by the NAD. To do so would be to give too much power to the auditors and too little to Parliament. The PAC must, if it is effectively to discharge its constitutional duty, be able to look into any matter of public expenditure of its own choosing. The committee would, therefore, retain and use as a matter of course the right to raise questions and initiate investigations itself. The pressure for such initiatives would come from a wide range of sources including topics raised in the House of Commons.

Usually the committee would find that the most convenient and effective way of pursuing these investigations would be to give a directive to the NAD. There ought, however, to be room for investigation to be carried out by other bodies of the committee's choosing, using any individual or group with a special expertise in a particular field.

There would be a number of advantages for proceeding in this way. In the first place it would bring fresh blood and fresh ideas into the investigative field which would generally help to stimulate thinking. This would be particularly good for the NAD, which would be presented with a form of competition, albeit somewhat limited, in the way in which it discharged its own responsibilities. Secondly, it would make the PAC to some extent independent of the NAD, and underline the fact that the committee was the principal in the organization and the NAD its agent rather than the other way around. Third, it would make extra investigative effort available without permanently increasing the staff of NAD.

There ought to be an unvarying rule in the public service that no one should make proposals for changes without putting a price tag on them and the proposals in these chapters for the NAD and the PAC ought to conform to that rule. If all the staff we have talked about were extra staff they would cost together with their ancillary services and overheads something in the range of £10–15 million a year. The most immediate question, therefore, is: is it worth it? According to the PSA spokesman in December 1976, that department was then saving about £12 million a year as a result of the savings on maintenance, and this figure, in the circumstances, is not likely to have been an exaggerated one. What it comes to, therefore, is that in one part of the works services budget, which in turn is one part of the budget of the PSA, itself a part of one department – in this fraction of fractions there has already been achieved an annual saving approaching the total cost of these new proposals.

It seems very unlikely, therefore, that at the worst the new organization could fail to pay for itself several times over. In reality it could be expected to perform considerably better than that. In any case, the extra 1500 staff for the NAD should be found from the 750,000 civil servants without adding at all to overall totals. I am not in favour of arbitrary percentage cuts for reasons which I will explain in a later chapter, but to the extent that it would be necessary to fill the NAD vacancies and provide some small secretariat for the PAC, the action would be justified in this case. Finding the staff initially and keeping them thereafter would be made both easier and cheaper in terms of overheads and travelling expenses if the NAD adopted a measure of regionalization for its extra staff. This would avoid the necessity for massive transfers of staff from the country as a whole to London. The auditors would be located near the places where their work would take them. On this basis the extra cost of these proposals would be only the costs involved in the extra services for the PAC, including the use of consultants and the fee for the examiners. For this a figure of £3 million per annum would probably be adequate.

18 The Official Secrets Act

Classification abuses. Executive order 11652 and its implementing National Security Council Directive of May 17, 1972, detail the requirements of strict adherence to classification and de-classification policies prescribed in those issuances. In particular they proscribe the use of classification to conceal inefficiency or administrative error, to prevent embarrassment to a person or a department, to restrain competition or independent initiative, or to prevent for any other reason the release of information which does not require protection in the interests of National security.

The wording if not the substance of this quotation indicates that it is not, sadly enough, an order which was made for use in the United Kingdom. The National Security Council referred to is the National Security Council of the United States of America.

It is difficult to believe that any responsible citizen in a democracy would wish to quarrel with the philosophy enunciated in this quotation. Yet the Official Secrets Act of 1911 which still governs the possession and communication of official information in the UK bestows rights on the Executive and penalties on citizens which are the exact opposite of the US law.

The first Section of the Act is unexceptionable. It lists offences of the kind which most people would expect a Secrets Act to deal with – entering prohibited places or making plans and drawings which might be useful to an enemy. In addition to specifying in detail what it is that constitutes a potential offence this Section makes it clear that the law is broken only if the person concerned acted as he did 'for any purpose prejudicial to the safety and interests of the State'. Under this section, in other words, guilt can be established only if action is coupled with felonious intent. There can be no doubt that the State needs these powers at least as badly in 1977 as it did in 1911, and if the rest of the Act was in keeping with Section 1 there would be no widespread demands for it to be changed.

The trouble comes from Section 2. First, having started as Section 1 did, with references to a 'prohibited place or anything in such a place' this Section goes on to bring within its scope *any* information of *any* kind which a person acquires as a result of 'holding or having held office under His Majesty'. Receiving unauthorized disclosures is also an offence under this section.

The second fundamental difference between Section 1 and Section 2 is that it may not be necessary to establish for Section 2 purposes that there was any unlawful intent.[1] The action by itself establishes the offence. It is, therefore, likely that a civil servant who without authorization tells his wife that his boss takes sugar in his office tea is committing an offence, and so quite probably is his wife for listening!

Such an all-embracing provision probably means that civil servants unknowingly breach it hundreds of times every day. One reason why these misdemeanours do not result in prosecution is that Section 8 of the Act specifies that a prosecution shall not be instituted except by or with the consent of the Attorney General. This is probably an adequate safeguard for those who believe in the wisdom of vesting in the Executive total discretion to decide what shall be done in matters which may be embarrassing to the Executive.

In 1971 the *Sunday Telegraph* and three other defendants were acquitted of charges brought under Section 2. In his summing up Mr Justice Caulfield said that the case:

may well alert those that govern us at least to consider if they have the time, whether or not Section 2 of this Act has reached retirement age and should be pensioned off . . .

Shortly after this the Government set up a committee under Lord Franks[2] to inquire into the working of the Act. The committee recommended that in place of Section 2 there should be a new Act which provided penalties for unauthorized disclosure of

1. The Franks Committee (see following pages) considered that there was 'still uncertainty on this point'.

2. British Ambassador, Washington, 1948–52. Provost of Worcester College, Oxford, 1962–76. Chancellor, East Anglia University, from 1965.

classified information relating to defence and internal security, foreign relations, currency and the reserves. Also covered, though in a different category, were information in connection with law and order, Cabinet documents, private information which had been made available to the Government in confidence, and official information used for private gain.[3]

These recommendations fall very far short of placing a statutory obligation upon governments to disclose information, but they would remove the most unsatisfactory features of the present law, and could therefore be expected to command a wide measure of support. So it appeared to be. The Conservative Government of 1972 generally accepted the Report and its recommendations but did not introduce a bill to give effect to it. The Labour Government announced in 1976 that a bill would shortly be introduced containing provisions generally similar to those of the Franks Committee recommendations, but this has still (1977) not yet appeared.

Much of the pressure on governments to reduce the element of secrecy in their deliberations and decisions has come from those who believe that a democratic society has the right to know what is going on, and indeed needs to know if it is to participate effectively in government. The arguments which support this point of view are widely available but have no place here. What then is the relevance of changes in the Act to this part of the book?

The answer lies in the quotation at the beginning of this chapter. The decision to forbid the use of secrecy to conceal inefficiency or administrative error in the USA was based on sure and certain knowledge of the dangers that secrecy can bring in its train. It is just as true in this country. There can be no shadow of doubt that the Official Secrets Act, as it is at present worded and used, contributes to the continuance of waste and extravagance on a massive scale in the public sector, and protects those who are responsible from the consequences of inefficiency, error and downright negligence. The reason for that is that the

3. The summary of the Franks Committee recommendations and some other facts used in this chapter are taken from 'Government Secrecy' by James Michael, *New Law Journal*, 19 May 1977.

use of the Act can be far more damaging than a total ban on the disclosure of information, however harmless to the State such a disclosure might be.

It is the possibilities for the selective use of the Act which are frightening. If, for example, there are ten factors affecting the proposition that $A = B$ and eight of them point to the conclusion that A does not equal B, while the other two factors indicate that there is a possibility that A does equal B, the Official Secrets Act can be operated in such a way that only the last two factors emerge. This in turn means that without anything untruthful being said an answer which is the opposite to the truth can be indicated as the reasonable one. It is not surprising that in evidence to the Franks Committee, Mr Justice Caulfield said that Section 2 of the Act 'could be viciously or capriciously used by an embarrassed Executive'.

There is no doubt that one of the reasons why waste and extravagance can flourish as they do in the public service in this country is that the operation of the Official Secrets Act prevents public servants and a great many others from speaking out as they would wish to do.

After the publication of the *Sunday Times* article of 19 December 1976, that newspaper was, to use its own expression, 'inundated' with answers to its invitation to people to send details of examples of waste which they had come across. Many of the letters were from civil servants, serving or retired, who applauded the article and went on to say that but for the Official Secrets Act they would themselves have liked to make similar contributions from their own experiences. The article in the *Daily Express* on 7 January produced 'a deluge of replies from readers'. The BBC Television programme *Nationwide* on 19 April 1977 produced a response which, according to the programme's managers, 'surprised even us'. But BBC Television ran into the same difficulty as the newspapers. Plenty of people wanted to say what they thought, but all of them were afraid of being quoted by name, and much of the material, therefore, was just not available for use.

The same was true of the letters and telephone calls which reached me at home. I did not quite get calls from Land's End to John O'Groats, but I came very near to it with one from central Cornwall and another one from northern Inverness-shire. Most of the people who got in touch with me were not members of the public. They were middle grade or senior staff of the public services who had reason in the past to be angered or outraged by the way in which the Official Secrets Act had prevented them from doing anything about obvious abuses which they themselves had uncovered. This indignation was at once a measure of the way in which the Act has interfered with proper administration in this country and a good omen for what may happen if these restrictions are removed.

There was no doubt that the indignation was genuine. One man had sat down to telephone long-distance and was going to work his way at his own expense through all the Chapmans listed in the Reading and district telephone directories. He was lucky that he reached me on the third call!

This book is concerned only with the financial consequences of unnecessary secrecy in the public sector, and there should be no room for misunderstanding on this point: while the Official Secrets Act is used as it is in this country, bungling and incompetence of all kinds can flourish undetected, and the taxpayer will pay dearly for this. The effectiveness of the NAD and the restructured PAC, described in the preceding chapters, will be assisted if these artificial hindrances to fair and accurate complaints by individuals, and most especially individuals in the public service, can be removed. There is no need to fear a flood of angry or cranky informers or people with imaginary grievances, though no doubt there will be one or two of these. As soon as the restrictions are lifted many of the events which now give rise to complaint will not happen.

Judging by experience in the USA, this removal of restrictions and their replacement by a positive right to demand information does not carry in its train any risks for the security of the State. The inter-agency classification review committee, in its report to the President dated 28 May 1976, says it believed it can be justifiably proud of its accomplishments in achieving a delicate balance between an informed citizenry and the protection of official information in the interests of national security.

One of the problems holding up a change in this law is the difficulty of framing legislation to provide in this country a legally enforceable right to demand information. There are difficulties though other countries seem to manage. But in any case it would be easy in the interim to remove the ban on the use of this type of information by those who already have it and do not need to demand it. It would be a pity if the pursuit of perfection in our version of open government prevented the removal in the meanwhile of a thoroughly bad piece of law.

Laws giving wider access to information are already enacted in several European countries and the Commonwealth, and are under discussion elsewhere. It is high time that steps were taken in the UK also to get rid of a device which can be used by the Executive to cover blunders, conceal extravagance and in general extend and perpetuate the kind of waste which this book is all about.

19 Parts for Early Treatment

If some or all of the proposals for change outlined in the preceding chapters could be agreed by Parliament in principle, what kind of timetable could be adopted and what kind of results could be expected to ensue?

It has become customary to say, and for many to accept, that these kinds of changes cannot happen overnight, and that what we seek is evolution, not revolution. But are these suggested changes so revolutionary? Much of what is being proposed is aimed at curing the kind of waste which, as the PAC said, ought to have been dealt with all the time.

The measures really fall into two parts. First, those which are designed to give the Civil Service and its management the opportunity to put things right for themselves. This includes making managers more realistically accountable, getting away from diffused responsibilities and management by committee and restating the responsibilities within the public sector for safeguarding the taxpayers' interests. All these changes, though essential, will achieve nothing by themselves. They must be supplemented, second, by the application of a sharp spur to set the reforms in motion. During biology lessons in schools before the war the standard demonstration of the working of some parts of the body involved taking a dead frog and applying electric currents to its muscles to cause it to twitch and jerk in such a way as to give a semblance of life. There are parts of the Civil Service which need a similar galvanizing effect. This could be achieved by the kind of investigations which could reasonably be expected from the NAD backed by the new PAC. If, in some cases, it seemed as if a form of violent shock treatment were being applied to some pretty dead-looking material, then so much the better.

There is no reason why it should take a long time to set up

this new galvanizing machinery. It would certainly lose some of its impact and impetus if it were allowed to be bogged down in endless discussions about trivia. None of the measures described needs much, if anything, either in the way of money or legislation to be put into effect. The exception might be the new arrangements for the PAC, and it will have several months' breathing space in any case before the NAD begins to produce its first results. There is no reason why all this machinery should not be working within six months, and if the Government wanted to do it quickly, a good start could be made in a matter of six weeks, rather than months.

Once the decisions in principle had been taken, the first steps should be to consult with the Civil Service staff associations and the trade unions representing industrial staff employed in the Government sector. This is not a matter of tactics or courtesy. Both groups have an absolute right to be consulted in these circumstances. The consultations would not relate to any matters involving new principles. Staff inspections both by departments themselves and by outside authorities, like the Treasury or more recently the Civil Service Department, are activities of very long standing. So are investigations and examinations by Exchequer and Audit Department, and there is no reason, therefore, why consultations at this stage should be a protracted business.

It must be borne in mind that the staff associations and the trade unions exist primarily to look after the interests of their members and the salaries of the officials of both groups are paid by subscription from the membership to safeguard themselves, not the public's interest. In the long term, of course, private and public interests coincide, and in my experience it was always recognized ungrudgingly that individual employees within the Government service, and the associations which represent them, have to have a proper regard for the public interest. But civil servants are human beings, and it is a fact that I cannot remember a single instance where a staff association proposed staff reductions. The most that could reasonably be expected from such bodies is the absence of active opposition. On the other hand I do not believe that any Government should accept the line that public sector staffs should not be cut in any circumstances. It should be enough to show that reductions can be justified, and can be carried out reasonably and considerately.

The two representative groups would be helped towards reaching a position of watchful neutrality rather than outright hostility by the way in which the proposals for economies would be researched, framed and put forward. The associations should be told that all proposals will be based on a thorough examination of all the facts and, special security considerations apart, consultation will be based on the disclosure of all those facts for examination and criticism. The implementation of plans for economies would be made only after there had been a reasonable opportunity for discussion, and if flaws in the proposals could be exposed and evidenced it would be in everyone's interests to make suitable modifications. While none of this amounts to a very agreeable offer for the representative bodies it ought to be infinitely preferable to them than the methods (especially overall arbitrary cuts) which governments of all kinds have tried to adopt in the past.

Arbitrary percentage cuts always miss their targets, whether they are applied in terms of staff numbers or money. They are exasperating for those to whom they are applied and often they produce a profound sense of injustice, which, because the wrong targets have been hit, is frequently justified. The alternatives now being proposed are rational decisions based on meticulously accurate evidence disclosed to everyone concerned. Economy measures built on this kind of foundation would command a very large measure of support both inside and outside the public service.

An essential prerequisite for winning even a neutral acceptance from the representative bodies would be safeguards for staff affected by these proposals. Staff must expect management to make reductions in staffing levels if this is what the situation requires. Equally management must expect staff to dig their toes in and fight hard if these reductions are imposed in an arbitrary or unsympathetic manner. After all, management must accept the responsibility (in some cases the word should be blame) for the need to make these economies. It is an intolerable position for staff to be told: 'You have been working here for the last fifteen years. We have suddenly discovered this Friday afternoon that we've been doing it all wrong and that you are not now needed. Don't bother to come next Monday.'

If anybody did that to me, I would be down at the gates on Monday morning with placards with the best of them. If management cannot accept the moral rightness of a reasonably sympathetic and considerate approach they will have to use it anyway because nothing else is practicable.

Without prejudging the results of the NAD activities, and leaving individual cases to be judged on the merits of the evidence, it would still be prudent to have some understanding with the representative bodies about the way in which matters would proceed if and when large-scale economies were found to be practicable in staffing levels, either industrial or non-industrial. I believe that the most useful preliminary step would be to agree on a procedure for natural reductions of staff which would largely avoid the need for redundancy.

Redundancy is an ugly and frightening word for employees. It was even at the time when the Southern Region surveys were in full swing, and the unemployment situation has worsened sharply since then. No manager can understand what is meant by redundancy until he has sat in a room full of men all worried, some of them hostile or bitterly angry, and discussed with them face to face proposals which he has initiated and which will lead many of them to face unemployment in the near future. The right to use redundancy proceedings must be retained by management as a last resort, but it can and should be avoided wherever possible. Large-scale redundancy can never be justified in the public sector in order to bring about a quick solution to a management problem.

Even in a fairly stable organization like the Civil Service it is surprising how many staff reductions can be achieved by natural wastage. People retire, die or fall sick, even sometimes find themselves jobs elsewhere. This can be supplemented in many ways by management. There is especially the use of measures which bring forward by agreement retirement dates for people nearing the end of their careers. The problem would be greatly eased also if departments could start to accumulate vacancies.

It would be possible then to start with a year or eighteen months of natural wastage in hand. Some part of any proposals for staff reductions could then be achieved painlessly merely by removing those vacancies from the approved complement of staff numbers. The principal difficulty in this way of proceeding is that it can quite reasonably be objected that action of this kind is prejudging the results of inspections. This may nevertheless be a price worth paying in order to reduce the redundancy problem. Alternatively, vacancies could be filled by temporary appointments. In a small way all these measures were used successfully in connection with the Southern Region surveys and no doubt in scores of other places inside and outside the Civil Service.

While these preliminaries were taking place the NAD would be preparing itself for its new and extended role. It would need to recruit staff from other departments and deal with the house-keeping arrangements: accommodation, communications and allied matters of logistic;

Here again, none of this need take much time and no excuses for delays should be accepted. In the past when the Government has given a clear lead and clear directives the Civil Service has acted quickly both in peace and in war time. The immediate task facing management and the NAD would be deciding where and how to start. It would be essential that they did not allow themselves to be daunted by the size of the problem facing them. They should not, in fact, be like the men set down at the beginning of the Forth Bridge with a pot of paint and a brush and told to get on with it. Their emotions should rather be those of fortunate men given the freedom of an Aladdin's cave filled with treasure stolen from and returnable to the taxpayer.

It would certainly do no harm at this stage if contributions and suggestions about economies of all forms could be sought from members of the public service and the general public alike. It probably would not produce anything very spectacular because of fears about the Official Secrets Act. But it would at least demonstrate a willingness to listen and to learn about prospects for savings, and it would be surprising if nothing useful was produced.

Having created in the last few chapters, at least on paper, the machinery which could dig out the facts and eventually produce economies, it would be worth considering next the type of programme which the NAD could tackle in its early stages.

It would be desirable to make a start without protracted discussion on long-term strategies and without even much pre-planning of individual inspections. A famous German general is reputed to have said that no plan, however good, survives the first encounter with the enemy. That applies to efficiency audits. It is better to get going and see what happens. Given the need to produce some savings of non-industrial civil servants to counter-balance the extra audit staff, a good starting point would be an attack on a malignant disease of public service staffing known as 'pyramidosis'. The symptoms are swollen staff complements accompanied by administrative flatulence. It's catching too! This is how it works.

If there are fifty staff doing similar jobs, they may need one supervisor or twenty. It depends partly on the nature of the work and partly on the staff and whether they constantly produce problems which require higher-level intervention or assistance. Professionally qualified people such as engineers or building surveyors, who in private practice might well be working without supervision for nearly all their professional careers, ought not to need much *professional* supervision. Nor, for different reasons in each case, should staff engaged on duties like repetitive clerical processes, driving, or welfare work. Scientific research, on the other hand, requires an abundance of higher-grade capacity. The effect of 'pyramidosis' is to inject into the organization layers of supervision which are not justified. Thus fifty staff – call them processors – who need only one supervisor will today have an organization chart which looks like this:

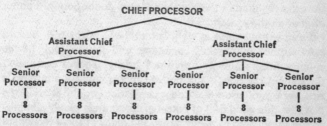

The chart should in fact look like this:

1 SENIOR PROCESSOR
|
50 Processors

It would be bad enough if all these unnecessary people just read a book or did crossword puzzles. But most are reasonably conscientious, and those who are not want to preserve appearances. So next it happens that each level has to start making regular reports to the next level up. The questions flow back down again and soon there is a need for typists, filing clerks and messengers.

If this pyramid is part of an organization which has counterparts elsewhere, there are opportunities for the little pyramids to coalesce, thereby providing even more and higher-grade processors. There are further opportunities still if the pyramids which are based on functions can be independent of, and additional to, some other management structure. If, for example, the fifty processors are part of a unit performing operations to which the processors contribute only a part, the unit will have its own management structure and may well include other functional pyramids. Either way there will then be almost limitless possibilities for clashes between management and the upper levels of the functional pyramids rushing to defend their special interests. Decisions which should take minutes drag on for weeks and months, while costs, in staff time and administration, soar upwards. The use of the accountable management structure is the best cure for this problem, provided the managers are given powers to lop off the tops of the pyramids. If the NAD made a determined onslaught it would save many times more staff than the extra required by the NAD itself, and do the Service a power of good in the process.

From extravagance in staffing the NAD might turn next to extravagance in physical conditions and take a look at the country houses already mentioned briefly. They are scattered throughout the length and breadth of the country and have a rich variety of uses. Such an examination would provide the NAD with a good deal of potential economy in purely administrative as opposed to policy terms, and many of these economies could be brought to a swift conclusion in consultation with the department concerned. No doubt there would also be a proportion of cases where departments refused to give up facilities which had been enjoyed for a long time. These would be suitable for consideration by the new PAC. The NAD would find that in the name of scientific research, defence, storage, training and other apparently sacrosanct causes quite considerable sums of money are being spent and have been spent for years in a way which merits a thorough re-examination from first principles.

What kinds of things would they find? To begin with all sorts of luxuries denied to most taxpayers. Expensive gardens and grounds; ornamental lakes; elaborate topiary; hothouses, conservatories and orangeries; sweeping lawns by the hundred; grassed areas in hundreds of acres; empty wasted land in thousands of acres; large buildings, expensive to heat, light and maintain; expensive panelling, moulded plaster work, gilded ceilings, mullioned windows; vast empty echoing marble-floored and pillared rooms; trout fishing and pheasant shooting.

The auditors will find some standard features in these expensive establishments. First, that they were provided regardless of cost in a society very different from the one in which we now live, for a tiny, privileged minority. Second, that these amenities continue to exist at a very high cost to the taxpayer and are still enjoyed by a tiny, privileged minority. Third, that a very great deal of the expenditure had nothing whatever to do, by any stretch of the imagination, with the official functions of the public service. Fourth, that the reason for this is that all these facilities were provided for millionaires and happened to be there when the Government moved in. Government employees have gone on maintaining these luxuries on much the same basis as was appropriate for the original owners.

By no means all the potential economies in the country houses will be in this area. Establishments which have been in existence for years in this type of environment attract excrescences (farms[1] and museums, for example), in the same way that sailing ships collect barnacles. The auditors would need to look at all the staff and money-consuming activities and consider how many of them are essential for the establishment to carry out its duties.

Such an investigation ought to produce results in three directions:

1. Economies in running costs which could be agreed with the department responsible.

2. The identification for Appropriation Accounts purposes of the costs of activities not essential to the functions of the establishment.

3. A statement of total costs for the establishment so that value-for-money judgements can be made.

Typical of the places at which the auditors would find themselves making inquiries of this kind would be the residential country retreat which is provided for padres of one of the armed services. Here a large old building, expensive to heat, clean and maintain, is surrounded by extensive ornamental gardens and grounds, also expensive to maintain. The auditors would need to get at the cost of this establishment, the whole cost, based on normal accountancy rules – not on civil-service methods – and consider with the users whether economies were possible. None of this should take long. Then the usage can be established. How many people are accommodated for how many nights? What is the cost per head? How does this cost compare with five-star hotel accommodation? Value-for-money comparisons would not necessarily stop there. At some later stage those responsible for defence policies and eking out limited allocations of funds might wish to consider how expenditure for this kind of establishment ranked with, say, the money needed for fighter aircraft or tanks, or improvements in service pay.

It is possible, therefore, that although the NAD would have no powers to do more than publish a statement of costs, departments might themselves decide to revise their policies before that happened. The Southern Region teams found very often that when they came to discuss wasteful practices, especially big ones, which had been going on for decades the department had by an

1. A desire to run farms (at the public expense, naturally) seems to be widespread in the public sector. The *Oxford Times* on 14 July 1978 carried a story and some pertinent editorial comment on the loss of £350,000 by the Thames Water Authority in its farming activities.

astonishing coincidence already had it in mind to take action and that the survey had merely anticipated something which was about to happen in any case. Auditors should always be suitably and even humbly grateful when this happens. It helps to give a tinge of propriety and respectability to their proceedings when their thinking is so much in accord with management!

After the lush pastures around the country houses an effective contrast would be provided by a look at the storage establishments, especially at the Ministry of Defence. There would be plenty of first-line economies to be found, and these could start yielding dividends quickly. Inefficient storage and handling of stores wastes a great deal of money in this country, both in the public and private sectors. Second, a longer-term process of rationalization, which would involve investing capital, would produce further savings which would more than justify the capital outlay. Third, in the even longer term, the basic philosophies of storage policies need to be re-examined in the light of conditions prevailing now, and it is here that the biggest savings of all would probably be found.

Next the NAD would turn its attention to the scientific and research establishments, which account for some £200 million a year and about 32,000 staff. It would be best to tackle these in three distinct parts. First, identify and implement standard management economies. This should be followed by the division of the residual expenditure between essential scientific/research expenditure, and staffing; and the remainder – expenditure on amenities and prestige. The third stage would be to take the expenditure analyses and to set these alongside an appraisal of what this expenditure had bought for the community in the last twenty years, and who precisely had benefited. The establishment concerned could make one such appraisal and others would be provided by that section of industry most concerned with the end product of the research. Assessments could also be made by other parts of the scientific community.

By themselves these would achieve nothing. The real evaluation would take place before the Public Accounts Committee with the experts being cross-examined by lawyers. The questioning should be directed towards determining not whether those asked would say that the end product was useful – no scientist is going to say that research is valueless – but rather whether it is worth what it costs and whether this is the best way of spending available limited funds. There are already advisory committees operating in this field.

The NAD could examine a more routine white-collar civil-servant activity – the collection of statistics. A number of government departments exercising a variety of powers, many of them compulsory and statutory, collect and process statistics of all kinds from the community. This is one of the growth industries in the government sector and currently requires a deal of official time and very much more time from those in the private sector who have to produce the data. The first line of inquiry by the auditors might be directed towards how much it costs to collect information from those parts of the community who do as they are instructed and answer the questions reasonably promptly and accurately. Given that it is necessary to collect statistics at all, it is possible that this inquiry will show that this part of the collection industry works reasonably well and there is not a great deal of room either for criticism or for improvement. But supposing something like 80 or 90 per cent of the potential suppliers of statistics answer reasonably and promptly, how much time and cost and effort goes into getting replies from the remainder? And are the results when the difficult and expensive sources of information are finally captured, and brought within the calculations, significantly different from the results produced by the inexpensive first category? Assuming that the second expensive category is necessary, is there some better way of collecting information from these reluctant subscribers than, for example, having civil servants touring round the countryside by car and paying calls on those concerned?

All these questions and more besides will relate to the execution of the policy by management and constitute the first line of inquiry by the NAD. In its new role it should then move on to examine the use which is made of these statistics. Of course they are put together, analysed, reassembled and issued in the form of reports. But this in itself is not making use of them. It is merely a change of form, and the auditors will need to know what use is made of them in the changed form. What happens as a result of the preparation of this data which would not happen otherwise? What evidence is there of any kind of government policy decision hinging on the information contained in these reports? Is there any evidence that government policy was deflected or changed as a result of what was revealed by these figures? It is likely that a dispassionate examination of the statistics-gathering process would show that much of it is a waste of time and money for the public, Government and Civil Service alike.

In presenting its purely factual report without suggesting conclusions or recommendations about policy the NAD would be doing no more than its duty if it reported equally factually the views of those in industry and commerce who are on the receiving end of the demands for information. The whole cost to the community – as opposed to the cost in civil-service terms – should be an essential part of the report and at this stage the NAD would bow out leaving the PAC to conduct hearings and take evidence from a variety of sources in the ways already discussed.

One of the convenient things about writing about waste in the public service is that there is no need to go searching around for the raw material. It arrives on the doorstep almost daily. While I was writing the preceding paragraphs an example of government data gathering reached me in my Welsh cottage. A circular letter explaining the need for information on travel habits was followed by a visit from a representative of the firm of consultants working on behalf of the Welsh Office. He brought with him travel diaries to be completed separately by every man, woman and child over five years old. The diary measures $8\frac{1}{2}$ in. × 6 in. and has twelve pages including two of detailed instructions for completion. It allows for 108 trips in seven days, each analysed under ten headings, with mode of transport also analysed under ten further headings. After completion the diaries were collected, again by hand. The data provided by these diaries will, no doubt, be used to provide, with the assistance of data-processing gadgets, a detailed report with a plethora of facts and conclusions. No one I have spoken to in our remote, thinly populated valley believes that anything will or should come of this. They also believe that if anything does it will not be in a form influenced by the bulk of these figures.

So many local people were ruffled and irritated by this questionnaire that I asked the Welsh Office to explain to me why so much information was being sought and gave as an example the question which asks retired people to state their last occupation. The only explanation forthcoming was that it might help to build up a picture of the kind of people we are. But my informant volunteered the fact that the Welsh Consumer Council had also questioned the way in which the survey was being carried out and its costs. A copy of the reply to the Council by the Department of Transport was sent to me. It is easy to imagine what a spirited defence would be put forward to justify a big survey on which big experiments were to be based. Does the reverse hold true? Not in the public service. Now it is the very fact that any future experiments are going to be small which becomes the justification for an expensive and detailed survey. The relevant paragraph reads:

Because we are necessarily dealing in very small numbers in measuring the impact of even the most ambitious experiments, it is essential to build up as full a picture as possible of the overall position before the services are introduced.

and:

... the Steering Committee's technical advisers give it as their considered professional judgment that in order to fulfil the objectives I have mentioned, exhaustive 'before' surveys are required in all the study areas.

How convincing it all sounds – at least it would but for two small snags:

(a) it emerges that the experiments have already started, without the benefits of the survey results. Those essential exhaustive 'before' surveys were, it seems, not quite so essential after all.

(b) After discussions between the Department of Transport, the Welsh Office, both at Ministerial and official level, the Transport and Road Research Laboratory, the firm of transport consultants carrying out the survey, the steering committee on road transport expenditure, local working groups, the Scottish Office and a number of other bodies, the two 'ambitious experiments' prove to be:

(i) using the empty places on school buses, and
(ii) using a post office van for an occasional passenger.

The foregoing proposals for looking into government statistics collection touches on the use of cars by civil servants, and another line of inquiry would be to extend this and inquire generally into the way in which civil servants use their cars for official purposes and what value for money the taxpayer gets as a result of official travelling. The NAD might start by finding out how many miles in a year a civil servant travels on average now compared with, say, ten, twenty or fifty years ago. If the amount of travelling has increased considerably, why is this? Has the nature of government work changed in such a way as to make it necessary for many more people to make journeys in order to carry out their duties? Official travelling should only be done if it is *essential* to the conduct of official business. The official expenses sheet stipulates this. Using sampling techniques, how true is this of the average journey? Would the public service be halted or even made much less efficient if travelling were cut by 50 per cent or even by 90 per cent, either as a result of an oil crisis or a government decision to impose such a cut for economy reasons? During the Suez crisis an almost total ban was imposed. Is there any evidence that that caused insurmountable problems? How much of the business carried out as a result of travelling could be as well, or nearly as well, executed by telephone calls? How much travelling has as its justification the kind of thing that is usually called 'showing the flag', 'keeping contact' and vague phrases of that kind?

A typical example of unnecessary travelling is described in the *Daily Telegraph*, 27 January 1976:

People in the property industry will have been amused, but not surprised, at the antics of the Government's Property Services Agency over the purchase of a £200,000 penthouse for our man (sometimes) in

Rio. The amusement will stem from the thought of 15 people travelling from the Southwark offices of PSA to Rio de Janeiro to inspect the property before paying too much for it. Because if the purchase followed the practice adopted by the PSA when it leases an office building in London at least 15 people from the agency will have had a look round. Recently an agent with a building in Victoria which he thought would be suitable for government use was surprised to find 12 people standing on the doorstep when he arrived to show the space. Such practice by the agency is by no means uncommon.

The NAD would not, of course, wish to limit itself to the United Kingdom. They would also want to examine travel abroad, and a similar array of questions presents itself for this purpose. Is there a lot more travelling abroad now than there was twenty or thirty years ago, and if so, why? Aircraft make it very much easier to travel, both at home and abroad, than used to be the case, but this improvement should merely make it easier to do what has to be done anyway and not in itself increase the amount of travelling. Again, using sampling techniques, it would be necessary to look beneath the ostensible reasons given for travelling to the actual achievements which stem therefrom. As a side issue it might be worth while finding out how many staff, especially senior staff, travel abroad on official business and just happen to end up somewhere near where they were going to be on holiday!

Expenditure by departments for prestige purposes and the need to account for this separately have already been mentioned, but the biggest spender by far in this field is the Diplomatic and Consular Service, which during 1975–6 cost the taxpayer around £140 million. Once again, a two-tier examination is needed. Are reductions possible while maintaining broadly similar policies? Second, having made the economies, what is the residual cost likely to be? Thereafter it would be for the PAC to consider what the United Kingdom gets in return for this massive expenditure. Is our status in the world governed by the stability of our currency and the growth in national productivity and similar considerations or by keeping up enormous embassies? Does an ambassador travelling in a Rolls-Royce, being run on money borrowed from other countries, carry more conviction about

our economic and political future than one travelling in a Mini?
Or is it that the more hard-up we are the more we have to keep up
appearances? With £140 million a year involved it would seem
worth while at least to take a fresh look at some long-standing
assumptions.[2]

This is equally true of the claims made for the importance of
overseas representation for the purposes of promoting exports.
This is a line which is argued vigorously these days, and commercial attachés have more of a case than many other diplomatic
staff. The justification for keeping them, however, should turn on
whether past commercial achievements justify government expenditure for promotional purposes; and, second, on how much
of this success is attributable to these promotional activities and
on whether it would not have come about in any case for other
reasons. There must be a point at which export orders can be
bought too dearly. While it is legitimate to consider future hopes
as opposed to past experiences, it is as necessary in this field as
in any other to balance the worth of the tomorrow which never
seems to come against cutting losses and writing off the past.

The list of possibilities for inquiry could go on and on. Each
of the suggestions made here will lead on to half a dozen others,
and we have hardly touched such richly potential areas as the
Ministry of Defence, which together with the armed services
would need a book all to themselves.

The NAD would have to expect to be unpopular in some
circles, especially in the early days, just for raising the spectre of
a hard-headed unsentimental investigation into public service
activities. It would, however, be essential that no part of the
public sector, with a few security exceptions, should be out of
bounds. No spending should be so hallowed by age or so recently
justified as to escape scrutiny. The fact that other investigations
in the distant or near past have found no cause for criticism
should not be accepted as a reason for immunity. Always the
questions must be: what does this organization do? How much
does it cost? Could what it does be done for a lower cost? Could
what it does be modified in some way so that the result, though

2. This paragraph was written before the publication of the similar
Think-Tank proposals.

still acceptable, costs less? And at the end, when all the answers are known to all those questions, the biggest question of all remains: is the end product, taking account of any economies which may be possible, worth what has to be paid for it, or could it be abandoned altogether?

Decisions to abandon policies altogether – for example, where the facts justify it, to close down a research establishment which has been going on for years – would be reached only after prolonged debate. Reductions, even fierce reductions, are not the same as abolition. They do not carry with them the same finality, nor the implication that all that has gone before is to be written off. Yet this disagreeable duty must be accepted sooner or later. The only alternative is the manifestly foolish idea that once created these projects should go on for ever regardless of change in the community they serve. Time and patience might solve the staff problems but still leave an establishment which represents a very large investment in terms of past researches and present buildings and services. Even so, it might make better economic sense to demolish it rather than pour money into it just because it seemed too good to let go to waste.

Except in minor cases it is very unlikely that the NAD would be the appropriate authority for making or even recommending a decision on this last aspect. It is likely, too, that it would not be appropriate for the Public Accounts Committee to reach conclusions about policy changes of this kind though it might find it possible and desirable in some cases to make recommendations. In the end, however, what the taxpayers' money is spent on is very much a matter for governments to decide.

This is a very long way from saying that neither the NAD nor the PAC has an important supporting role to play in this field of policy-making or policy-changing. Unless government expenditure is to be regarded as completely open-ended, capable of substantial increases indefinitely year after year, policy must increasingly become a matter of priorities. It will not be enough to say that something is moderately desirable or even very desirable. Increasingly it must be a case of asking: if this desirable expenditure is to be permitted, what other kind of expenditure must go to the wall?

For these purposes it is essential that government has before it a continual stream of accurate information about the cost of what it is buying. In a large number of cases merely to state the cost will be to state the answer. In others, if the conclusion is less obvious, it will at least be possible to see what is being bought and what, in consequence, is being forgone, so that the community as a whole, not just the Government, can be aware of the priorities which are being used to determine the allocation of the community's resources.

Most of all, though, the reduction of waste which the NAD and the PAC would bring about will make it less necessary to discard worthwhile policies for lack of money, and this must be a course of action which commends itself alike to Government, Opposition and taxpayers.

Part IV

More about the Wasting Sickness

20 Public Concern about the Disease

The first edition of *Your Disobedient Servant* was published on 9 May 1978. On the evening of 8 May, Granada Television used its current affairs programme *World in Action*[1] to provide a thirty-minute documentary which dealt with a number of issues raised in Part I of the book and also with some elements from Part II. On the evening of 9 May, BBC2, in the *Man Alive* programme,[2] covered a range of examples of waste of money in the public sector, devoting about half its time to the PSA maintenance and car service economies, and to the weaknesses in the civil-service and PAC procedures for control which these examples revealed. Both programmes made significant contributions to the evidence in favour of reform of these procedures. In the process, they gave a rare opportunity for the taxpaying public to see at first hand the problems, human and procedural, which need to be dealt with if control of public spending is to be more effective.

Discussions with the television authorities had begun in February 1978 and were made more complicated by the fact that it is unusual for two programmes covering much the same ground to be transmitted so close together. This was followed by a period of intensive research, preparation and recording, which went on until the weekend before the broadcasts. Not for the first time, I was taken aback by the amount of energy and care put into the investigation of every word which was recorded and by the enormous scale of the editing and discarding that led finally to the programmes seen by the public. If errors do creep into this type of programme (and they did not in the case of these two), it is not for want of care on the part of the production teams, nor, more importantly, for any lack of desire on the part of the

1. Producer, André Singer; researcher, Stephen Segaller.
2. Producer, Alan Patient.

authorities to present a completely objective and accurate report.

It was as a consequence of this critical and questioning approach, and the reappraisal of the arguments put forward in the book, that *World in Action* decided that on one vital question it would try to use its resources to take the investigation a stage further.

The matter at issue was the way in which Sir Robert Cox, the accounting officer of the PSA, had dealt with the implied criticisms in the C and AG's 1975 Report on the Appropriation Accounts 1973–74 (Appendix 1, and see also pp. 80–88). These criticisms dealt with the effectiveness with which economy measures had been applied in the rest of the United Kingdom as compared with the Southern Region. They were the most important part of the C and AG report because of the significance which Exchequer and Audit Department obviously believed they had for the rest of the department. This was the issue, therefore, which, when the brief for the accounting officer (see pp. 79–80) was being prepared, could have been expected to engage the close attention of the PAC and for which in consequence even greater care than usual would be needed in establishing the facts. In the event, the criticism was effectively disposed of, and all further questioning on this point brought to an end by Mr Cox's explanation that there was a special circumstance in the Southern Region – that large numbers of troops had been moved out to the north – which made it possible for that region to make economies. The same opportunities, said Mr Cox, were not available elsewhere.

Because this was vital not only to the particular case but in general to the credibility of the Public Accounts Committee's investigatory role as an effective defender of the taxpayer's interest, I devoted almost the whole of Chapter 8 to a detailed examination of this and other points of evidence. The difficulty I faced in writing this chapter was that while I was sure that the evidence given by Sir Robert Cox on this point was completely inaccurate, I was quite unable to prove it. The Official Secrets Act made it impossible for me to get at the facts, and I was, therefore, obliged to draw attention to the unsatisfactory nature of the

answer by bringing out the consequential difficulties and incon-
sistencies which arose if it were accepted as accurate.

World in Action concluded that this was not a matter of opinion
but of verifiable fact, and that it should be possible on this
fundamental point to establish whether the department was right
or I was. Granada Ltd decided that this was a sufficiently
important matter of public interest to warrant seeking the assistance of a Member of Parliament. Accordingly, in early April Mr
Michael Thomas, Labour MP for Newcastle upon Tyne East,
put down for the Minister of Defence a series of Parliamentary
questions designed to get at the truth. The answers made it
crystal-clear that the evidence given by Sir Robert Cox had been
inaccurate, and that this had been known to the PSA and Sir
Robert since March 1977. The detailed consequences and the
events which followed from this as far as the PSA and the PAC
were concerned are dealt with in Chapter 22. Meanwhile it made
it possible to justify ending the programme with the statement
that what was needed was a public inquiry to establish all the
facts and, among other things, to reach an estimate, based on the
department's own admissions, of the cost to the taxpayer of the
delays in carrying through the economy measures.

The BBC decided to examine the rather wider issues which it
saw as being involved in these matters. One of the problems I
had tried to tackle was the 'entrenched lethargy' that prevents
change in the Civil Service and in this connection the role played
by the higher Civil Service.[3] I dealt at some length with the proposals made by the Fulton Committee and the lack of success
which the Government had had in implementing the proposals
for reform. I also dealt with the English Committee's Report,
made some ten years after the Fulton Committee.[4] It is very easy
to say that the Civil Service, or senior civil servants in particular,
resist proposals for reform; it is extremely difficult to prove such
statements, especially as civil servants rarely appear in public to
give their views on these matters, and opportunities for questioning them are even rarer. It was, therefore, a matter of rather more
than passing interest when *Man Alive* were able to interview Lord

3. See Chapter 13.
4. See the Postscript to the First Edition.

Armstrong (who as head of the Civil Service had presided over the non-implementation of most of the Fulton Committee Report). The public were able to see and hear at first hand how proposals for reform, and those who make the proposals, are viewed by the higher Civil Service. Lord Armstrong had two comments to make about the members of the Fulton Committee: the first was that 'they can be stupid'; the second was that their average age was 'rather high'.

It is, of course, a matter of opinion whether the members of the committee and their recommendations were stupid, although a very brief study of these individuals' achievements gives no support for Lord Armstrong's assessment. The question of age, being purely factual, is more easily dealt with. At the time of their appointment to the Fulton Committee the average age of the twelve members was 53·6 years. At the time when Lord Armstrong was dismissing the committee as being rather elderly his own age was sixty-four.

The average age of the English Committee, which by and large endorsed the findings of the Fulton Committee, was 46·5 years (in 1976), and, being unable to dismiss them on grounds of senile decay,[5] Lord Armstrong changed the line of his attack. The committee had spent over a year on their work; they interviewed over one hundred witnesses, many of them of high standing in their professions; they held forty-three meetings – twenty-eight of them to hear evidence from witnesses or groups of witnesses, and fifteen deliberative meetings. The minutes of evidence ran to three volumes of close print. Lord Armstrong's comment, nonetheless, was 'They haven't studied it, they don't really know what went on, and they're looking possibly at the wrong things.' A little later on, talking about the questions of accountability and management, which are the vital questions in any review of proposals for reforming the Civil Service and making it more efficient, Lord Armstrong, tiring of disposing of the committees one by one, said 'I'm not at all sure that either the Fulton Committee *or* the English Committee really knew what they were talking about on that subject'.

In my dealings with the BBC, during the preparation of the *Man Alive* television programme, I became aware that the produc-

5. But were they perhaps too young?

tion team had some misgivings about the way in which I might view Lord Armstrong's comments about me, which were both offensive and inaccurate. They need not have worried. I believed, and this was overwhelmingly supported by the letters and telephone calls which reached me in the following weeks, that Lord Armstrong did more in two or three minutes of spontaneous and unrehearsed comment to shed light on the way the higher Civil Service think of Parliament and the public than any number of official reports and books could possibly do.

In addition to the two television programmes and a number of radio broadcasts about the book, it was given generous coverage by the Press. The national dailies and weeklies were joined by local newspapers and also by professional journals with a specialized interest in one or other of the fields covered. The combined estimated audience for the television programmes was twenty millions; for just one of the sound broadcasts eight millions[6]; and the combined circulation of the big newspapers is fifteen to twenty million. No doubt there was a good deal of overlapping between these groups (some unfortunates must have had three or four or more accounts of the wasting sickness and its symptoms), but it was still an extensive coverage, mostly concentrated into four or five days, and one result was predictably a steady flow of letters and telephone calls from individuals and organizations. There is no information available to show how far public interest in a subject of this kind can be measured by the level of this type of response. People who are knowledgeable in these matters tell me that there is no meaningful correlation between the two things. This is moderately comforting, since at the time of writing (August 1978) I have received only 727 letters from individuals and organizations, which is a good deal fewer than I had expected.

The second unexpected (to me at least) though gratifying feature of the correspondence was that nearly all the writers were drawing on their own first-hand knowledge of the public sector, and with one exception their experience and conclusions matched mine. Perhaps, on reflection, it was to be expected that only those who agree with me would write, and therefore too much should not be read into this aspect of the public response.

6. *The Jimmy Young Show*, 10 May 1978.

Rather more predictably, there were no dissenting views at all in the letters from members of the general public.

One depressing characteristic of the majority of the letters was the writers' obvious fear that if they expressed criticism of the way in which the public services worked this would in some way bring retribution upon them. This is not surprising when it comes from people still serving in some part of the public sector, but a surprisingly large number of those who had long since retired were equally apprehensive. So also were numbers of those who had never been in the public service but were merely expressing their views as users or observers of one or other of the services. However ill-founded these fears may be, they are obviously very real to the individuals concerned – and this in a country which claims it has had freedom of speech for centuries. If I had had any doubts about the need for changes in the Official Secrets Act and for legislation for freedom of information they would have been dispelled by this correspondence.

Because of these fears, in seeking permission to quote from letters I have received, I undertook to publish the writers' names only if they have agreed to this.

One of the most interesting letters was from Mr Alan Plastow,[7] who was well placed to judge the validity of comments on the public service generally and the PSA in particular. In the period 1968 to 1970 Mr Plastow was on secondment from the Manpower and Productivity Service of the Department of Employment and was in control of a mixed Ministry of Public Building and Works/Department of Employment team which carried out a feasibility study for the purpose of advising civil servants on improving efficiency. Mr Plastow says that when he read the reviews of my book 'memories of the staggering inefficiencies came flooding back', and he recalls how 'in desperation' he wrote a criticism of the way in which civil servants got to the top. This criticism included the statement that 'getting work done cost-effectively [was] something which never even figured in measuring the Civil Servants' contribution to the nation'.

Another well-placed commentator was Alex Henney, who

7. Now Group Personnel Controller for May and Baker Ltd, Dagenham, Essex.

tells me that he recently completed two years' secondment to the Department of the Environment as an assistant secretary[8] to work on the housing policy review. His experience, he says, confirmed the validity of findings which argue that our present systems 'provide a cosy, formal and tidy way of taking the wrong decisions'; and he speaks of 'the unimportance of being right' and the use of secrecy and anonymity to prevent wrong decisions being brought home to particular individuals; and of politicians and administrators 'taking the smooth with the smooth and achieving consensus at the taxpayers' expense'.

Norman Fuller of North Mundham, West Sussex, writes with the advantage of having spent the last seventeen years as the representative of an international office equipment corporation dealing, in his case, solely with government departments, ranging from Whitehall headquarters down to the smallest unit. His experience confirms my criticisms of the fundamental weaknesses of the Civil Service organization, although, like me, he feels that attacks on individual civil servants are often misguided and unjustified.

Some of the best-documented and most forthright comments came from retired members of the Royal Air Force and the Army. The letters came mostly from senior grades (up to General in the Army and Air Vice-Marshal in the R A F), and from them I have selected one from Group Captain (Retired) T. W. G. Eadey because he makes a point which I found very noticeable when I was talking to the Press. He says 'the scandalous waste of public money is on so colossal a scale that it ceases to be credible and no one believes it. It must be measured in billions not millions'. I too found that if I said what I really feared about the scale of waste it tended to be counter-productive. No one, however well-disposed generally, would take me seriously. Group Captain Eadey, like all my other correspondents from the armed services, makes it clear that he has no grievances against the service of which he says he is proud to have been a member. His quarrel is solely with 'the Ministry' (that is, the Civil Service).

Arthur Silkin (no relation to the Minister) spent the last five years of a life-time career in the Civil Service as a lecturer in

8. See Figure 1 (p. 19) for the status of an assistant secretary.

public administration at the Civil Service staff college. He was, he says, 'frequently dismayed by the empire building, or, more precisely, the empire maintenance of officials who are reluctant to admit that fewer staff may be required than was formerly the case, or that certain jobs may no longer be necessary, as well as the by no means infrequent under-employment of staff, often for lengthy periods.'

Another correspondent wished to remain anonymous because he said his son was about to enter the Civil Service and he did not wish to prejudice his boy's prospects. He based his criticisms on his lengthy experience in an organization on the fringe of the Civil Service, from which he was also able to observe some of the operations of the National Health Service. In this limited field he estimated that one small malpractice alone was costing tens of millions of pounds a year up and down the country. He tried to interest his MP in this matter but got nowhere, and his final judgement is 'The decision makers are members of a closely knit coterie who are so finely attuned to one another that decisions need never be discussed but go through on a nod and a wink; nothing can ever be pinned down on anyone; they are loyal not to the public whose servants they are supposed to be but only to each other.'

A second correspondent who felt obliged to remain anonymous is a civil servant in the Department of Health and Social Security. He gives, as an example of over-manning, the fact that in his part of the organization there are three sections who are for all practical purposes doing exactly the same work. In this one small example of waste, he says, the salaries for the unneeded staff are approximately £80,000 per annum. Salaries are, of course, only a part of the gross total cost of a civil servant, and my correspondent goes on to say 'I have illustrated only one item of waste – I can assure you that it is just the tip of the iceberg.'

The *Daily Express* said (on 16 May 1978) that its review of the book had 'released a flood of supporting evidence from tradesmen, MPs and readers', and it printed some examples. I think the best was one reported on 16 June when a junior civil servant with twelve years' service gave his account of his career to date.

After he had continually complained that he had little or nothing to do, he was sent on sick leave while the problem was sorted out. 'In the end I was off work for six months until the following Easter. Just before that Christmas the Civil Service doctor examined me from top to toe and agreed that I was very fit, but he too said I wasn't to go back to work until the problem of finding something for me to do had been sorted out.' This problem must have been sorted out, because at the end of the article this man describes his current situation as follows:

There are three Clerks in [my] present office, they chat, they browse through five newspapers a day each, they play football among the desks to pass the time, [they] just talk all day and generally try to keep themselves amused. One of them talks about his garden most of the day . . . he is not lazy, it's just that he's got absolutely nothing to do – we don't get any phone calls and no one comes in with any work.

The other bloke sits at his desk all day, day after day, typing with one finger. He gets no phone calls, gets no paperwork to deal with and no paperwork comes from him.

We never talk about it or ask him what he's up to although I know it's not his job. No one ever asks each other what they are doing because everyone's sitting there all day with nothing to do hoping that no one finds out.

Any assessment of the significance of correspondence and other forms of criticism of this kind must inevitably contain a measure of judgement and opinion. It seems reasonable to assume that any large organization contains within it a handful of malcontents who will seize any opportunity to air grievances, imaginary or otherwise. On this I can only say that the letters I had did not give the impression of coming from people with a grievance. Except for a tiny minority, they were from people who had gone on to make a success of careers elsewhere or who had retired with mainly pleasant memories of careers lasting, in most cases, for many years. As far as I can judge, they seemed to be genuinely concerned to do something about improving a situation which worried and dismayed them. Their motives appeared to be only to help the public service and the community as a whole.

But brief extracts from a small sample of the letters can give only the flavour rather than the full range and gravity of the indictment of the public service which these responses provide. I decided therefore to devote the whole of the next chapter to a detailed account of a particularly serious case of waste which one letter-writer had brought to my attention.

21 A Serious New Case

In the 1940s and 1950s Hertfordshire County Council embarked on a programme of new school building. Shortages of materials and skilled labour, coupled with the urgency of the need for extra school places to cope with the post-war 'bulge', made it necessary to devise new techniques and methods of working, not only in terms of physical construction but also in relationships between users, contractors and the professional staffs. The work was the responsibility of a team led by the county architect.

It must have been a team of formidable abilities, because when, at the end of the 1950s, it was time for them to move on, its members became chief architects in no fewer than five major government offices: the Ministries of Education; Housing; Environment; Health; and the National Building Agency.

William Tatton-Brown had been a deputy county architect in the Hertfordshire team and he went to the Ministry of Health in 1959 as Chief Architect just as the National Health Service hospital-building programme was getting started. The letters I am using in this chapter relate to his experiences during and immediately after this long spell in the top professional post of the organization, responsible for a multi-million-pound programme. The two letters, dated 6 and 22 August 1978, were written after Tatton-Brown had read the first edition of this book. He says: 'I agree with every word you say . . . my experience very much ties up with yours at Reading . . . The absence of anyone in charge and the way that the administrative machine worked practically doubled the cost of hospitals.'

Tatton-Brown's experience complements my own in a most interesting way because it relates to capital expenditure on a large-scale government building programme. In his case it was complicated by the three-tier administrative set-up of the

National Health Service, consisting at that time of Hospital Management Committees (which looked after patients), Regional Hospital Boards (which built the hospitals) and the Ministry of Health (which allocated the money). Soon after Tatton-Brown took over, the Nuffield Provincial Hospital Trust set up a fellowship to study the question 'Why do hospitals take so long to build and cost so much?' and this was won by his wife, Aileen Sparrow.[1] She was based on the Building Research Station, and she was given access to the Ministry's files and allowed by the Regional Boards to sit in on the briefing of architects and engineers on project teams responsible for designing new hospitals. Visits to existing hospitals and conversations with people running them were separately arranged to find out the views of the users. It very soon became clear that the cost of hospitals rose because no single individual was in charge of the building project as a whole. The system was for experts remote from the field of action to recommend what should be provided, each in his own sphere, and the Treasury would foot the bill, subject to the money being available. The more authorities that had to be consulted or placated, the greater the delay and the greater the cost, and the more impossible the designer's usual task of revising plans to meet a cost target by a given date. But when hospitals spent their own limited funds, contact between the different specialists involved was close, and everyone was conscious of the pressing needs of patients. In these circumstances economical use was made of money and other resources.

Tatton-Brown was able to persuade his colleagues at the Ministry to put his wife's theories to the test. It was agreed to short-circuit the usual system and put a single doctor in charge (Dr Harrington) with instructions to build two 'best-buy hospitals' – not the best possible but the best value for money while providing an adequate standard of service for the needs of the local community.

The resulting hospitals, Frimley and Bury St Edmunds, were a resounding success. They cost little more than half the cost of any other hospital built till then,[2] and patients and staff were

1. Exhibitioner, Somerville College, Oxford, 1930–33; read Politics, Philosophy and Economics. ARIBA, 1938. Assistant Editor, *Architects Journal*, 1942–3. Nuffield Research Fellow, 1963–7.

well satisfied. Why were they not repeated? In the early seventies more money became available. But instead of building more hospitals, sights were raised, 'improved standards' were sought and as the machine took over costs soared up. By the mid-seventies they had reached such a peak that the whole computer-ized hospital programme had to be recast, and, what was worse, those buildings that had been completed were in some cases left partially empty – too expensive to staff and use as intended. The analysis contained in Aileen Sparrow's report[3] had turned out to be only too correct.

Allowing for the fact that her report dealt with capital invest-ment projects and my work was mainly in the field of day-to-day expenditure, there was, as we have noted, a marked resemblance between both the problems and the fundamental changes needed in the administrative machine to solve them, while the scale of the savings possible on new hospital buildings was even greater than those I made.[4] But the most striking parallel of all comes at the end of the story.

'The fate of the research workers', writes Tatton-Brown, 'who comes up with unpopular findings is not a happy one. Her report although printed was never allowed to see the light of day.' For 'research worker', substitute managers, administrators, directors of any other civil-service title, and the proposition still holds good.

The report was not contested on a basis of fact. It was studied for two years, during which time every individual example of inefficiency given to illustrate the inadequacy of the system was dealt with and corrected. It was then said to be out of date. But the main thesis of the report, that the *system* was responsible for wasting vast sums of money, was never dealt with. The evidence was merely suppressed.

Except for saying that the bureaucratic machine had taken over again, Tatton-Brown makes no comment on arrangements for controlling public expenditure which can allow this kind of

2. At 1975 prices, the approximate cost per bed was £13,500 in the 'best-buy hospitals', compared with £23,300 in the 'computerized hospitals'.

3: BRS Internal Note IN 65/70, Production Division: 'The Hospital Planning Process 1963–6', by Aileen Sparrow.

4. For example, at 1975 prices the hospital capital programme rose from £286 million in 1970 to £376 million in 1973.

thing to happen. Similarly he does not say where the responsibility lies either for weaknesses in the procedural machinery or for failures in operation. Nevertheless the story of the hospital building programme raises yet again these fundamental questions, which must be asked and answered if there is to be change for the better. Here was a programme involving thousands of millions of pounds of taxpayers' money which had been intended to provide an essential part of a vital public service. The shortage of money which bedevils this same service is something that by now every family in the land must be aware of, and a good many have suffered from. Yet it was not only that nearly half the money spent on new buildings was wasted. This same wasted capital expenditure produced in turn continuing wasted expenditure on running costs which will go on (at increasing rates) for the life of the buildings.

Were Ministers ever made aware of this? The size and gravity of the waste suggests that they certainly should have been. Is it possible that Exchequer and Audit Department could have remained ignorant of waste on this scale? If they were aware of it, why were the facts not made known to Parliament and the Public Accounts Committee? If they were not aware of it, is this not further evidence that, as they are at present constituted, the PAC and E and AD are almost completely ineffectual in safeguarding the public interest?

The exact size of the waste has been difficult to determine. Changes in the way appropriation accounts are presented, uninformative wording of accounts and the effects of inflation combine to obscure the facts. For the ten years ending 1977–8, however, it seems likely that the actual capital expenditure in England, Wales and Scotland on hospital building was around £2370,000,000. At 1978 prices this probably means expenditure equivalent to well over £3500,000,000. Mr Tatton-Brown's findings would therefore indicate that waste in these ten years alone was probably something over £1,500,000,000.

The next chapter returns to this problem with a re-examination in detail of the workings of departmental, PAC, and E and AD relationships in the light of up-to-date information on the issues first discussed in Chapter 8.

22 Case Study No. I: Further Examination and Disagreeable Medicine Administered!

For accounting officers appearing before the Public Accounts Committee there is one over-riding imperative – to be sure that their evidence is completely accurate. They are not required to be eloquent or witty; or to be sufficiently in command of the facts to be able to give answers quickly and without reference to documents and advisers. If, after such consultation, they still do not know the answer they can put in written evidence later; and if they give an answer which subsequently they find is wrong, they can amend it at leisure by putting in a written correction before the proceedings are published. Everyone understands the difficulty of their situation, and due allowance is made for it. Indeed, as we noted in Chapter 8, the question is whether in the light of all this there is much real point in proceedings of this kind.

By April–May 1978 Sir Robert Cox, who had known since March 1977 that his evidence about troop movements was inaccurate, but who had decided to remain silent (for the reasons given in Para. 12 of the Second Special Report, Appendix 14), was being forced to come to terms with the unwelcome knowledge that it was inevitable that very soon either my book or the television programmes or both would make this fact public.

Consequently, on 2 May 1978, Sir Robert wrote to Mr Edward du Cann, Chairman of the PAC, saying that 'there was one factual inaccuracy in my answers and it is only right that I should let you know about this'. The letter, which is reproduced in full as Annex A to the C and AG's report (see Appendix 8 below), makes it clear that it was written because the television authorities, as a result of my forthcoming book, might be going to question the accuracy of some of the evidence given in 1975. Sir Robert went on to say that it was the statement about troop movements that was incorrect, but what his letter did not say was that the PSA and Sir Robert himself had known about this error for over a year.

Mr du Cann acknowledged this notification on 5 May 1978. He said that he accepted Sir Robert's explanation that there had been no intention to mislead the committee and that he would discuss the position with the C and AG and with the PAC. But he went on to say that, in his view, the inaccuracy had not affected the PAC's recommendations.

This relaxed view of what was involved seemed to have undergone a change by 10 May, because the C and AG was then asked to investigate and report further on the matter to the PAC. It is not possible to gauge with certainty from the published papers the extent to which this change was brought about by the TV and Press comment and how much it was due to the reaction of the members of the PAC, who, judging by later events, took a more serious view of the matter than did the Chairman. But my guess is that both factors played a part.

The C and AG duly produced his report for the PAC, which is reproduced in full as Appendix 8 below. This report, together with other material, including the first edition of this book and television and Press comment, formed the basis of two further examinations of Sir Robert Cox on 12 June and 10 July 1978. Those proceedings are reproduced in full as Appendixes 9, 10 and 14 of this edition, and taken in conjunction with all the other statements on this subject (including the 1975 evidence and reports), they make fascinating reading. For anyone who is concerned with the way this country is governed and administered (at least in matters involving money) they provide a series of real-life insights into the strengths and weaknesses of the existing system. Because I believe that in this sense these documents speak for themselves I do not propose to discuss them in great detail. Instead I suggest that they are read at this stage, and that the remainder of this chapter is used as an aide-mémoire to help focus attention on matters of particular importance.

The first of these is the way in which the PAC discharged its obligation to the taxpayer. I believe that most readers of the proceedings on 12 June 1978 will feel that the questioning was much more effective than in 1975, and that the truth was being pursued with vigour and skill. Indeed, as I discovered later that day, there were moments when even hardened lobby correspondents shared my feeling that for once we were seeing part of the great machinery of democracy working in the way it should. This was made possible by the fact that the PAC had before them at that stage fairly limited and straightforward issues, on which they had sufficient information to enable them to go beyond superficial questions and answers. This happy state of affairs did not last long, and by 10 July they were once again losing their way in a welter of figures. Nevertheless, it was encouraging while it lasted, and gives some indication of how effective the committee could be if it was supported by an adequate audit and inspection organization, and by committee assistants who could conduct the examination of official witnesses (see Chapter 17).

The PAC's considered judgements on all these matters is contained in the Second Special Report (Appendix 14). If the Committee's role at this stage is to be assessed fairly, it must be understood that dignified and reserved language, with a fair measure of understatement and detachment, is its accepted style. If the PAC had reported to Parliament on the charge of the Light Brigade they would most probably have summed up rather as follows: 'This manoeuvre was possibly not, in the view of some participants and observers, a complete and unqualified success; and it is possible to argue, though admittedly with the benefit of hindsight, that some improvements in communications could be made. Nevertheless, we are satisfied not only that everyone involved acted with the best intentions, but that in the event neither the outcome of this battle, nor the campaign as a whole was materially affected.' The words in Para. 10 of the Report, '. . . we are unable either to accept or to reject the PSA's opinion that the alteration to the earlier draft of Sir Robert's brief was made in good faith . . .' must be read against this traditional background.

Mr du Cann was questioned in the BBC TV interview about the practice of using this very lofty style. He defended it vigorously, saying that there was no need, when making criticisms, to use the language of the gutter. No doubt many politicians, of all parties, and the higher Civil Service would, like Mr du Cann, see no possibility between those two alternatives. That is not true for the majority of taxpayers, who use neither Parliamentary circumlocution nor gutter talk. One of the changes that Select Committees may have to make if they are to regain public confidence is to make themselves more intelligible to people who are not members of the governing elite, but who merely have the unavoidable obligation to pay the bills.

The flavour of olympian detachment which the PAC imparts to its activities is not limited to its language. Observing (Para. 7 of the Second Report, Appendix 14) that if they had pursued their questioning on the comparison between Southern Region and the other regions they would no doubt have been critical of slowness in those others, the committee goes on to say that their main conclusions, which were directed towards the future, were unaffected. I doubt whether many taxpayers would endorse this forgiving philosophy. It is all very well to look to the future and hope for improvement, but one constituent in bringing about such changes must be the deterrent effect of delving into past weaknesses and failures and commenting on them publicly.

All in all, after a promising start the PAC seemed to lose some of its impetus. Reporting this, the *Economist* on 17 June 1978 said that Sir Robert was lucky that Mr du Cann was such a toothless old tiger. The taxpayer may feel that this description would more fairly describe the PAC as an organization in its present form, which is a pity when it has both the power and the opportunity to equip itself with sharp new fangs.

One section of Sir Robert Cox's evidence, and the PSA's supporting memoranda, which would have greatly benefited from more effective examination was the remainder of his 1975 explanation of the reasons why Southern Region's economy measures produced different results from the rest of the country (see Chapter 8). Sir Robert listed three reasons, one of which – the troop movements – was now admitted to be incorrect; the other two were different timing – Southern Region started sooner – and greater enthusiasm for economy measures in the Southern Region (Q. 1318, Appendix 2).

In an article published in the *Sunday Times* on 18 June 1978 the PSA's assertion that Southern Region's early start had been an important factor was attacked as factually incorrect. The newspaper said, and I agree, that in fact the other regions had started very soon after Southern[1] but had failed to press on diligently with the surveys. The PSA objected to this judgement, although everything in Para. 22 of their memorandum (Appendix 11, Section III, 'Sunday Times article of 18 June 1978') seems to support the newspaper's case (and mine) rather than otherwise. However, in this instance readers may judge for themselves. Table 1 gives the PSA's own account of the dates on which teams were set up in the regions, and of progress thereafter.

Table 1

| | 1968–9 | | 1969–70 | | 1970–71 | | 1971–2 | | 1972–3 | | 1973–4 | |
	T	S	T	S	T	S	T	S	T	S	T	S
South East	1	1	1	1	2	6	2	5	2	2	2	8
Scotland	1	1	1	4	–	–	1	4	1	4	1	1
London	1	2	1	1	1	1	1	1	1	1	1	1
North East	1	5	1	2	1	2	1	3	1	3	1	4
Wales	–	–	1	2	1	3	1	2	1	1	1	2
Midland	1	2	1	2	–	–	2	4	2	5	2	7
North West	1	2	1	2	1	4	1	4	1	4	–	–
Southern	2	5	3	8	3	7	3	7	1	3	1	4
South West	1	1	1	1	6	7	5	9	3	7	2	11
Eastern	1	1	2	2	2	5	2	6	2	2	–	–

T = Number of Teams   S = Number of Surveys

This shows that all the regions except Wales started their surveys in the same year as I did, that is, in 1968–9. My start over them was measured in months. Secondly, it shows that the other regions either failed to appoint more teams; or disbanded those

---

1. Southern started in May–June 1968; the remainder (except Wales) in October–November 1968.

they had; or worked very slowly (see London, for example); or contrived a mixture of those factors. The PSA seemed to think that admitting this disproves the criticism that 'The real difference was that most other Regions progressed only slowly after they had started.' To the *Sunday Times* and to me, these same facts make the case for the criticism.

It is a pity that the PAC did not have an opportunity to see these figures. They were supplied to Granada TV (who made them available to me) and to the *Sunday Times*. It would therefore have been a simple matter to include this analysis with all the other material given to the PAC in June–July 1978. Perhaps the PSA felt that in this instance it would be better and safer to give the PAC not the actual figures, but rather the Departmental View of what those figures meant?

This analysis also brings to light another inaccuracy in the statements made by PSA to E and AD in 1974–5 and reproduced in the C and A G's report (Para. 32, Appendix 1). According to that report the PSA had said that Midland Region shared with Southern a high level of savings from the surveys because both regions had started earlier, before other management initiatives took effect. In fact the analysis in Table 1 shows, first, that Midland started when everyone else did (in 1968–9) but, more importantly, made such slow progress that by 1970–71 they were sharing bottom place and had in fact stopped survey work altogether.[2]

Early starts proving to be illusory, this leaves only Sir Robert's third and last explanatory factor – a greater enthusiasm in Southern Region. In reality, of course, this is not an explanation at all; it is merely a different way of saying that there was a lack of enthusiasm in the other regions. This failure, especially having regard for the instructions issued by successive Ministers, is the basis of my criticism of the way matters were handled in PSA. Mr du Cann (Q. 1318, Appendix 2) made a good start on this in 1975. He did not ask *if* there had been a difference in enthusiasm. He asked, as you will see if you refer back to Appendix 2, *why* this was so. It was of course the only question that really went to the heart of the matter. He never did get an answer.

2. They were to catch up later; see p. 73.

Mr John Watkinson alone seems to have seized upon this, and at the hearing on 10 July 1978 (Appendix 10, Qs. 3807–17) he pressed Sir Robert hard for an explanation. He did not get very far. Three times (3807, 3815 and 3817) when Mr Watkinson must have thought that he was about to get conclusive answers Sir Robert replied that he was not in the department at the time, and once (3817) that he did not know the people concerned.

These answers, together with some other facts which emerge from the evidence, oral and written, have a significance which goes beyond the operations of PSA. As we saw earlier, especially in Chapter 12, the PAC has invented for itself a mythical system in which, since accounting officers are held to be personally responsible for everything that happens in their departments, they alone are called to account by the PAC, and no other witnesses are considered necessary. Let us now re-examine these theories in the light of what actually happened.

1. On 12 June 1978 (Q. 3213, Appendix 9) Sir Robert Cox agreed with Mr du Cann that he gave 'a slightly free interpretation of the information and the brief that was in front of [him]'.

2. Dealing with the factual inaccuracy in his evidence he said that he had accepted what was put in front of him, that is, in the brief (Q. 3214).

3. He went on to admit that it would have been sensible to have the statement in the brief checked, but that this had not been done by him (Q. 3214). It emerges from the answers to the following questions that no one checked it.

4. The error remained undetected, as far as Sir Robert Cox was concerned, because of ignorance of the subject (Q. 3220).

5. He accepted (Q. 3229), and the committee confirmed that it was their view too (Para. 12 of the Second Special Report, Appendix 14), that a material error in evidence should be notified to the committee upon its discovery. This was not done.

6. It would have been sensible for Sir Robert to consult the committee Clerk, or the C and A G, on this matter. He did not do so.

7. The factual error in the evidence led to a considerable misleading of the committee (Q. 3252, Appendix 9); to the heat being

taken off the other Regions (Q. 3283); and to the committee not pressing Sir Robert Cox further (Para. 5, Appendix 14).

8. As we have already noted, three times during the 10 July hearing Sir Robert was obliged to say, when the questions became pressing, that he did not know because he was not there and once that he did not know many of the people concerned.

9. A variety of information (Appendix 11) was submitted by the PSA to the PAC after the hearing on 12 June 1978. There was adequate time and every facility for PSA staff to get these facts right. In view of what had already happened about factual inaccuracies it is reasonable to suppose that, if anything, rather more than the usual degree of care would have gone into their preparation, and that very senior staff in PSA would have scrutinized and been responsible for them. One paragraph of the memorandum related to land disposals, and as soon as the questioning on this started (Q. 3795, Appendix 10) Sir Robert had to say that there was a factual error in the figures and he made a correction. Even then, it was not right; it had to be corrected yet again in a footnote.

10. The Minister responsible for PSA, Mr Ken Marks, stated in an interview with *World in Action* on 2 May 1978 that the PSA had known of the troop movements error for a month or two. In fact, as we have seen, the error had been known about since March 1977.

11. Sir Robert Cox said (Q. 3325, Appendix 9) that he had 'got into a muddle about car hire charges' at the 1976 hearing (see Chapter 9).

This list contains only the inaccuracies and errors of judgement that have been admitted. Considering that accounting for building maintenance and associated activities is by any reasonable test a somewhat humdrum routine business, not really requiring intellectual giants to understand it, is this not a dismal record for a major Government department? Yet Sir Robert Cox's integrity has never been in question. No one had ever suggested that he is less competent than his fellow accounting officers, or that the PSA is more inefficient than other Government departments. Does not the obvious fault lie in the system which persists in asking the impossible of accounting officers, and insists on perpetuating an absurdity? A fault obvious, that is, to anyone outside Parliament and the PAC?

The functions and responsibilities of E and AD and of the Comptroller and Auditor General are closely linked with those of the PAC and the accounting officers (see Chapter 15). When the PAC took the opportunity to ask the C and AG about his functions in connection with the scrutiny of departments' evidence, it appears to have been satisfied with his answers. Should it have been? The C and AG says (Para. 13 of the Memorandum dated 5 June 1978, Appendix 8) '. . . my staff did not attempt to substantiate what had been said about redeployment of military resources. It was only one of a number of arguments and points relating to the PSA's actions and it seemed unlikely to have any material effect . . .' But it was not just one of a number of points. The PAC describes it (Para. 5, Appendix 14) as 'so telling a point', and elsewhere members of the committee make it abundantly clear that they *were* misled, and that the course of questioning and investigation *was* changed by it. So the defence that it didn't really matter cannot be substantiated.

But that is not the end of it. The C and AG goes on to say (in the same paragraph of his Memorandum, Appendix 8) that he should not expect, indeed should not permit his staff to spend time checking all details of evidence. Such concern for civil-service time, and therefore taxpayers' money, is admirable. But should there have been such a problem of checking and using staff time? As I said in Chapter 8, E and AD had already spent a lot of time in 1974–5 finding out all about maintenance economies, and getting the department's explanations for the differences between Southern Region and the others. The troop movement explanation was not given then, and no reference to it appears in the E and AD summary of the department's explanations (Appendix 1, Para. 32). Should not E and AD have checked the validity of this 'so telling' point when it suddenly appeared out of nowhere for the first time at the 1975 hearing? Surely this was evidence which, to use the C and AG's own phrasing (Para. 12, Appendix 8), was at variance with, or added to, their existing knowledge of the case, and which therefore his department would seek to substantiate?

One of the great strengths of the defensive positions of the

Civil Service is that the public soon gets tired of protracted investigations and analysis. The media cannot afford to bore their listeners and readers. Even with a book like this, there are limits to the extent to which the reader can be asked to follow a painstaking and detailed analysis of tables and figures. I therefore propose to comment in detail on only one or two further items arising from the memorandum put before the PAC (Appendix 11).

A good deal is made of the amount of land given up, compared with my statement (p. 40 above) that only about 5 per cent of the possible reductions had been disposed of. The PSA interpretation, which was accepted by the PAC, was that I was referring to 5 per cent of the survey teams' proposals. This is not what I said. If you look at the passage referred to, I said that we gave up only about 5 per cent of *the possible reduction*, not 5 per cent of the survey recommendations. This is not just a matter of wording. A few paragraphs earlier, I had said that we did implement all or nearly all the suggested economies, which clearly could not have been asserted if we had failed on 95 per cent of the land proposals. What happened was that we quickly found that giving up land (especially when it was owned by other departments) was one of the subjects best left (see p. 63–4) to be dealt with separately. I do not blame the PAC, but I find the PSA's misreading of this section very surprising in view of the enormous amount of time and energy they put into reading the first edition.

On the Government Car Service, the PSA, obviously feeling that it had a good case, actually volunteered a statement to the PAC (reproduced in full as Section IV of the Memorandum, Appendix 11). This states that my book made no allowance for the cost of alternative means of transport for other departments and that I had overestimated both the length of delays and the annual saving.

As to the first point, I made no allowance for alternative transport for the simple reason that in Southern Region we found that these alternative costs were negligible and could be disregarded. Perhaps the Southern Region's greater enthusiasm for maintenance economy in general, which Sir Robert Cox admitted (Q. 3296, Appendix 9), made itself felt here too?

On the second point – the amount of annual saving, which in turn indicates the amount of past waste – I had available only the figures from the PAC hearing (Appendix 2). These figures were limited to savings outside London, and the only clue to the total savings was a brief reference in a newspaper article. Since then, evidence has been published on economies in the use of cars given by the Civil Service Department. This shows that a potential saving of £600,000 per year has been identified, with the possibility of more to come.

As to the length of the delay, this same evidence shows that on 17 May 1976 (four years after the Southern Region action, and four and a half years after the basic study was completed), very little in the way of implementation had occurred, and no reference is made to any actual reductions in numbers of cars or drivers. Further studies were still going on. I reiterate with confidence, therefore, that six years is the minimum possible delay, and I suspect that completion will take seven, eight or possibly more years.

The amount of avoidable waste therefore is not £450,000 for six years, as I have said; it is something over £600,000 for a period of over six years.

And PSA have again overlooked the fact that these estimates of time during which taxpayers' money was being squandered through incompetent management show only part of the truth. The waste did not suddenly begin in 1972. It had been going on for as far back as our records went – and it did not suddenly start then either!

Finally, I think it is worth taking a look at the PSA's attempt to show that Southern Region did not, after all, produce results so much better than those of other regions (see Appendix 11, Para. 14 and Annexes B and C). There is a good deal of juggling with figures, including doing things (Para. 13) which are 'not a completely accurate measure of savings'. These figures purport to show that Southern Region's percentage expenditure reduction between 1967–8 and 1973–4 was 28 per cent and some other regions did nearly as well. Ignoring all the other factors such as boundary changes and changed responsibilities, this is probably true. But it is not realistic to ignore these other factors.

For example, not only was it not true that the number of soldiers was being reduced in Aldershot; it was confirmed by the Garrison Commander, Major-General Mans, that between 1969 and 1972 '. . . the reverse was the case, and I can recall we were constantly being hard put to find places to house people . . . I have taken a certain amount of trouble to check on this . . .'[3] In another programme General Mans said that in Aldershot by 1972 the Army was 'bulging at the seams'. It was to get worse, and we had to bring into service hutted camps that had been empty and near-derelict for decades.

Another reason why comparisons of gross expenditure provide a misleading picture is that in Southern Region we had a large proportion of new buildings for the Army. In the late 1960s and early seventies we were faced with colossal bills for making these new buildings habitable. Roofs leaked like sieves, and so did door and window frames; cracks developed so that the occupants of married quarters could drop coins from the flats above to those below; drains were laid running uphill; concrete powdered away. There is no secret about this, nor did it apply only to Southern Region; but our maintenance expenditure figures were distorted, and comparisons with others therefore disturbed, by the fact that we had more expenditure on this account than all the other regions added together. Although the buildings had been MPBW/PSA HQ projects, the millions of pounds needed for the remedial work fell for the most part on regional maintenance budgets.

However, now that the figures have been published, they make interesting reading. Annex B shows that the overall reduction in maintenance expenditure for the department between 1967–8 and 1973–4 was 16 per cent. Southern Region's figure, even without making any allowance for its extra burdens, was 28 per cent, nearly double.

PSA points out that the national average would have been higher but for the low figures in London and the North West. Quite right: without those two regions, the average reduction would have been about 20 per cent. This is another way of saying that the department agrees that one fifth of the money it had been

3. Extract from the official BBC transcript of *Man Alive*, 9 May 1978.

spending had been wasted. Is anyone going to be so churlish as to point out that all the measures attempting to end this situation started, by an astonishing coincidence, soon after Southern Region began to prove how much waste there had been?

It is fortunate, too, that although PSA did not use them, better figures than these imperfect comparisons of gross expenditure are now available. Although the survey report recommendations tended to understate the value of savings (see p. 37), they did at least deal with real places, actual budgets, and specific proposals, instead of 'adjusted' figures and comparisons that are not of like with like. The figures for six out of the first seven surveys in Southern Region have been made available to me and are given in Table 2. (I believe the figures for the later surveys were not much different.)

Table 2

	Principal client department	Pre-survey expenditure	Recommended economies	Economies as % of expenditure
Bicester	Army	500,000	199,500	39·9
Haton	RAF	320,000	91,655	28·6
Bletchley	Civil	350,000	159,125	45·4
Bordon	Army	440,000	156,845	35·6
Roads and Ranges (Aldershot)*	Army	275,000	219,250	79·7
Hurn	Civil	135,000	109,425	81·0
TOTAL		2,020,000	935,600	46·3

* This is the depot which was responsible for a number of the 'uneconomic undertakings' referred to on p. 41, and both the undertakings and the depot were closed down completely. The percentage saving in this case was therefore not typical.

This shows the percentage of savings the teams were producing; and incidentally it demonstrates how much truth there is in the suggestion that defence spending yielded far bigger savings than civil.

The last set of figures that I want to comment on are those for directly employed labour. The PAC asked for them during the hearing on 12 June 1978, and they are shown in Para. 10 of the

PSA Memorandum (Appendix 11). In Para. 15 the PSA are at pains to make the point that other regions made reductions in DEL by methods other than surveys, but since their figures show the *total* reductions achieved by all methods, this hardly seems relevant. And, while it is of no great importance, the suggestion in this paragraph that reductions had begun before 1967 is not significant. Numbers of DEL were not being reduced before 1967: they were dropping slightly – which is not at all the same thing – because the department was finding it impossible to recruit to fill vacancies caused by natural wastage.

The numbers of DEL (from Para. 10, Appendix 11) for March 1967 and December 1973 (when I retired), with the reductions shown as a percentage of the 1967 figures, are given in Table 3.

	March 1967	December 1973	% reduction
		Table 3	
Scotland	3,208	2,475	22·8
North West	2,343	1,933	17·4
North East	2,661	2,104	20·9
Eastern	2,863	2,010	29·7
Midland	2,929	1,818	37·9
Wales	1,732	1,367	21·0
South West	4,835	3,628	24·9
South East	4,082	2,695	33·9
London	5,615	4,033	28·1
TOTAL			
(excluding Southern)	30,268	22,063	27.1
Southern	3,781	1,794	52·5

There is one other statement in the C and A G's memorandum (Appendix 8) which I cannot leave without comment. This appears in Para. 9 and relates to a draft brief not submitted to the accounting officer. A statement in this appears without qualification (and by implication is regarded as more accurate than the amended version of the brief) that 'There was local resistance to change, particularly among Army Commanders, who were used to a "personal" service by DEL'. This is a particularly unjust criticism. Certainly, as I said in the first edition (see p. 63 above), at the beginning of our surveys we had to persuade the services that what we were proposing to do and our methods of doing it made sense. Thereafter, from Army and RAF staffs at all levels (we had only one naval depot), we had wholehearted co-operation and drive in the pursuit of economy. I believe that the taxpayers' interests were well served by all the service people I worked with, and, directly contrary to what is said in the draft of the PSA brief, this was most notably true of Army commanders.

Acknowledgements

In addition to those to whom acknowledgement is made in the text, I should like to thank the following public servants for their help during my time as regional director, 1967–74:

Army Staffs
Generals commanding Aldershot District: Major-General Bernard Penfold, CB, MVO; Lt-Gen. Sir Alan Taylor, KBE, MC; Lt-Gen. Sir Terence McMeekin, KCB, DBL.

Staff Officers in Aldershot District: Colonel (now Brig.) R. A. Lister; Colonel (now Brig.) S. H. Chapman.

PSA Staff in Southern Region
Members of the teams: J. J. Andrews, M & E engineer; R. V. Stagg, higher executive officer; J. A. Bosley, higher executive officer; W. J. Bradley, quantity surveyor; E. H. Forest, building surveyor; R. Gamlin, M & E engineer; I. McNaughton, M & E engineer.

Trade Union Officials
Len Whitwell (TGWU), Trade Union Secretary, Southern Region joint industrial Whitley Committee; Members of the Southern Region joint industrial Whitley Committee.

I have also to acknowledge help with the information used in this book from the following:

The *Sunday Times* (especially the Insight team, including Peter Kellner and Tony Rocca); *Daily Express* (Jeremy Gates); *Daily Telegraph*; *Berkshire Mercury*; *Reading Evening Post*; *Dorset Evening Echo*; *Works World* (later *DOE World*); Reader's Digest Association Ltd; *Municipal and Public Services Journal*;

Economist; *Aldershot Weekend News*; *Sandhurst Midweek News*; *Illustrated Carpenter and Builder*; *Financial Times*; BBC Television, *Nationwide* (especially David Green and David Graham); Westward Television; BBC South, *Today*; Radio BRMB (Birmingham); Beacon Radio (Wolverhampton); Public Interest Research Centre, Monroe House, 9 Poland Street, London, W1; and HMSO for kind permission to quote the official documents printed in the Appendixes.

And finally to C. W. Reid (Under-Secretary for Finance, Ministry of Public Building and Works, 1954–6, retired 1956), who first encouraged me to attempt to do something about waste in the Civil Service.

Postscript to the First Edition

In Chapters 10 and 11 I quoted from evidence that was being given early in 1977 to the House of Commons Expenditure Committee on the Civil Service (the 'English Committee'). The Report[1] from the committee, including its recommendations, did not appear until September 1977, too late unfortunately to be taken into account when the rest of this book was being written.

The committee began taking evidence on 3 May 1976 and went on doing so until 9 May 1977. During that time it heard from an impressive list of expert distinguished and authoritative witnesses, including fifty-one in Washington and Paris, two ex-prime ministers (Sir Harold Wilson and Mr Heath) and Lord Fulton. It also heard from some civil servants. It was presented with 101 memoranda and reports from a variety of official and non-official bodies.

The Report is a major step forward in the continuing process of attempts by Parliament to improve the Civil Service and I commend it to anyone who is seriously interested in this topic.

Recommendations and the committee's supporting comments are conveniently summarized in Volume I of the Report. About half of those recommendations deal with recruitment, pay, pensions and training. These are matters which are for the most part outside the scope of this book, which in turn covers matters not dealt with by the committee. There is, however, a substantial overlapping area, and it is interesting to compare the two sets of conclusions reached by such different methods. (Paragraph numbers relate to the Report; page and chapter numbers to this book.)

1. Eleventh Report from the Expenditure Committee, Session 1976–77. 'The Civil Service' (Stationery Office).

Areas of general agreement

1. *The failure to implement the Fulton Report*, Para. 74; (Chapter 11) The committee clearly considers that this is so self-evident that it requires neither argument nor detailed comment. It merely refers to it in passing: '. . . with the evaporation of Fulton enthusiasm, and the virtual shelving of the report . . .'

2. *Accountable units*, Para. 93; (Chapter 11, pp. 116–22)
The committee recommends a determined drive to introduce accountable units. It makes two comments in this connection:

We do not believe that the Fulton proposal of accountable units has been taken sufficiently seriously in the Civil Service.

We find it hard to understand Lord Armstrong's opinion 'I do not feel unhappy about what I tried to do in that area'.

3. *Reduction in the size of accounting officers' responsibilities* (Para. 95; Chapter 12)
The committee says that accountable units in government should be scaled down to the size most conducive to effective informed control by the officer in charge.

4. *Public accountability* (Chapter 17)
The committee wants to bring more civil servants to be directly answerable to Parliamentary Committees for management decisions. It does not see that this infringes ministerial responsibility, involves civil servants in politics, or generally presents any great problem.

5. *Reducing costs by policy changes*, Paras. 64–70; (Chapters 16 and 17)
The committee makes two recommendations on this subject:

We recommend the inauguration of a programme of regular surveys on the possibilities of reducing costs through policy changes.

We believe that Parliament should be regularly informed of potential savings from policy changes, in order that it may have sufficient knowledge for informed debate and criticism. We do not think that the disclosure of such information could be construed as political activity by civil servants. We therefore recommend that the Government devise methods by which they could continually report the options in this respect to Parliament.

6. *Parliamentary control over expenditure*

The committee says: 'A reappraisal of the entire apparatus of Parliamentary control of expenditure is overdue' (Para. 107; page references are not appropriate: much of Part III is devoted to this).

7. *Fundamental weakness and ineffectuality of the Civil Service Department,* (pp. 113–14 and 117)

The committee makes a number of comments on this, all very much to the point. The following are examples:

It [the CSD] has lost its original drive. [Para. 73]

We do not believe that the CSD . . . has a prominent part to play at the centre of Government . . . it has lost its *raison d'être.* [Para. 74]

The relationship [of the CSD with other Departments] has not been satisfactorily defined; the sovereignty of each Department in efficiency matters has seriously inhibited the work of the CSD. [Para. 113]

8. *Efficiency and other checks to be imposed upon departments,* Para. 118; (p. 147).

The committee's recommendation is that management services and staff inspection should be placed on the same basis; 'i.e., their entry should be compulsory, though not their recommendations'.

9. *Personal risks to civil servants who propose economies,* Para. 117; (pp. 53, 123).

My suggestion that people may suffer as a result of proposing economies might seem alarmist, but the committee did not think so. In the context of staff inspectors, but clearly having a wider application, it says inspectors 'have no means of imposing recommendations which are unpopular with senior management *bearing in mind they may even place their careers at risk*' (my italics).

10. *Incentives for staff* (pp. 108–9).

The committee makes two recommendations:

We should like to see more . . . of relating pay and promotion to performance. [Para. 129]

We recommend that one US system should be introduced as soon as possible. This is the speeding up or withholding of increments. [Para. 130]

The committee, however, took the view that, subject to this speeding up and slowing down, automatic increments should continue. I am opposed to this.

11. *Need to extend the role of Exchequer and Audit Department*, Paras. 154–6; (Chapters 15 and 16)
The committee begins with an unequivocal statement: '. . . we are of the opinion that by comparison with other countries our system of public audit is out of date' (Para. 153), and goes on to advocate an audit department much more like the General Accounting Office of the US.

12. *Exchequer and Audit Department to monitor efficiency of all departments* Para. 156; (Chapter 16)
The committee recommends 'that the E and AD should be empowered to conduct audits of the management efficiency and effectiveness of all that it audits financially'.

13. *Appointment of the Comptroller and Auditor General*, Para. 158; (p. 154)
The committee feels that the present system for appointing the C and AG is wrong: 'the field of recruitment [i.e. from the Civil Service] seems to us to be unduly limited'.

14. *Power to require E and AD to carry out an investigation*, Para. 160; (p. 162)
The committee believes that it is wrong that no one can oblige C and AG to initiate an inquiry and proposes an Amending Act so that it becomes clear the E and AD 'should initiate enquiries if requested to do so by the House [of Commons] or one of its Committees'.

15. *Committees of MPs to be more specialized*, Para. 161; pp. (158–9)
Noting in passing that the House of Commons 'has, almost accidentally, lost control of the process of appropriating expenditure', the committee recommends that committees should

be created, each of which relates to only one department of state. That differs from this book (though in detail rather than in principle), since I propose sub-committees for related groups of services and departments.

16. *Cost comparison with the private sector*, Para. 102; (p. 156)
The committee points out that in the absence of competition, tenders from the private sector and comparisons with overseas are useful checks, and concludes that '... comparisons with the private sector should be normal practice ... [wherever] feasible'.

17. *Accounting to Parliament*, Para. 100
The committee asserts that 'the accounts that Parliament is presented with simply do not correspond to the realities of public expenditure' and recommends that changes be made despite all that this would involve (pp. 139–42).

The committee advocates changes different from those I propose on pp. 140–43. It recommends Appropriation Accounts linked to accountable units, Para. 100. The committee does, however, agree on the need for analyses to be presented to Parliament which show what past programmes of expenditure have achieved (Chapter 16).

18. *The Civil Service college*, Para. 16; (p. 156)
'We do not consider that it [the College] has been wholly successful ... a view apparently shared by its former Principal, Mr Grebenik.' Mr Grebenik added 'Amen' (a heartfelt one, I suspect) to a report on the college which said:

> It is as though the same institution were expected to combine the roles of All Souls and an adult education centre, with some elements of technical education and teacher training thrown in for good measure.

Areas of disagreement

1. The committee disagrees with the proposals in this book on only one important aspect (in addition to the points of detail already referred to). The committee, referring yet again to the 'impotence' of the Civil Service Department and its 'disappointing performance', concludes, as I do, that the responsibility for

monitoring efficiency and for staff inspection should be taken away from the CSD. The committee recommends that these powers be transferred to the Treasury, Para. 85. I have proposed that they go to the New Audit Department.

Both systems would work, but I am still of the opinion that the NAD would be the better choice for four reasons. First, the areas of scrutiny will be mostly those where policy is not in question, but only the manner of its execution. The Treasury on the other hand is very much involved with policy.

Second, in those cases where policy is in question, albeit by implication only, there is much to be said for an objective report on costs being made (by the NAD) for consideration and appraisal elsewhere, and the Treasury would certainly be involved in this latter process.

Third, the Treasury has a responsibility for the strategy of the control of public expenditure and the shaping of policies which can best be discharged if it sits above the sort of exchanges likely to be involved in audit activities. Lastly, the mechanics of audit and inspection – entry into departments, on-the-spot inspections, and the investigation of cases – are much more in keeping with the traditions and experience of E and AD than they are with the Treasury.

2. The committee makes a recommendation on one matter that I do not. It suggests that the Prime Minister and the Leader of the Opposition should jointly consider the rule that no Administration sees the papers of its predecessor of a different party, Para. 152. The disadvantages of the present arrangement are described in Chapter 7 at the point where it prevented me from briefing Mr Channon adequately about the past, even though there was no difference between the wishes of the Ministers of the two parties. There is no doubt that a change in this rule would be a useful step towards better control over the Civil Service. It is mortifying that, after repeatedly urging that nothing must be accepted without challenge, it did not occur to me that this rule was an obvious candidate for scrapping. Truly, it is easier to preach than to practice!

*

More important, perhaps, than individual recommendations and comments is the underlying impatience of the committee with complacency and inactivity, coupled with its refreshing determination not to be soothed or persuaded by civil-service witnesses. Since it was largely thanks to the Press that it became possible to write this book I think it would be appropriate to use their headlines as a final summary of the committee's views, and as a fitting conclusion to this postscript.

The Times: 'Civil servants' powers must be curbed.'
Daily Telegraph: 'MPs suspect civil servants of deliberate delay.'
Daily Mirror: 'Shake up bowler brigade, urge MPs.'
Sun: 'The Pinstripe saboteurs.'
Financial Times: 'Public unease about the Civil Service.'
Daily Mail: 'The Puppet Masters of Whitehall.'
Guardian: 'Civil Servants "the masters".'
Evening Standard: 'Whitehall Wreckers.'

October 1977

Appendixes

Appendix 1

APPROPRIATION ACCOUNTS 1973-74

Appropriation Accounts of the sums granted by Parliament
for Civil Services, Classes VI–XI, for the year ended 31st March
1974. (pp. v–vii)

CLASS VI, VOTE 7. CIVIL ACCOMMODATION SERVICES, &c.,
UNITED KINGDOM
CLASS VI, VOTE 8. CIVIL ACCOMMODATION SERVICES, &c.,
OVERSEAS
CLASS VI, VOTE 9. DEFENCE ACCOMMODATION SERVICES, &c.

Maintenance and Operating Expenses

24. During 1973–74 the Property Services Agency of the Department
of the Environment spent £116m. in the United Kingdom and £49m.
overseas on maintenance and operating expenses of buildings and
fixed installations of government departments and establishments.
They employed approximately 14,000 industrial staff in the United
Kingdom on maintenance and 8,000 on such duties as stoking, plant
attendance and storekeeping. Their staff carried out about 40 per cent
of all maintenance and repair work and contractors did the rest.

25. The Agency, or their predecessors, have delegated to their
Regional Offices and Directorates and through them to Area Offices and
some 280 Depots in the United Kingdom, the main responsibilities for
the control of maintenance and operating expenditure and methods of
work. Similar arrangements operate in the six overseas Regions except
in Hong Kong where the cost of maintaining any properties occupied
by British Forces is borne by the Hong Kong Government. In recent
years the Agency have commissioned management consultants to
advise on operational procedures to improve productivity, introduced
a productivity bonus for industrial staff to secure flexible working, and
carried out maintenance economy reviews at Depots to ensure that

maintenance responsibilities are clearly defined, maintenance standards are adequate and not higher than necessary and the most economical working methods are used.

26. In 1968 the Southern Region carried out exploratory maintenance economy reviews at Depots in their Region by independent teams of one administrative and two technical officers, and these had shown that maintenance expenditure could be reduced without any appreciable lessening of the service given and that economies of 17·5 per cent in one Depot and 16 per cent in another could be achieved. Therefore the Agency decided to extend the surveys to other Regions. A review in 1969 indicated that the surveys had been generally worthwhile but that there were marked differences in the results achieved in the efforts made by different Regions; Southern Region had used three full-time teams, Wales had still to start. A report to Ministers in March 1970 stressed the importance of the surveys to the economic running of Depots and the need for a standardised survey method.

27. In 1971 the Agency instructed Regions to press ahead with the surveys and gave general guidance on the selection of teams and the conduct of surveys so that reviews would be comprehensive and teams' recommendations soundly based. They suggested that at least two teams per Region were needed for the work to be completed in a reasonable time, and instructed Regions to submit annual reports on the results of the surveys.

28. An analysis of the results of maintenance economy reviews completed by 31 March 1973 showed that some 140 Depots, with a workload of £42·5m. and 13,000 industrial staff, had been surveyed and that economies recommended and accepted amounted to £6·4m. of which £5·3m. were annual savings. Potential savings of an additional £2·8m. were under discussion. Capital expenditure of £1·1m. had been incurred and the staff costs of the surveys were £0·7m. Corresponding information for reviews completed by 31 March 1974 was not available when my officers examined the position.

29. The Agency informed me that it was difficult to quantify the savings in every case or to distinguish between savings attributable to particular maintenance economy reviews and to general management initiatives, but that the savings had been substantial. They had arisen mainly from the elimination of unnecessary servicing, reduced ground maintenance, better planned working arrangements and methods, and heating and fuel economies. As a result of the measures taken and

because some work had been transferred to contractors, the Agency's directly employed industrial staff had been reduced by nearly 30 per cent from 31,000 in 1968 to 22,000 in 1973.

30. By March 1973 after about half the Depots in the United Kingdom had been surveyed, two Regions had virtually completed their programme, while the Directorate of Works, London, had done only about 10 per cent of theirs. More than half the savings mentioned in paragraph 28 above had been contributed by two of the ten Regions, Southern and Midland. The total number of survey teams in operation had fallen from 18 in 1971 to 15.

31. In reply to my inquiries the Agency informed me that they were satisfied that reviews had been conducted with as much urgency and thoroughness as other calls on their resources allowed. Because of lack of resources at headquarters formal arrangements to co-ordinate and disseminate information on uneconomic practices revealed by the reviews had not been introduced but the results of the reviews were circulated and acted upon within Regions. The Agency did not consider that there were large potential savings remaining untapped. The Depots surveyed had been those, primarily in the Defence estate and particularly old barrack areas and large airfields where the original requirements for buildings and facilities had changed, where large numbers of industrial staff had been employed. Subsequently they had achieved further reductions in directly employed labour through policy directives and improved management methods. The early reviews had led to large savings in fuel consumption, and since then the Agency had secured further economies from the use of better control equipment and improved operating instructions to technical staff in Depots.

32. The Agency told me that the high level of savings in the Southern and Midland Regions had reflected the early start of maintenance economy reviews in those Regions before other management initiatives had taken effect; also in the Southern Region there were many Defence establishments which had employed a large number of industrial staff. The Agency said that progress by the Directorate of Works, London, had not been as fast as they would have wished. Staff resources had permitted only one review team to operate and it was under strength for eight months during 1973–74. However, the results of earlier reviews had been summarised in 1973 and circulated to all area officers in London and every effort would be made to maintain progress in the Region.

33. The Agency said that they thought that, in general, the scope for special maintenance economy reviews in home Regions had considerably diminished and that for the future a continuous review of the maintenance effort should be seen as a normal part of management. Potential savings disclosed by previous reviews would be followed up and any large establishment that justified an individual review would be surveyed.

34. In reply to my inquiry on overseas Regions the Agency stated that they considered that their close working relationship with the Ministry of Defence, and the constant pressure on overseas expenditure with frequent Defence policy reviews, had ensured that the Defence estate overseas was not over-maintained. Recent visits by headquarters' staff had confirmed this except in certain areas where they thought some rationalisation could produce worthwhile economies. They had decided to conduct special reviews of expenditure on the Defence estate in Germany and Gibraltar, but saw no need to do so in other Regions.

Appendix 2

FOURTH REPORT FROM THE COMMITTEE OF PUBLIC ACCOUNTS

together with the Proceedings of the Committee, part of the Minutes of Evidence, Appendix and Index. Session 1974–75 (pp. 244–248)

APPROPRIATION ACCOUNTS (CLASSES VI–XI: CIVIL) 1973–74

CLASS VI, VOTE 7. CIVIL ACCOMMODATION SERVICE, &C., UNITED KINGDOM

CLASS VI, VOTE 8. CIVIL ACCOMMODATION SERVICES, &C., OVERSEAS

CLASS VI, VOTE 9. DEFENCE ACCOMMODATION SERVICES, &C.

Maintenance and Operating Expenses of Government Properties

Chairman:

1314. We will now turn to the third and last subject that we should like to discuss with you, that is to say, paragraphs 24 to 34 of the Comptroller and Auditor General's Report on maintenance and operating expenses. Could you very kindly define for the Committee exactly what is the maintenance and operating work which we are considering?——(Mr *Cox*) It is very wide and very varied. We are responsible for the estate management of all the civil estate of the Government – I am not speaking about the Crown Estate but of Government departments – and also of the Services and the Ministry of Defence. This brings under our umbrella in the United Kingdom something like 22,000 different properties on the civil side, representing about 55 million square feet of offices, 14 million square feet of stores, and about 25 million square feet of miscellaneous buildings like research establishments and museums. On the Defence side, we have got about 12,000 properties to look after and 90,000 married quarters. The Defence estate is very varied, comprising airfields, barracks, camps, dockyards, the whole of Salisbury Plain, and lands and foreshores over which farmers may have rights or, conversely, where the military have rights of their own. For all this we have the task of physical maintenance, such as painting and repair, heating, looking after grounds, cutting of grass, and negotiating for and looking after the farms which form a large part of the military estate. Also, in a much wider sense, we have the task of seeing to it that the estate is managed in a sensible fashion. For example, if there is a demand for new accommodation, we first look to see whether the demand cannot be met from within the existing estate, but on maintenance as narrowly defined, it is really the whole job of looking after this enormous property.

1315. Everything except new capital work, basically, you might say?——Ranks as maintenance, yes.

1316. Can I take your attention to paragraph 24, please? I see from that that your own staff carry out something like less than half of the maintenance and repair work. I have no judgment as to whether it is right that you should do 100 per cent. or 5 per cent., but how do you make the decision as to whether or not to use your own staff or to use contractors?——The practice we follow is that we use our own staff where there is a particular reason for doing so; for example, where there are continuing and continuous operations to be looked after, like stoking and looking after boilers, and where there are security considerations, which require that it should be our own people operating within a given area. This also applies in areas where it may be difficult to get contract work done and in areas, conversely, where there may be a very high level of building activity and where we need to ensure that we have a nucleus of our own staff to look after urgent needs. We also look at costs. The general principle is that having looked after those essential needs which I have mentioned, we then carry out a costing operation on a sample basis from time to time to ascertain whether it is cheaper to work with our own labour or whether we should use contractors. The current result of this is that about 60 per cent. of our work is done by contractors and about 40 per cent. is done by our own labour.

1317. I now turn to the subject of economy – paragraph 28. Have you got any figures for savings later than those that you quote in that paragraph?——That paragraph gives figures up to the 31st March,

1973. To bring it forward to the end of the financial year that we are discussing today, 1973–74, the corresponding figures are that the total saving from reviews carried through amounts to £6·8 million in annual savings, and £1·2 million in non-recurring savings, making a total of £8 million, and there are still about £1 million worth of ideas being discussed.

1318. Those are healthy figures. One matter that surprised me, at any rate, was the differences that there seemed to be between regions in their enthusiasm for economy reviews? Why was that?——I think that it was not simply a matter of enthusiasm; it was also a matter of opportunities and timing. The region which stands out in our figures is the Southern Region, which started this work in 1969 and achieved substantially higher savings than any of the other regions. I think that there are two or three main reasons for that. The first is that they started sooner, before a number of other management initiatives took place which in themselves made economies in maintenance and which therefore fell to be registered in different ways and were not available when the other regions came in later on. Secondly, there was a greater opportunity. One of the most effective ways of achieving maintenance economy is to reduce the number of buildings and the areas to be covered. The Southern Region covers, among other things, the Aldershot area, and in the years immediately before 1969 there had been substantial re-deployment of military resources. There had been a lot of staff moving north. Consequently, there were quite a number of opportunities in the Aldershot area and in the Southern Region generally for proposing to the Army that there should be economy in the use of buildings, that buildings which were only partly occupied could be closed, and that there should be a reduction in heating in buildings that were no longer used or no longer fully used, and I think that it is fair to say that with the enthusiasm that was shown, full advantage was taken of these opportunities. Other regions did not have the same possibilities because the same re-deployments had not taken place. I think, on the whole, the figures show that most of the regions produced broadly similar results. They produced, in total, savings of round about £½ million, with two or three exceptions. On the one hand there was the Southern Region, which showed a much higher figure. On the other hand there were the North West Region and the London Region, which showed substantially lower figures, and I think that there were special reasons in each case for those lower figures.

1319. I do not want in any way to detract from what has obviously been a substantial, and I would think, successful effort here, but if I can take you to paragraph 29 while there are a number of reasons stated there for savings, they seem to me to be just the sort of things that management should have been putting into effect all the time. Can you give the Committee your version of why that had not happened before these drives?——I think, possibly, that it is a question of priorities at any one particular time. One important factor is that the nature of the organisation changed substantially in 1963 when the then Ministry of Public Building and Works took over the whole of the Defence works responsibilities. This produced an entirely new management structure and a new set of responsibilities. This, I think, took a certain amount of digesting, but then, given the new set up, the opportunities were there and were taken.

1320. I was a bit surprised when in paragraph 31 you said that you were unable, because of lack of resources at your headquarters, to disseminate information on uneconomic practices. What is the position on that now?——The position now is that we are going to have annual reports for each of the regions which cover not only the results achieved but the methods by which they were achieved. I would say, on the other hand, that most of the things, as you have just pointed out, were not very sophisticated devices. Going back to your client and saying 'Do you really need to use that building? Can you reduce your direct labour force? Are the painting periods sensible painting periods?' is not dealing with very complicated or sophisticated things. They are ideas which could be exchanged around the table by the Regional Directors at their regular meetings, and by informal contacts.

1321. What is the situation in London?——The situation in London is that we are not satisfied. There is a chronic difficulty there in that we find it extremely difficult to get staff of the sort that we need to carry through this work, and there is a heavy burden of urgent work. We therefore have not done as much as we would like. We have only one team operating at the moment and a great deal still remains to be done. In fairness to the London Region, however, I would say that it has made better progress in other areas. For example, it has carried through and completed the reorganisation in management terms of its maintenance organisation, which few of the other regions have yet finished, so that it is gaining on the swings what it has lost on the roundabouts. But I would accept that this is not satisfactory and we need to press on here.

1322. Do you want to say anything about the reviews that you are undertaking in Germany and Gibraltar?——These have just started and I really have not got a great deal of information about what progress they may be making.

Mr *Hordern*

1323. May I ask about one or two of the notes which appear in the losses statement under Vote 7 on page 41 of the Appropriation Accounts, Classes VI to XI? What is the extra contractual payment of £1·4 million in settlement of a claim arising from the contract for the erection of government offices in Horseferry Road?——(Mr *May*) This was the settlement of a claim arising from the contract for the erection of the government offices in Horseferry Road, Marsham Street. We had a claim for £3·3 million due to difficulties and changes that arose during the process of that very prolonged building project. We negotiated a settlement with the contractors, and finally, although they had claimed £3·3 million, we were able to settle at something just over £1·4 million.

1324. Thank you. There is one other point which I am sure you will need notice of. That is, what is the Department lending £17,000 to a county council for? That is on page 46.——That is on Defence accommodation?

1325. Yes?——The Department is planning to build quarters for naval ratings and the local authority were having to borrow £100,000 to provide site services.* It was agreed that, with Treasury approval, we should make a loan to the local authority, repayable over a period of years to help meet the cost, and the figure that you see there is the sum that was paid by the local authority as their annual payment.

1326. As their annual payment?——Yes.

1327. What is the total sum involved?——They borrowed £100,000.* They had to borrow £100,000 and our loan was £50,000. We made a loan of £50,000.

1328. Why should the Department be lending money to county councils at all? Why should not the county council be borrowing the money themselves in the normal way?——As you said earlier, we might need notice of some of the consequential questions here. I think that

---

* *Note by Witness:* The references to £100,000 were related to an earlier proposal in the same area. The £50,000 loan to the County Council was to help with road works.

they must have had difficulty in raising the money at the time. This arose essentially because of a demand that we were placing. We were building a very large number of houses, and it was we who were imposing the burden on the Services, and I suppose they felt that we ought to help them out in their difficulty, and with the agreement of the Treasury that is what we did.

1329. Perhaps I could ask the Treasury witness whether this is an unusual event, that the Department should lend money directly to local authorities in this way?——(Mr *Jones*) To my knowledge, in my field, yes. (Mr *Kemp*) Yes, I think it an unusual event. (Mr *Cox*) It is very unusual.

Chairman

1330. I think for the convenience of everybody that it might be better, rather than answering this particular matter ad hoc, which I know puts everybody in a difficulty if there has not been notice, if you would let us have a short note?——Certainly.

Chairman] Then we can take the circumstances, Mr Hordern, if that is convenient.

Mr *Hordern*] Yes, it would be particularly helpful, especially from the Treasury, because I should like a note to see just how often this occurs.

Chairman] I think we would like both the particular and the general, if we might, perhaps a note from the Treasury and a note from you, Mr Cox. You will obviously want to co-ordinate them.†

Mr Orbach

1331. I should like to know what stimulated this special review of expenditure in Gibraltar and Germany. They are two entirely different establishments. Is there any special reason?——(Mr *Cox*) We have been doing this in the home regions in the United Kingdom for some time and we were left with the question whether we should look at our overseas regions. Of the overseas regions Germany and Gibraltar were the only two where there seemed to be a profit for a variety of reasons in undertaking this exercise. In Hong Kong we do not meet the expense. Singapore we are going to leave early next year. In Malta we are due to leave in 1979, and Cyprus is clearly not the place at the moment for

† Not printed.

undertaking an exercise of this sort, so that then left Germany and Gibraltar.

Mr *Crouch*

1332. The only question that I should like to ask is exactly how you institute these maintenance economy reviews. I am not unimpressed by what you have achieved, but I am impressed by the enormous amount of expenditure that you find yourselves still saddled with. I wondered whether the reviews were, as it were, an instruction on paper to regions and depots and elsewhere to carry out, or whether you sent an inspecting team round to these 22,000 places?——No. The maintenance reviews are undertaken by teams from the regional offices, consisting of one administrative officer and two technical officers. They go round on tour. They have got a schedule of things to look at and cover and they do this. But I would, if I might, try to avoid resting on these as our only method of achieving maintenance economies. We have had a whole number of improvements operating over the last few years, including basically the whole reorganisation of our maintenance system in the regions, a number of steps to secure better planning and control of our direct labour force, a productivity agreement that we have entered into with them, a new system of planned maintenance of the mechanical equipment that we maintain, a much more sophisticated fuel saving programme than we had when these maintenance reviews were first started in 1969, and a number of other things which, in total, I think, produce a notable effect on maintenance costs as well as these maintenance economy reviews.

1333. When these inspecting teams have gone round they must have been armed with very valuable information that they have gained for themselves?——Yes

1334. Do you have an exchange of information between these teams? Do they report to each other?——The information is more specific than general. It is a question of looking at particular buildings and groups of buildings that we maintain and seeing what needs to be done there, whether more is being done than is necessary, whether the buildings themselves still need to be used, and whether the grass needs to be cut so often. It is that sort of thing.

1335. What I meant was that presumably there might be different standards developed from one area to another, and by reporting back to the centre and by one team learning from another, they might realise that their standards were different. I wondered if you had come across that?——Yes, these things do come back eventually through the Regional Directors to the regular meetings that they have among themselves, but I would say that there are indeed, and there must be, different standards in some things. Obviously, paintwork needs different treatment for different types of building in different types of area.

Chairman] Mr Cox, the Committee is much obliged to you. Thank you very much indeed.

Appendix 3

FOURTH REPORT FROM THE COMMITTEE OF PUBLIC ACCOUNTS

together with the Proceedings of the Committee, part of the Minutes of Evidence, Appendix and Index. Session 1974–75 (pp. xv–xvii)

CLASS VI, VOTE 7. CIVIL ACCOMMODATION SERVICES, &c., UNITED KINGDOM
CLASS VI, VOTE 8. CIVIL ACCOMMODATION SERVICES, &c., OVERSEAS
CLASS VI, VOTE 9. DEFENCE ACCOMMODATION SERVICES, &c.

Maintenance and Operating Expenses

23. During 1973–74 the Property Services Agency of the Department of the Environment spent £116 million in the United Kingdom and £49 million overseas on maintenance and operating expenses of some 34,000 properties, comprising offices, research establishments, museums, storage depots, barracks, airfields and dockyards, and some 90,000 married quarters. They employed approximately 14,000 industrial staff in the United Kingdom on maintenance and 8,000 on such duties as stoking, plant attendance and storekeeping. Their staff carried out about 40 per cent. of all maintenance repair and operating work and contractors did the rest. In some circumstances there were particular reasons to use their own staff, but the general principle followed by the Agency was to adopt, in the light of sample costings, whichever method was the cheaper.

24. The main responsibilities for the control of maintenance and operating expenditure and methods of work

[margin notes:] C. & A.G.'s Report (Classes VI–XI: Civil) Paras. 24–34 Q. 1314

Q. 1316

are delegated to Regional Offices and Directorates, and through them to Area Offices and some 280 Depots in Q. 1332 the United Kingdom. In recent years the Agency have introduced a number of measures to secure better planning and control of the direct labour force, including a productivity agreement, a new system of planned maintenance of mechanical equipment and sophisticated fuel-saving methods.

25. They have also carried out maintenance economy reviews at Depots to ensure that maintenance responsibilities are clearly defined, maintenance standards are adequate and not higher than necessary and the most economical working methods are used. An exploratory maintenance review was first carried out in 1968 by the Southern Region. This had shown that maintenance expenditure could be reduced without any appreciable lessening of the service given and that economies of 17·5 per cent. in one Depot and 16 per cent. in another could be achieved. Therefore the Agency decided to extend the surveys to other Regions. A review in 1969 indicated that the surveys had been generally worth while but that there were marked differences in the results achieved and in the efforts made by different Regions. A report to Ministers in March 1970 stressed the importance of the surveys to the economic running of Depots and the need for a standardised survey method.

26. In 1971 the Agency instructed Regions to press ahead with the surveys and gave general guidance on the selection of teams and the conduct of surveys. They suggested that at least two teams per Region were needed and instructed Regions to submit annual reports on the results. By March 1973 after about half the Depots in the United Kingdom had been surveyed, two Regions had virtually completed their programme but the London Region had done only about 10 per cent. of theirs. The total number of survey teams in operation had fallen from 18 in 1971 to 15.

Q. 1317   27. The Agency informed Your Committee that an analysis of the results of maintenance economy reviews completed by the end of 1973–74 showed economies amounting to £8 million, of which £6·8 million were annual savings and further possible savings of £1 million were under discussion. It was difficult to quantify the savings in every case or to distinguish between savings attributable to particular maintenance economy reviews and to general management initiatives. The savings had arisen mainly from the elimination of unnecessary servicing, reduced ground maintenance, better planned working arrangements and methods, and heating and fuel economies. As a result of the measures taken and because some work had been transferred to contractors, the Agency's directly employed industrial staff had been reduced by nearly 30 per cent. from 31,000 in 1968 to 22,000 in 1973.

28. More than half the savings mentioned had been contributed by two of the ten Regions, Southern and Midland, with Southern Region contributing the highest   Q. 1318
saving. The Agency told Your Committee that Southern Region had started the reviews sooner than the other Regions and before a number of other management initiatives aimed at achieving maintenance economies had taken effect; also, military resources in the Region had been substantially re-deployed which had provided opportunities for reducing the number of buildings and areas to be maintained. The same opportunities had not existed in the other Regions which had, with two or three exceptions, each produced savings of about £½ million.

29. The Agency told us that they were not satisfied with   Q. 1321
progress in the London Region. There was difficulty in getting the right staff for the work, only one review team was currently operating and a great deal remained to be done. The Region had however made better progress in other matters and had completed the re-organisation of their maintenance organisation. They intended to press ahead with the reviews in the London Region. We trust that the Agency will pursue this work energetically, so that all possible economies may be secured as early as possible.

30. The Agency considered that in general the scope for special maintenance economy reviews in Regions in the United Kingdom had considerably diminished and that in future a continuous review of the maintenance effort should be seen as a normal part of management. They had not had the resources at Headquarters to introduce formal arrangements to co-ordinate and disseminate information on uneconomic practices revealed by the reviews but the results had been circulated and acted upon by Regions. They told us that they now required each Region to prepare an annual report to show the results achieved and the methods adopted which would be considered and ideas exchanged at regular meetings of regional directors and by informal contacts.

Qs. 1320, 1335

31. Your Committee are glad to note that substantial savings have been achieved by maintenance economy review teams in the United Kingdom, but it seems to us that many of the ideas for economies were of a type that management should have been putting into effect all the time. We also think that resources should have been found at Headquarters to disseminate information on uneconomic practices to all Regions. We agree that in the future the review of maintenance work should be a normal task of management, but we look to the Agency to take steps to satisfy themselves that uneconomic practices are persistently sought out and eliminated by their local offices and depots, and that all possibilities for significant savings are publicised throughout the Organisation.

Qs. 1319–20

32. The Agency had not introduced maintenance economy reviews in overseas Regions at the same time as in the United Kingdom, because they had considered that their close working relationship with the Ministry of Defence, and the constant pressure on overseas expenditure with frequent Defence policy reviews, ensured that the Defence estate overseas was not over-maintained. The Agency told us, however, that special reviews had just started in Germany and Gibraltar, the only Regions overseas where conditions made them appropriate, but they could not yet say what progress was being made.

Qs. 1322, 1331

We will be surprised if there is not scope for substantial savings on Defence estates overseas as there was at home and we trust that the Agency will ensure that the reviews now in train will be energetically pursued.

Appendix 4

APPROPRIATION ACCOUNTS 1974–75

Appropriation Accounts of the sums granted by Parliament for Classes X–XV and XVII for the year ended 31st. March 1975. (pp. xliii–xliv)

CLASS XIV, VOTE 1.
OFFICE AND GENERAL ACCOMMODATION SERVICES

Use of the Government Car Service

145. During 1974–75 the Property Services Agency of the Department of the Environment incurred expenditure of £1·7m. on the operation of the Government Car Service. The fleet consists of some 480 cars, ranging in size from 850 cc. to 3·5 litre saloons, of which about 60 are self-drive. Nearly half of the fleet is based in London and used mainly by Ministers and senior civil servants. The remainder operate under the control of the Agency's Regional Directors. Departments may use the service where they consider this essential to enable work to be carried out effectively and economically or if public transport would involve a disproportionate loss of official time, but the Agency can refuse a request if they consider it cannot properly be met.

146. In 1971 the Directorate of Management Services of the Department of the Environment examined the use of the 19 cars and 16 drivers based in the Southern Region. They reported in September 1971 that, on a six week sample, over 80 per cent of the car usage was by three Departments. The cars were generally booked by the day to make circular tours with a number of stops for, mainly, junior officers of the Department of Health and Social Security to visit claimants in their homes, the Inland Revenue Department to collect taxes and make property valuations, and the Department of the Environment to inspect construction and maintenance work. The annual cost in the

Southern Region was £40,000 and the report stated that between £5,000 and £9,000 a year would be saved if hired cars or taxis were used in every instance, between £21,000 and £23,000 if self-drive cars were used and £29,000 if all officers had and drove their own cars. As a result the car service in the Region was withdrawn during 1972 and Departments made their own travelling arrangements.

147. Car services continued to be operated in the other Regions. In May 1973 the Agency asked eight Regional Directors whether it might be worth considering the use of hired in place of official cars, since Southern Region had discontinued their car service without real inconvenience, although they recognised that local circumstances would vary. None of the Regional Directors favoured complete abolition of the service in view of its use for visiting Ministers, senior civil servants and overseas visitors, and five saw little value in a detailed investigation. The North West Region, with the largest car pool, favoured an investigation because their main users were junior staff on visiting duties. Because the views of Regional Directors were mixed the Agency eventually decided to obtain a report on actual experience in the Southern Region. The report was presented in June 1975 and was being considered when I made my enquiries.

148. My staff had examined car requisitions and log sheets covering at least a month in 1974–75 and found that about half the journeys outside London Region were made by junior staff. Journeys were often for short distances with long waiting periods and chauffeurs sometimes drove further without a passenger than with one. As this pattern of usage was similar to that which had led to the abolition of the car service in the Southern Region I asked about the consideration given to the matter in other Regions.

149. The Agency informed me that although the investigation in the Southern Region had strongly suggested that withdrawal of the car service would yield significant cost savings, the annual cost of regularly hiring cars was potentially greater than providing them through the car service, although hiring was cheaper when demand was intermittent or met short-term peaks. They had thought it prudent to confirm that savings had materialised in practice and without loss of efficiency before extending the experiment in the Southern Region more widely. Experience in the Southern Region over the past two years had confirmed that, apart from a minimum provision of chauffeur-driven cars, it would be cheaper to make greater use of self-drive cars, with hired cars being used to meet peak demands. The Agency considered that

most Regions needed a minimum number of chauffeur-driven cars to cater for the needs of visiting Ministers and senior officials and Southern Region had been unusual in that respect because visiting Ministers normally travelled direct by car from London. When the Regional cars were not otherwise committed, it was economical and sensible to use them for journeys even by relatively junior staff.

150. The Agency told me that the issue of a Government Car Service went beyond their responsibilities and had been referred to an inter-departmental committee which had been set up at their instigation in June 1975 under the chairmanship of the Civil Service Department to review the arrangements of all Departments for the use and operation of transport services. The enquiry into the car service was expected to be completed in early 1976. The Agency meanwhile, when replacing cars in provincial pools, were using smaller, cheaper vehicles.

Appendix 5

SIXTH REPORT FROM
THE COMMITTEE OF PUBLIC ACCOUNTS

together with the Proceedings of the Committee, part of the
Minutes of Evidence, Appendices and Index. Session 1975–76
(pp. 339–342)

APPROPRIATION ACCOUNTS (VOLUME 3), 1974–75

CLASS XIV, VOTE 1. OFFICE AND GENERAL ACCOMMODATION SERVICES

Use of the Government Car Service

Chairman

2380. Let us turn to paragraphs 145 to 150 of the Comptroller and Auditor General's Report, on the matter of the use of the Government's car service. I am sure that it is the view of the Committee that those who have a job to do, and a very responsible job to do, should have all the tools that they need. Do not think, please, that there is any prejudice against the use of motor cars – quite the reverse. If somebody could prove to us that double the number were needed, I have no doubt that the Committee would be only too willing to agree to that. But when we look at paragraph 146 of the Comptroller and Auditor General's Report we see that substantial savings were made by withdrawing the Government car service from the southern region in 1972. So that there was a proved economy. That being the case, why was it that the PSA did not insist at that time on similar reductions or, at any rate, planning for similar action in other regions?——(Mr *Cox*) I think that there are two points here. One is that we felt that we had to satisfy ourselves that the economies made in the southern region were genuine in the sense that clearly there was a saving for the PSA Vote, but we had to be clear that the additional expense incurred by other departments in making other arrangements did not exceed that saving, and did not make it impossible for the departments concerned to do their jobs properly. Secondly, we had to be clear that the conditions in other regions were similar, or sufficiently similar to those in the southern region to justify similar steps there. Those things we have now done and we are now embarking on substantial economies in all the other regions.

2381. When did you start the action that you are describing to reduce the car pools in other regions?——There has been a successive series of requests first of all from the southern region and then from other regions to estimate what savings could be made, or had been made. Last June we had the report from southern region which convinced us that it was certainly possible, and safely possible, to make savings, and in November all the regional directors were asked to make proposals for cutting down the car pools in their parts of the country. They proposed reductions from 172 cars to 101. We went back at them again and got further reductions agreed, down to 87. We recently notified the trade unions that we were going to embark upon these economies, and they are now being implemented. We hope to implement them over the course of the next two years.

2382. You do not think, do you, that from the withdrawal from the southern region in 1972 to implementation over the next two years by 1978 is a very long time to take for this exercise to be completed?—— I agree. What happened was that the first stage after withdrawal from the southern region was a first inquiry from the other regions, but at that time the regional controllers were not in favour of complete abolition. There was at that time a certain amount of administrative difficulty because the Agency had recently been set up and there was a good deal of reorganisation going on. The supplies division of the Agency, which runs the Government car service, was being turned over to a system of accountable management in preparation for the setting up of a trading fund which came into force in April this year. It was not clear to people at that stage just how the financial arrangements would work, and who in fact was going to be the client of this accountable unit of management and the subsequent trading fund. This, I think, caused some hesitation in pushing this through, but I accept that it could, and should have been, possible to have followed up the southern region experiment more quickly than was the case.

2383. It is very good of you to be so clear and frank with the Committee. All that is much appreciated. Just to underline the point a bit, if the withdrawal was made from the southern region in 1972, it must have been done for a good reason. Someone must have been very clear that this was going to result in a substantial saving, or at any rate that the chances of doing so were good. In those circumstances it seems to me particularly surprising that it took so long to deal with the other regions?——It was done as the result of a thorough management survey which costed out the operation in the southern region. I think that the two valid reasons for delay were, first, as I have said, the need to be certain that we were not simply inflicting higher costs upon other departments as a result of our savings and that they could continue with their work properly without the use of the Government car service and, second, unlike the southern region, there was, and there remains a clear need in all other parts of the country for at any rate some element of the Government car service to look after Ministers and senior civil servants visiting regions in the course of their duty. In the southern region this was not necessary because it is so close to London that if a Minister visits, shall we say, Reading, he would normally travel in his car from London and there is no need for a regional pool to look after him. If he is going to Newcastle he will travel by train or by air and will expect to be met, and will need to be met, by a Government service car.

2384. You cannot tell me that 107 Ministers travel all at the same moment, however?——Eighty-seven was the figure that we got down to, and that covered six regional offices in Scotland and Wales. In Scotland, of course, there are special needs because of the presence of Ministers, so that the number is not all that high in that respect and, of course, it will be looked at with the progress of this experiment.

2385. It says in paragraph 150 that there is an inter-departmental committee which was set up last year to review the use and operation of the whole field of Government transport services. Has the committee made any recommendations?——The committee has finished the first stage of its work and has made certain recommendations, and these are now being considered inter-departmentally because they affect departments going far beyond my own. I am not clear what the result of some of these is going to be, but certainly we are starting to implement straightaway certain recommendations, mainly concerned with the use of smaller and cheaper vehicles. We are going to use Minis for our despatch service, and we are moving down from some of the larger cars in the fleet which have got automatic gearboxes to manually operated, smaller cars.

2386. I should like, finally, to put a question to you, Mr Kemp. This is not a major area of Government spending, and I do not want to pretend that it is, but it is in the public eye, obviously, and therefore to some extent is a sensitive matter. It does seem from what Mr Cox has very frankly said to the Committee that the opportunity for useful economies was overlooked for some time. As you know, Mr Kemp, and as Mr McKean also knows, there comes before the Committee a whole succession of items of this style, of which perhaps the latest example in the Committee's mind may well be the failure of the Home Office to adjust fees over a very long period of time. I mention that because we were looking at it when we were looking at Excess Votes, so that it is quite a recent occurrence. What I think the Committee wants to know from the Treasury is this. What steps can the Treasury take, what steps does the Treasury take, to make sure that some of the smaller areas of expenditure, or of revenue for that matter, are frequently and effectively examined to see whether savings can be made?——(*Mr Kemp*) I do not want to go into the question of fees and charges again.

2387. No, I did not mean that specifically; I am talking about the general area?——As a general proposition we come up against the difficulty that departments and their accounting officers are there to handle things and there is a limit to what the Treasury, as such, can do by way of getting involved in detailed management. But there is an annual opportunity at the time of the estimates, when the appropriate Treasury divisions examine with the appropriate spending people the proposed expenditure, and those exercises should cover even smaller items, not perhaps specifically, but on the basis that savings have to be found; and an incentive is given to the department to look for savings in these areas.

2388. I wonder if the Committee have the feeling that that examination is always made effectively. Do you think that it is always made effectively?——I do not think that I would like to say that it can always be made effectively in all cases. We are frequently looking for something that one does not know is there. That is why I mention fees and charges specifically. Fees and charges are common to a number of departments so that we can indeed, as Mr McKean has told the Committee, set up machinery to look at those. The Government car service, on the other hand, is special to the PSA, and there will be other special areas of activity, special to other departments. But I should like to say that I hope the Treasury people who look at these things get to know what their departments are doing and can pursue these areas.

2389. I agree, of course, that the Treasury does not want to get into the area of management. I am not suggesting that, but what the Committee do want to see is that people are reminded of their responsibilities. You are really saying that that happens?——I am saying that it should happen, certainly. As I say, there is an opportunity for it to happen, and I hope that it happens.

Mr *Orbach*

2390. You mentioned the fact that discussions had gone on with the trade unions. I presume that this is because some people might be declared redundant, but surely most of these people are young, or of middle age. Could they not be transferred to some other job in the service?——(Mr *Cox*) It is possible, but, obviously, since we are removing quite a number of jobs, we need to consult the unions and consider what the consequences are. The trouble is that these are redundancies at particular places.

2391. Yes, I appreciate that, but there are not so many at any particular place, are there?——That is true.

2392. Five or six people, or seven or eight people, surely?—— Indeed. We hope that we can do this without redundancy, but we need to consult the unions.

Mr *Ovenden*

2393. We are told in paragraph 150 of the Comptroller and Auditor General's Report that the Agency – I assume that that is the Property Services Agency – when replacing cars in provincial pools, are using smaller, cheaper, vehicles. Can I assume from that that you are not adopting that policy in London?——We are now adopting that policy in London.

2394. You are now, but at the stage when this report was made I take it, that it was only the policy in the provinces?——That is so. We were doing a certain amount of experimental work in the regions, trying out some smaller cars in the regions before their use in London. Also, the nature of the job is a bit different in London, where a very high percentage of the work done is for Ministers.

2395. Are you assuming that work done for Ministers requires bigger cars?——I should think that certainly for senior Ministers a bigger car is what people would expect, and indeed, it is what is provided.

2396. I think that that is something of a matter of opinion, but I will not dispute it at this stage. We are told in this report that the cost of the Service in 1974–75 was £1·7 million and that the fleet was 480 cars. Have you any idea of the total mileage covered by those cars in the year 1974–75, or have you an estimate?——We could let you have a note, but I am afraid that I have not got the figure with me.

2397. It would be useful because I wanted to try to calculate what the cost per mile was. It would appear that the cost per car was something between £3,000 and £4,000 per year, which would point, I think, to a very high cost per mile. Would you say that 50 pence would not be far off?——I am sorry; I recall that I have got a mileage figure. I think that the average mileage figure is round about 11,000.

2398. For each vehicle?——Yes.

2399. But it would only be carrying official passengers for part of that time?——Yes.

2400. So that the cost for the effective part of the mileage would still be extremely high?——That is right, yes.

2401. Still approaching something like a figure of 50 pence? That would not, perhaps be an unreasonable figure?——This could be so, but the detailed work that we did on the southern region showed that even allowing for our costs, it was cheaper still to carry officials around than for them to use public transport, particularly in areas where public transport is not all that good. You have to think, for example, of the case of the social security officer or of the tax inspector, with a number of calls to make in a day in an area where public transport may not be very good. We found that the wages costs very soon exceeded the transport costs.

Mr *Costain*

2402. I have a great deal of sympathy with you over this. It is a terrible job to run a car pool in a firm, never mind in a Ministry. With the increase of wages for chauffeurs and the fact that there is so much waiting time for chauffeurs, does it not warrant another look at whether chauffeurs are really as necessary as they used to be?——This is the heart of the solution to the regional problem. We examined all the different ways of replacement, and what appears to be the cheapest and most cost-effective way of dealing with the problem is for people to drive their own cars and to claim an allowance for doing so. That is all right for the kind of use that we are replacing in the regions. It is not so possible, of course, in large cities, particularly in London, where parking makes this absolutely impossible, or, of course, in providing for the needs of Ministers and perhaps very senior officials.

2403. Consideration has been given to getting estimates from hire firms to see whether any sort of deal could be done?——Yes, we have done this. This, indeed, was part of the southern region examination. This was clearly shown to be more expensive than using the Government car service.*

Chairman.] Mr Cox, I am sorry that we have taken up so much of your time, but the Committee is grateful to you for your great helpfulness.

* *Note by witness:* The 1971 Survey in Southern Region indicated in fact that use of hired cars would result in savings but, on current information, on an hourly basis during the normal working day the Government car service tends to be cheaper than private hire, though overall costs may be higher because of the need to provide a continuous service.

Appendix 6

SIXTH REPORT FROM
THE COMMITTEE OF PUBLIC ACCOUNTS

together with the Proceedings of the Committee, part of the
Minutes of Evidence, Appendices and Index. Session 1975–76
(pp. xxvii–xxix)

CLASS XIV, VOTE 1. OFFICE AND GENERAL ACCOMMODATION SERVICES

Use of the Government Car Service

C & A G's
Report
(Volume 3)
paras
145–150 64. During 1974–75 the Property Services Agency of
the Department of the Environment incurred expenditure of £1·7 million on the operation of the Government
Car Service. The fleet consisted of some 480 cars, ranging
in size from 850cc to 3·5 litre saloons of which about
60 were self-drive. Nearly half of the fleet was based in
London and used mainly by Ministers and senior civil
servants. The remainder operated under the control of
the Agency's Regional Directors. Departments may use
the service where they consider this essential to enable
work to be carried out effectively and economically or if
public transport would involve a disproportionate loss of
official time.

65. In 1971 an examination by the Department of the
use of 19 cars and 16 drivers based in the Southern
Region showed that, on a six week sample, over 80 per
cent. of the car usage was by three Departments. The
cars were generally booked by the day to make circular
tours with a number of stops for, mainly, junior officers

of the Department of Health and Social Security, the Inland Revenue Department and the Department of the Environment. The annual cost was £40,000 and it was calculated that between £5,000 and £9,000 a year would be saved if hired cars or taxis were used in every instance, between £21,000 and £23,000 if self-drive cars were used and £29,000 if all officers had and drove their own cars. As a result the car service in the Region was withdrawn during 1972 and Departments made their own transport arrangements.

66. Car services continued to be operated in the other Regions. In May 1973 the Agency asked eight Regional Directors whether it might be worth considering the use of hired in place of official cars, since Southern Region had discontinued their car service without real inconvenience, although they recognised that local circumstances would vary. None of the Regional Directors favoured complete abolition of the service in view of its use for visiting Ministers, senior civil servants and overseas visitors, and five saw little value in a detailed investigation. Because the views of Regional Directors were mixed the Agency decided to obtain a report, which was presented in June 1975, on the actual experience in the Southern Region.

67. The Comptroller and Auditor General's Report stated that his examination of requisitions and log sheets for Regions outside London had shown a pattern of car usage in 1974–75 similar to that which had led to abolition of the service in the Southern Region. About half the journeys were made by junior staff and they were often for short distances with long waiting periods and with chauffeurs sometimes driving further without a passenger than with one.

68. The Agency informed Your Committee that they had reviewed the situation in the Southern Region to check whether the abolition of the car service had led to higher costs in other Departments than the savings to the Agency and whether the Departments had been able to do their work properly. The report in June 1975 had

Q. 2380

Q. 2381

convinced them that reductions were possible so, in November 1975, Regional Directors were asked to put forward proposals, which had led to agreements to reduce the number of cars outside London from 172 to 87 during Q. 2382 the next two years. The Agency accepted that they could and should have conducted the exercise more quickly, but there had been uncertainty and hesitation following the establishment of the Agency and the development of new systems of accountable management for the Supplies Division which ran the car service.

69. Your Committee consider that the time between the abolition of the Southern Region car service in 1972 and the agreements to halve the car fleets in other Regions by 1978 was excessive. We think that the Department and Regional Directors should have realised from the outset that substantial economies were possible. Q. 2383 The Agency informed us that most Regions need a car service for visiting Ministers and senior officers. We accept this, but we look to the Agency to press ahead quickly with the reductions now decided upon and to make sure that no further opportunities are lost to make all justifiable economies.

70. The general issues of a Government Car Service went beyond the responsibilities of the Agency and an inter-departmental committee, under the chairmanship of the Civil Service Department, was set up in June 1975 to review the arrangements in all Departments for the Q. 2385 use and operation of transport services. The Agency told us that the committee had finished the first stage of its work and had made certain recommendations which were being studied. Some recommendations, mainly concerned with the use of smaller and cheaper vehicles, were being implemented straight away. We expect the inter-departmental study to be quickly concluded and all possible economies to be promptly implemented.

71. While the car service is not a major function of the Property Services Agency it involved sizeable expenditure and it has been shown that useful economies can be made. There may also be activities in other Departments which may escape proper economy reviews because they are not

central to the Department's main functions and Your Committee stress the need for all Departments to seek out and effect economies over the whole range of their activities.

Appendix 7

SIXTH REPORT FROM THE COMMITTEE OF PUBLIC ACCOUNTS

together with the Proceedings of the Committee, part of the Minutes of Evidence, Appendices and Index. Session 1975–76 (pp. 343–344)

TREASURY MINUTE ON THE FOURTH REPORT FROM THE COMMITTEE OF PUBLIC ACCOUNTS, 1974–75

Mr W R Cox, CB, Chief Executive, and Mr G May, Principal Finance Officer, of the Property Services Agency, Department of the Environment, called in and further examined.

2412. To go on to paragraphs 23 to 32 on the matter of maintenance and operating expenses, how far did you get with the maintenance economy reviews for the London area?——We have made a certain amount of progress there. We still have staff difficulties, but we have had one special team working through London and we have also been using the area management officers to supplement the work of that team. We have already run through six districts out of the 29 in London, and we hope to complete three more soon. We have economies totalling about £600,000 under discussion and consideration, and there will be more to come.

2413. What about the reviews in Germany and Gibraltar? Have you made savings there?——We have made progress there, too. In Germany we have formed two maintenance economy review teams which started looking at the Düsseldorf and the Bielefeld depots. There was a pause in that work because soon after we started on this the results of the Defence Review became known and there was then a major re-structuring exercise of the command in Germany which we had to cope with as a matter of priority, but we have got the two teams operating again now. They have finished work on the Düsseldorf depot, they are continuing with Bielefeld and they are going on to Hildesheim now. The work that has been done so far shows us that we can expect savings running into six figures in relation to the depots that we have looked at already, and when we come to complete Germany as a whole, where there are twenty depots, we should certainly be up into the millions in savings.

2414. I think that the Committee will be very pleased to hear what you have had to say. It is, in effect, therefore, a justification of the assertion in the Treasury Minute that uneconomic practices are sought out and eliminated locally. That is proving to be the case?——Yes.

2415. Of course, the question that comes to my mind – I hope that it is not an unreasonable one – is, why on earth is all this not done automatically without your having to sit on people and seeing that it occurs?——I think that the answer is that a fair bit is done in the ordinary course of business, but a special initiative of this kind does produce exceptional results, particularly in the early stages of a review of this kind.

2416. What are the sort of uneconomic practices that have been eliminated that we are talking about?——They are related mainly to the use of buildings, heating, painting, the maintenance of ground, and that kind of matter.

Appendix 8[1]

*Memorandum by the Comptroller and Auditor General
on the Fourth Report from the
Committee of Public Accounts, 1974–75 (pp. 40–44)*

ENQUIRY INTO EVIDENCE GIVEN TO THE COMMITTEE OF
PUBLIC ACCOUNTS OF SESSION 1974–75 BY THE PROPERTY
SERVICES AGENCY OF THE DEPARTMENT OF THE
ENVIRONMENT RELATING TO MAINTENANCE AND
OPERATING EXPENSES

1. On 14 April 1975 the Committee of Public Accounts (PAC) of Session 1974–75 examined the Accounting Officer of the Property Services Agency (PSA), Mr W R (now Sir Robert) Cox, on the subject of property maintenance and operating expenses, to which my predecessor as Comptroller and Auditor General (C&AG) had referred in paragraphs 24 to 34 of his Report on Classes VI to XI of the Civil Appropriation Accounts for 1973–74. The C&AG's Report described how maintenance economy reviews had been started in 1968 in the Southern Region of the former Ministry of Public Building and Works (which was succeeded in 1972 by the PSA) and had produced substantial savings in cost. It showed that up to 31 March 1973, despite instructions from headquarters, the progress made in carrying out reviews and achieving savings in other PSA regions had varied considerably; and it summarised PSA's answers to the questions which the C&AG had asked them.

2. On the basis of the information in the C&AG's Report PAC asked the Accounting Officer about PSA's policy towards the use of

1. Appendixes 8–14 are all taken from the Second Special Report from the Committee of Public Accounts. At the beginning of each appendix the relevant page numbers in the Report are added in square brackets after the Report's subheading.

Where the text of the Report refers to the first edition of this book, the page numbers have been altered here to those of this edition.

Directly Employed Labour (DEL); the apparent variation between regions in enthusiasm for economy reviews; the extent to which economies should have been initiated by management rather than by special reviews; the way in which reviews were conducted and information on potential economies disseminated throughout all PSA regions; and the progress made in regions at home and overseas which had been slow to start economy reviews.

3. The PAC's Fourth Report 1974–75, paragraphs 23 to 32, summarised the evidence contained in the C&AG's Report and derived from the Committee's examination of the Accounting Officer and stressed the need for PSA to press ahead energetically with reviews in the London Region, Germany and Gibraltar. The Committee thought that many of the ideas for economies were of a type that management should have been putting into effect all the time and that there should have been better dissemination to all regions of information on uneconomic practices. The Committee looked to the PSA to ensure in the future that uneconomic practices were persistently sought out and eliminated as a normal task of management and that potential economies were publicised throughout the Organisation.

Admission by the Accounting Officer of PSA of an Error in his Evidence

4. The former Regional Director of the PSA's Southern Region between 1967 and 1974, Mr L C Chapman, subsequently wrote a book entitled 'Your Disobedient Servant', about his campaign to reduce the cost of property maintenance. This was published on 8 May 1978. On 2 May 1978 the Accounting Officer of the PSA, Sir Robert Cox, wrote to the Chairman of the Public Accounts Committee to inform him that questions to the PSA by television interviewers in preparation for programmes on 8 and 9 May 1978 about Mr Chapman's book had indicated that the accuracy of some of the PSA's evidence to the Committee on 14 April 1975 was likely to be challenged. The Accounting Officer stated that he had made one factual error in his evidence by including in his answer to Q. 1318 an incorrect statement that there had been a substantial redeployment of military resources in Southern Region and that a lot of staff had been moving north; and he tendered his apologies to the Committee.

5. The Chairman replied on 5 May accepting that Sir Robert Cox believed his statement to be correct at the time he made it and that he had no wish to mislead the Committee. The Chairman brought this

correspondence before the Committee who asked me on 10 May to report further on the matter.

6. The texts of these letters are at Annex A and the text of Question 1318 and the answers to it is at Annex B.

Investigation of the Error

7. My staff received the full co-operation of Sir Robert Cox and his staff in carrying out this investigation; and they were shown all the relevant briefing papers for the Accounting Officer's examination on 14 April 1975, to which they would not normally have sought access.

8. The PSA's files recorded that they had learnt of the error in the Accounting Officer's evidence in March 1977, after a newspaper reporter had mentioned to their Press Officer that Mr Chapman (who had figured in a *Sunday Times* article about his economy campaign in December 1976) might challenge the Accounting Officer's evidence to PAC about the reasons why Southern Region achieved greater savings than other regions. The PSA accordingly investigated the basis for the Accounting Officer's answer.

9. The Accounting Officer's statement about a re-deployment of military resources towards the North was based upon information in his brief which read:

'In addition there was a trend during the relevant period for the Ministry of Defence to concentrate its facilities elsewhere than in the South which made the time for review in Southern Region most opportune'.

In addition a draft answer to a possible question included the sentence

'Prior to 1969 there had been considerable changes in the Defence Estate, particularly in Southern Region'.

When enquiring into the grounds for these statements in March 1977 PSA were unable to obtain any evidence either from their own records or from the Ministry of Defence that military facilities had been concentrated elsewhere than in the South. They found, in fact, that an early draft of the brief not submitted to the Accounting Officer had stated:

'There can be little doubt that in 1968 Southern Region had more scope for economy than most regions. This was due to traditional reasons mainly inherited from the absorption of the Army Works Organisation in 1963. There was local resistance to change, particularly among Army Commanders, who were used to a "personal" service by DEL. The Army rebuilding programme had also left several old barracks and buildings under-occupied which were continuing to be maintained and heated'.

Their enquiries showed that this passage had been changed to the wording eventually included in the Accounting Officer's brief at the suggestion of the Director of Home Regional Services, who had since retired. The PSA concluded, therefore, that the mis-statement had arisen from this Officer's faulty recollection of knowledge acquired during his previous tenure of the post of Regional Director, Southern Region.

10. Although the PSA thus recognised in March 1977 that the Accounting Officer's evidence had contained an error of fact, they did not consider that it materially affected the general theme of the Accounting Officer's answer. The answer had drawn attention to the fact that Southern Region had initiated the special type of economy review, which they had pursued with enthusiasm, whilst other parts of the PSA had relied more on other methods of securing economies; and it had expressed the view that the extent and circumstances of the Defence Estate in Southern Region had offered at that time considerable opportunities for economies. The PSA accordingly decided to defer action until such time as Mr Chapman formally challenged the point, as he subsequently did in his book.

11. My staff satisfied themselves that the findings of the PSA's internal enquiries were supported by the evidence in the relevant briefing and other papers. They also noted that the statement included in the earlier draft brief (paragraph 9 above) was consistent with the earlier observations recorded in the Exchequer and Audit Department's files and with the information summarised in my predecessor's report to Parliament.

Responsibility of the Comptroller and Auditor General for checking Evidence to PAC

12. Although the C&AG has no formal responsibility for verifying evidence given to the Committee my Department are supplied with proof copies of the evidence, and they seek to substantiate any statements which are at variance with, or add to, their existing knowledge and which appear to be sufficiently material to the matters under

consideration to influence the conclusions and recommendations of the Committee. If a statement proves to be significantly wrong or likely to mislead the Committee they ask the Department to inform the Committee so that the corrected information can be taken into account and the record amended as appropriate. Such corrections are not infrequently made at the proof stage on the initiative of the Accounting Officer's own Department; it is understandable that permanent secretaries may not always recollect or present detailed information entirely accurately in the course of a long, quickly moving and sometimes complicated personal examination.

13. In the case of the answer to Q.1318 on 14 April 1975 my staff did not attempt to substantiate what had been said about redeployment of military resources. It was only one of a number of arguments and points relating to the PSA's actions and it seemed unlikely to have any material effect on the critical view which the Committee were likely to take of the PSA's management. They would therefore have seen no need to devote staff resources to carrying out investigations to verify its accuracy; and although I was not myself responsible at that time I should add that I have no reason to dissent from that judgement. I should not expect, indeed I should not permit, my staff to spend time checking all details of an Accounting Officer's evidence except in the circumstances indicated above.

DOUGLAS HENLEY

5 *June* 1978.

ANNEX A

PROPERTY SERVICES AGENCY
CHIEF EXECUTIVE SIR ROBERT COX, KCB
2 MARSHAM STREET, LONDON, SW1P 3EB
May 2, 1978.

The Rt Hon Edward Du Cann MP
Chairman
Public Accounts Committee

Dear Mr Du Cann,

I think you have been approached, as we have here, about television programmes connected with the forthcoming publication of a book by Mr Leslie Chapman, who was formerly Director of the Southern

Region in the Ministry of Public Building and Works and subsequently PSA.

It seems that one of the issues the television companies may wish to raise is the accuracy of the evidence I gave before the Public Accounts Committee three years ago (Fourth Report, Session 1974–5, Questions 1314 to 1335). I am in some difficulty about this as neither the publishers nor the author have been prepared to let us see a copy of the book before publication and I am, therefore, not entirely sure just what points of criticism are to be made.

It is nevertheless clear to me that there was one factual inaccuracy in my answers and it is only right that I should let you know about this and offer you my apologies.

The issue centres on Question 1318 where you were trying to establish the reasons for the differing results secured by different regions in the pursuit of management economy reviews. In my reply I was trying to make three points. First, I was accepting the implication of your question that there was greater enthusiasm in some regions than in others. Secondly I was saying that the early timing of the Southern Region initiative had some effect on the way the score was kept; and thirdly I was trying to make the point that the Southern Region at the relevant time offered good opportunities. In this last connection I mentioned that there had been a substantial redeployment of military resources and that a lot of staff had been moving north. It is this statement which was incorrect, though I need scarcely say to you that I believed it to be correct at the time I made it. There was indeed some reduction in military strength in the Aldershot area during the relevant period, but this was I think due mainly to a general run down in the size of the Forces. It is very difficult to disentangle events which took place some 10 years ago, but in spite of this factual inaccuracy I think I would still wish to stand by my general judgement that the nature of the estate being managed by the Southern Region and the circumstances at the time were well suited to the type of initiative that was launched there.

My colleagues and I take considerable pains to ensure the accuracy of answers given to your Committee. It is a matter of very considerable regret when a mistake of this kind occurs and I should like to repeat my apologies.

Yours sincerely,

ROBERT COX

From: Rt. Hon. Edward du Cann, MP

HOUSE OF COMMONS
LONDON SW1A 0AA
May 5, 1978.

Dear Sir Robert

I much appreciated your letter of 2 May and I will, of course, report its contents to the Select Committee on Public Accounts.

Like you, I have not seen Mr Chapman's book. I have, however, given interviews to the Granada television company and to the BBC about our meeting of three years ago. The interviews dealt with the work of the Public Accounts Committee in general as well as with the particular discussions we had at that time. This was, of course, before I received your letter.

I entirely accept that you believed that the information you gave to the Select Committee on Public Accounts was accurate in every respect at the time you appeared before the Committee. Of course I also accept that there would be no wish for the Committee to be misled in any way.

I am grateful to you now for making the position clear. I will of course discuss this correspondence further with the Comptroller and Auditor General and with the Committee. It is my view, however, that the corrected information which you are now giving to the Committee in relation to what was said in paragraph 28 of their 4th Report 1974–75 would not have affected our main recommendations in paragraph 31 of the Report in question which were, as you know, critical.

Yours sincerely
Edward du Cann

Sir Robert Cox, KCB,
Property Services Agency,
2 Marsham Street, SW1P 3EB.

ANNEX B

1318. Those are healthy figures. One matter that surprised me, at any rate, was the differences that there seemed to be between regions in their enthusiasm for economy reviews? Why was that?——I think that it was not simply a matter of enthusiasm; it was also a matter of opportunities and timing. The region which stands out in our figures is the Southern Region, which started this work in 1969 and achieved substantially higher savings than any of the other regions. I think that there are two or three main reasons for that. The first is that they started sooner, before a number of other management initiatives took place which in themselves made economies in maintenance and which therefore fell to be registered in different ways and were not available when the other regions came in later on. Secondly, there was a greater opportunity. One of the most effective ways of achieving maintenance economy is to reduce the number of buildings and the areas to be covered. The Southern Region covers, among other things, the Aldershot area, and in the years immediately before 1969 there had been substantial re-deployment of military resources. There had been a lot of staff moving north. Consequently, there were quite a number of opportunities in the Aldershot area and in the Southern Region generally for proposing to the Army that there should be economy in the use of buildings, that buildings which were only partly occupied could be closed, and that there should be a reduction in heating in buildings that were no longer used or no longer fully used, and I think that it is fair to say that with the enthusiasm that was shown, full advantage was taken of these opportunities. Other regions did not have the same possibilities because the same re-deployments had not taken place. I think, on the whole, the figures show that most of the regions produced broadly similar results. They produced, in total, savings of round about £$\frac{1}{2}$ million, with two or three exceptions. On the one hand there was the Southern Region, which showed a much higher figure. On the other hand there were the North West Region and the London Region, which showed substantially lower figures, and I think that there were special reasons in each case for those lower figures.

Appendix 9

MINUTES OF EVIDENCE TAKEN BEFORE THE COMMITTEE OF PUBLIC ACCOUNTS

Monday 12 June 1978 (pp. 1–21)

Members present:

Mr Edward du Cann, in the Chair

Mr A P Costain	Mr Maurice Orbach
Mr David Crouch	Mr John Ovenden
Mr John Evans	Mr Robert Taylor
Mr Hugh Jenkins	

Sir DOUGLAS HENLEY, KCB, and Mr C J CAREY, called in and examined.

Examination of witnesses

Sir ROBERT COX, KCB, Chief Executive, Mr G MAY, Principal Finance Officer, Mr W J SHARP, Controller Property Services Agency Supplies, and Mr L A BALDWIN, Financial Controller, Finance, Property Services Agency Supplies, Property Services Agency, Department of the Environment, called in and examined.

Chairman

3211. Sir Robert, the Committee is glad to welcome you again. What we would propose, if it is agreeable to you, is to take items 3, 1 and 2 on the agenda, in that order. If you will allow me, I propose to put all my questions to you in one group, as it were, for personal reasons of which you are aware and when I have to leave the Committee Mr Costain is very kindly going to take my place. Let us begin with the Fourth Report of the Committee of Public Accounts in the session 1974–75. I am sorry that we have got to go back over all these matters but, obviously, it is important that we should do so. We have before us in this Committee the Memorandum* by the Comptroller and Auditor General on the evidence which you gave to the Committee of that year on maintenance economy reviews. Is that Memorandum by the Comptroller and Auditor General a fair statement of the relevant facts so far as the PSA is concerned?——(Sir *Robert Cox*) Certainly.

3212. The Memorandum indicates that one of the reasons for the Southern Region having achieved such high savings up to 1973 was not that there was a sudden movement of troops away to the north or to anywhere else, but rather that the Region contained a preponderance of army establishments which traditionally had been uneconomic in their use of directly employed labour and buildings. Would it be fair to put to you that perhaps that might have been the main fact to bring out in answer to the question that I put to you, No. 1318, on 14th April 1975?——Certainly. I think that it would have been a much more important consideration because the other statement, as you know, I think, is not correct.

3213. Yes. Thank you very much for making that plain, and, of course, I reiterate what I have already said to you in answer to the letter which you were good enough to write to me as Chairman of this Committee, that we absolutely accept that there was no deliberate intention to mislead the Committee. That is understood. Going into this matter in a little more detail, the answer that you did actually give me to Question 1318 seems a slightly free interpretation of the information and the brief that was in front of you. Do you think that what we now think would be the appropriate answer was what the brief really meant?——I am in some difficulty here because the Comptroller and Auditor General has quoted from an earlier draft of the brief which I did not see or consider at the time, and all I had in front of me for the purpose of dealing with this part of the issue was the quotation which you have seen. I certainly accept what you say, that the words that I used in front of the Committee were a free interpretation of that phrase. The reason for that was that I believed that the words that I used in front of the Committee were the practical explanation of what that phrase meant in actual terms. I was wrong, of course, because those things did not take place, and the underlying phrase was not correct, but that was why I expressed myself in the way that I did. I believed that I was explaining in straightforward language what the brief meant.

3214. I quite appreciate that you did not see that earlier draft, and

* Appendix I [Appendix 8 above].

there is no reason why you should have done, but it is quite clear, I think, that the fundamental cause of the inaccurate statement was the fact that that earlier draft was changed, and changed, apparently, on the strength of a senior official's memory. It seems to me that the alteration had the effect of suggesting that the opportunity to make savings arose only during Mr Chapman's time as regional director and had not existed before. Why was not the correctness of that recollection checked against substantive evidence?——I had no particular personal reason to question the brief that came before me on that particular point. I had no personal knowledge of troop dispositions at that time and consequently I accepted what was put in front of me. I would accept that it would have been a sensible precaution to have had that statement checked, but it was not done at the time by me.

3215. Is it not the usual habit, as I should have thought was common practice in the Civil Service when an Accounting Officer appears before the senior Select Committee of this House of Commons, for the evidence which he has given – which is necessarily given, perhaps in relation to a whole series of subjects with a lot of questions being asked—to be checked by the staff after the evidence is published?—— Yes, certainly. The proof of the evidence goes back to the experts concerned and it is checked before it is returned to this Committee.

3216. Was it checked in this case?——The proof of my evidence was sent back to the directorate concerned and no comment was made upon this passage in my experience.

3217. I did ask you, Sir Robert, if it was checked?——I have no personal knowledge that it was checked by any particular individual. It was certainly sent to the directorate concerned.

3218. Yes. Are you satisfied that there was no neglect of duty by any member of the PSA's staff?——I do not think so. I think that this was simply a matter of faulty recollection at a time when the staff briefing me were already looking back to a period some ten years before and not, as is usually the case, to the year of account which immediately precedes the examination.

3219. So that you have not thought that there was any matter here which warranted disciplinary action?——I would not think so. It is perfectly possible to make mistakes of this kind, and I think that such a mistake was made here.

3220. Why do you think that the error was not detected?——So far as I am concerned, because of ignorance of the subject.

3221. I should have thought that it was a matter of fairly obvious fact whether there had been substantial troop movements from one area of the country to another?——Yes, it could indeed have been checked. I think that here also, there was the point that the directorate dealing with the evidence was a directorate covering the whole range of maintenance affairs and not simply Defence affairs, and consequently it did not have as close a contact with the Ministry of Defence as some of the rest of us.

3222. Would you look at paragraph 8 of the Memorandum in particular? That reveals that the PSA were warned in March 1977 that this piece of evidence might be challenged?——Before answering that question, may I modify what I have just said?

3223. Yes?——There was, I am reminded, an attempt to check numerically on this statement, but at the time when the brief was being prepared this attempt was unsuccessful. It was not possible to obtain either confirmation or denial in numerical terms of the statement.

3224. At the time that you were before the Committee?——At the time when the brief was being prepared, yes.

3225. But afterwards there would be leisure, would there not?—— Yes, indeed, but I think that the point is that as the matter was expressed before the Committee, it did represent the belief and view of those concerned with this matter in the Agency, so that I do not think that they would have had any particular reason or motive to undertake a further check at that point. They would have been looking at what I had said to see whether it confirmed their beliefs and they would have told me and would have moved me to get a correction had I been wrong.

3226. I know that if we had different information we should probably not have changed our conclusions. The conclusions that we came to, as you know, were critical of the PSA, but it seems to me such an elementary matter of fact, as to whether the number of troops in a particular part of the United Kingdom had changed or not over a period of time. I must tell you that I really am surprised that a matter of this sort should not be picked up in the ordinary routine examination of evidence after you came to see us. Do you think that it is unreasonable that I should be surprised?——No, indeed, not, and I was extremely surprised myself when the error came to light.

3227. Let us talk about the timing of it. I was beginning to say to you that it came to light in fact inside your Department in March 1977?—— That is right.

3228. You very kindly wrote to me at the beginning of May this year, fourteen months later. Why was this Committee not advised at the moment when the PSA discovered that perhaps there was an inaccuracy?——I think because at that stage we did not consider that this particular point, taken in the context of the evidence as a whole, the Committee's Report and our follow up action, was of such critical importance as has been attributed to it recently. When one reaches the proof stage of dealing with evidence, there are very clear rules of guidance about what one can, and should, do, and one can follow them. But so far as I am concerned it is quite unprecedented to discover an error so long after the date at which the evidence was given. This was some two years after the hearing of the Committee. The Committee had reported, we had had the follow up the second year round, and it was only after that stage that the error came to light. Given that situation, there are obviously no rules to follow. I do not see how there can be rules to follow. One has to use one's discretion and common sense. Clearly, there could be some very minor errors that one would not wish to trouble the Committee, or anybody else, with. The length of time that has elapsed obviously must be a relevant consideration, as must also be the relevance of the point being made by the witness to the Committee and its continuing relevance in the light of the Committee's Report, and the action that one is taking in order to follow up the Committee's recommendations. Having thought about all this, it seemed to us that this was an error which, though regrettable, was not of such great significance that it had to be reported to the Committee immediately. We knew that it was one which would come to light and that it would have to be dealt with, and it seemed to us to be right to deal with it when it came to light in the context in which it came to light – as, indeed, I did.

3229. You did not speak to the Comptroller and Auditor General or to the Clerk, or have any of your staff speak to the Comptroller and Auditor General's Department and just mention it to them in passing, or have any of your staff speak to the Clerk?——Not at that stage. Clearly, it would have been a sensible thing to do.

3230. You do know, do you not – it is appropriate that I should underline the point – that this Committee sets the utmost store on receiving information from Government departments that is accurate? Mistakes can be made, of course, and they happen, and this Committee always adopts, as it properly should, an attitude of understanding and sympathy when mistakes occur. There are vast Departments of State, immensely complex, and although the accounting officer has responsibility, it may well be that there will be a multitude of detailed matters with which he cannot be familiar. But it embarrasses the relationship between the Committee and accounting officers when mistakes are not acknowledged, and I am bound to tell you that the Committee does take a most serious view of a mistake which is known and about which the Committee is not then informed, because a cynic might take the view, 'Oh, well, the Department perhaps hoped that the mistake would never be discovered and the Committee would never know about it'. You can see that difficulty, can you not?——I can see that difficulty. In the present case I do not think that there was any prospect that the matter was not going to come to light. The information was already in the hands of the Press.

3231. Sir Douglas, may I ask you, what is your normal practice and the practice of the Exchequer and Audit Department in scrutinising the evidence which is given to this Committee?——(Sir *Douglas Henley*) The normal practice is to look through the evidence very carefully in relation to the lines on which we think that the Committee is likely to report and, of course, if there are any points in the evidence which my staff or I know to be significant, we check them, as necessary. Indeed, if there was something that was not particularly significant and we happened to know about it, we should draw it to the attention of the department and the accounting officer and would normally expect them to correct it. As I think I mentioned in my Memorandum, it is the case of course, that departments themselves, on their own initiative, do correct evidence if they find subsequently that there is some inaccuracy in it. Having said that, I am bound to say that I would not expect, and as I have said in my note, I would indeed not permit, my staff to spend a great deal of time checking detailed evidence which I, or they, did not think was highly material. Clearly, a matter of judgment may be involved, but, as the Committee will appreciate, we do know quite a lot about the background of the material which comes before the Committee normally, so that we are in a good position to make a judgment. Secondly, it is a very time consuming and, if I may say so, an expensive business, to spend staff time on checking a great deal of detail if we do not think that it is necessary. So that my short answer is that I do not think that we want any changes in our procedures and that on the whole I think that we cope with this kind of thing reasonably well.

3232. What you are really saying to the Committee is that you follow up anything that you think is in any way suspect but that on the whole you rely upon departments. That is basically the position, is it not?——

Yes. We rely on departments and on our own background knowledge of the significance of different aspects.

3233. When did you first know about this particular error?——I do not want to mislead the Committee; that is the very last thing I want to do.

3234. You of all people must not mislead the Committee!——I think that I should have notice of that. I think that someone told me at the time when Mr Chapman's book came out that there was a problem here, but I am not quite sure about that.

3235. Yes, but what I am really looking for – and I appreciate that you may want to check your answer before you give it – is whether or not you knew about this matter before that time. The answer, I think, is no?——Not before that time, no, certainly not. (Sir *Robert Cox*) I do not wish to make too much of a point of this, but I did in fact, I think, mention this informally to the Comptroller and Auditor General a week or two before I wrote to you – not very long before I wrote to you – and sought his guidance on the exact timing of the letter.

3236. Yes, thank you very much. I am quite sure that those conversations were taking place. What I wanted to establish from the Comptroller was whether or not anyone in your Department had been in touch with him as far back as March, 1977. That is what I was asking?——No . . .

Mr *Crouch*

3252. Sir Robert, may I go back to the first point, namely, the discrepancy that you have written to the Chairman and the Committee about? I remember this occasion very well, as I took part in the questioning of you on that occasion, and I have refreshed my memory, of course, by referring to what went on. Looking back to Question 1318, and taking note of your letter to the Chairman of 2nd May this year, in which you, as it were, corrected what you said in answer to Question 1318, do you not appreciate that your misleading of the Committee on that occasion, at least by my reading of it, was very considerable? If I may elaborate upon that, when the Chairman asks a question of the chief witness, the Accounting Officer, other members of the Committee are guided in their subsequent questions by the answers that he gives to the question. Many of us prepare our questions, having studied papers beforehand, and we tend to strike out a lot of questions rather than have a repetition of answers when a question has already been answered. On that occasion your answer to the Chairman was, in my opinion, very full, and it was subsequently, as you went on, elaborated, and it certainly made me feel that you had given a very full explanation of why there were special reasons in the Southern Region for them to have achieved considerable success, rather than other regions. Do you not agree with me in my summary of the feeling that I got from your answer?——(Sir *Robert Cox*) I certainly accept that what I said there was incorrect. Obviously, it is not for me to say what interpretation individual members of the Committee drew from it. There are two things that I would say. First, what I said I believed to be correct. Second, there were, in my view, other reasons for believing that the Southern Region had, if not the easiest wicket, certainly an easier wicket than some other regions which appeared rather poorly in the figures, notably the North-West Region and London. To that extent I do not think that I was misleading the Committee if I led them to think that the Southern Region did have a more profitable field to plough in this particular area than some other parts of the Agency.

3253. I accept what you say because, looking back at your answer on that occasion, that is how I interpreted it. I did interpret it a little further then than from the way that you have described it now. You used a phrase – and I am quoting what you said in 1975 – 'There had been a lot of staff moving north. Consequently, there were quite a number of opportunities in the Aldershot area and in the Southern Region generally for proposing to the Army that there should be economy in the use of buildings, that buildings which were only partly occupied could be closed, and that there should be a reduction in heating in buildings' and so on. You went on to say, 'I think, on the whole, the figures show that most of the regions produced broadly similar results'. I tried to find out, when I questioned you in Question 1335, because I was interested in this discrepancy, whether we could not have benefited in other regions from the success in Southern Region. We are concerned in this Committee to find out success as well as failure. Your answer prompted me to think that there had been a success in Southern Region, and I accepted, if my memory serves me correctly, and I think that it does, that there was a very good reason why Southern Region had been able to achieve savings – that troops had moved north, as I understood it. But I wondered whether the advantages of the success that had been achieved in the Southern Region had been made known to the other regions, and that is why I went on to ask in Question 1335: 'What I meant was that presumably there might be different standards developed from one area to another,' – I was trying to penetrate your answer – 'and by reporting back to the centre and by one team learning from another, they might realise that their standards were different. I wondered if you had come across that.' I was trying to find out then, without any of the hindsight that we now have that there was an error, whether there was something to be learned from what had been going on in the Southern Region, but we did not have the advantage of learning that there had, other than that the regional officers met?——Yes. There certainly was, and arrangements were made, and were built up gradually, for the exchange of information about the improvements that could be made. This was done.

3254. I have been a little disturbed to hear today that when you found that there was an error, you thought that it was not necessary to report it to the Committee of Public Accounts immediately, yet if you have listened to me this afternoon, one member of this Committee at least, and I am sure that there are others, was actually misled in subsequent questioning by this error. It was very important to me, as I think about it now. I did not know about it then, but I am trying to make a point to you?——Indeed.

3255. When you said to the Chairman this afternoon that you had thought that it was not necessary to report to the Committee of Public Accounts immediately, I would say to you, why not? Is the Committee of Public Accounts of so little consequence in your estimation?—— That was certainly not the view I formed. As I was trying to explain to the Chairman, my belief was that the error, though most regrettable, was not critical in relation to the whole of the general tenor of my answer. What you have said, obviously, would weigh very much with me.

3256. I must say to you that I accept, of course, without reservation, the statement that you certainly had no intention of misleading the Committee, and I accept, too, that you did not think that it was of such seriousness, but I have been trying to say to you this afternoon that, seeing it from my side of this Committee room, it was serious. Do you see what I am saying?——Indeed. I do not, obviously, want to labour a situation where, clearly, there was an error made, but it did appear to us that it was not incorrect to say that in Southern Region at that time there were good opportunities. The particular reason which has attracted so much attention recently was not correct. This was a part of the country, where there was a high proportion of expenditure on the Defence estate, in particular a high proportion on the military estate, and experience has shown, and the records show, that these are the areas where it was possible to make good and profitable savings by this kind of method. I do not say this in any sense in criticism of Southern Region; on the contrary, the opportunities were there and they took them, and it was right that they should have done so. But there were certain other parts of the country which, by implication, were being criticised, where the situation was quite different and where the same opportunities did not arise. To that extent, I still believe that there was some foundation for the argument that I was trying to put before the Committee.

3257. Yes, some foundation, but in your letter to the Chairman of May 2nd this year you said, 'There was indeed some reduction in military strength in the Aldershot area during the relevant period, but this was I think due mainly to a general run down in the size of the Forces'. When I see that, I realise that perhaps we could have had greater savings in other regions?——The point here, of course, is that such run down as there was in the Aldershot area was not special to the Southern Region; it was more general. I am certainly not attempting to say that similar things could not have been done in other parts of the country with a high proportion of expenditure in the Defence estate, and indeed they were. For example, in Southern Region there was, over a period, a reduction of 29 per cent. in maintenance expenditure on the Defence estate, but there were four other regions which did, in fact, achieve an economy of 25 per cent. It was not a black and white picture. I come back to the two difficult regions, the North West, where on the mainland there was a largely civil estate, (and there was the Northern Ireland commitment building up, which was part of the North West's responsibility) and London, where only 25 per cent. of the estate was military estate, and where such of it as there was did not for the most part, offer the kind of opportunity as existed in the more rural parts of the country . . .

Mr *Orbach*

3263. May I come back to the main issue of the error, that was stressed by the Chairman? Your letter covers the whole question, and we are satisfied that you were wrongly advised, and that the memoranda which were presented to you were in fact not examined later. The statement made in the Report of the Comptroller and Auditor General is to the effect that part of your brief was changed at the suggestion of the Director of Home Regional Services. Are we correct in assuming that? That part of your brief was prepared by him?——(Sir *Robert Cox*) So I understand, yes.

3264. Subsequently to that, he never made any reference to it when the proof of the Committee's documents was available. I was almost going to say 'conveniently', but he has since died?——No, he has retired.

3265. He has retired; I beg your pardon. What sanctions have you got against an officer of your Department who is guilty of giving you a statement that is quite incorrect?——If he were still a serving civil servant various disciplinary sanctions would be open, but that would depend on whether one took the view that this was an error made deliberately or by inadvertence.

3266. Yes, I accept the latter, but suppose that it had not got to the stage where we had heard something about it from the Press and a book had been published, and that you are the unfortunate defendant, without necessarily having been responsible for the words that you uttered. What action could you take if he had not retired? What action would you take, in spite of the fact that it may have been given in good faith? There was a second opportunity when the report appeared in proof for him to correct the statement that he had submitted to you?——May I make one preliminary observation? I do take responsibility for the words that I uttered. I think that this is an essential personal part of the responsibility of an Accounting Officer who appears before this Committee, and I do not want to duck that issue at all. So far as the second stage that you have mentioned is concerned, I do not think that it is in essence any different from the first stage. My understanding is that the officer concerned believed the insertion that he caused to be made to the brief, to be correct. I expressed this in the Committee in words for which, as I say, I must take personal responsibility, and unless he had thought that I was going beyond what he believed to be correct, there would have been no cause for him at that stage to call for a correction. In other words, I think that the two things go together. If you have a situation where a brief is incorrectly prepared deliberately, and then the proof is not corrected, the two things are part of the same story. But there was no reason, I think, for him to come to a different view between the two stages.

3267. I do not want to hammer this, but I do think that you are not helping the Committee or yourself by the answer that you have given. What you have said is that you accepted the statement that was presented to you as part of the evidence that you should present to this Committee, and that, although it was later discovered to be incorrect, the individual who was responsible did not take the opportunity to direct your attention to the fact, he believing that it was correct, too. This is what you are saying is it not? He believed that whatever he had written in his memorandum was a correct statement?——He believed it, yes.

3268. But belief does not come into this; this is a question of accountancy and of your responsibility. He has, of course, delivered you to the gods, or to the devils if you like – whatever you like to call us – in this unfortunate position. What can you do with regard to an individual like that, even though he thinks that he is doing the right thing but has not taken the trouble to ascertain the facts? Is there any sanction that you can take against him on that basis?——I take it to the situation that he has retired and had retired before this error was discovered. I do not think that there is anything that one could do in these circumstances.

Mr *Orbach*] Except chop his head off!

Mr *Jenkins*

3269. I was not a member of the Committee in 1975 and therefore, referring again to the main subject of the discussion this afternoon, I should like to look a little wider, rather than at the particular questions in which I took no part at that time. Is it not the case that in certain circumstances it is the plain public duty of a senior civil servant to mislead the public and anyone else? For example, in time of war, the nature of the strength or weakness of Her Majesty's Forces must not be revealed. In times of financial crisis the Treasury has to pretend sometimes that things are quite other than they are. So that it is in fact a question of confidentiality – that a senior civil servant has a plain public duty on occasion to say things that are other than the truth. Is that not so?——In the wartime context, I would accept that.

3270. Even in the case of financial stringency, if the pound is in a weak condition, everybody concerned has a plain duty to present it as stronger than is the case, sometimes. Is that not so?——I have never been in such a position, but I will accept your point.

3271. Arising from that has there not grown up in the Civil Service a tradition which spreads far beyond questions of security – a tradition of confidentiality, of secrecy, of degrees of confidentiality, under which facts are regularly concealed. We will not say at the moment that they are misleading, but facts are regularly concealed?——I do not think so, except in the kind of context that you have just been describing. There may be points of time at which one reveals information. There may be matters still under discussion before Ministers which have not been decided and there may be returns of one kind or another which are published at given intervals and which one should not reveal before. Apart from that, I do not recognise the kind of situation that you are describing.

3272. Do you not recognise that documents passing from department to department, whichever departments they are, are under various degrees of confidentiality?——They may be, yes.

3273. So that in fact, the whole business of concealment is part of the Civil Service myth?——I would not treat it as concealment; I would regard it as confidentiality which may apply to public or any other business.

3274. Whatever word we use, it is keeping the public in the dark, is it not? That is what the whole business is about?——I do not think that that is the purpose.

3275. No? It may not be the purpose; it is, however, the practice, is it not?——We are under certain instructions in relation to the conduct of our business, and authorisation may have to be given for the revealing of certain facts and figures at particular times.

3276. This is precisely where I am trying to take the questioning – away from the question of personal responsibility to a questioning of the system under which all civil servants, whether they like it or not, have to work. Is there not in fact a tradition of confidentiality, of secrecy, arising historically, which is carried forward into the Civil Service, by which civil servants are under the necessity, and are told so from the beginning to preserve confidentiality?——This is so, I think particularly in relation to certain aspects of the work, some of which you have mentioned.

3277. Thank you very much. The point that I am getting at is this. Is it not the case that this need to preserve confidentiality may on occasion, at some stage in the Civil Service, lead to the concealment of error for the sake of the people concerned rather than for the sake of the public interest?——I would hope not.

3278. You would hope not, but in the nature of things, human beings being what they are, it is probably so, is it not?——I hope not.

3279. You hope not. Well, we must leave it at that, but the evidence which has been before us in this matter suggests, does it not, that in your own department it has been so?——If the implication here is that the concealment of this particular error was intended to be permanent, I really do not think that this is so. This information was known to be in the hands of the Press and known to be in the hands of those who were campaigning on this subject, and it was inevitably going to become public.

3280. Do you feel yourself that perhaps, because of this tradition of concealment, for very good reason, the whole question of the tradition of keeping matters rather close under wraps ought to be re-examined?——I have no personal knowledge of this, but, as the Committee will know, there is a review of the Official Secrets Act in progress.

3281. Finally, do you think that now we are moving more towards what we like to call open government, it being generally recognised nowadays that the public has, perhaps, a wider interest which has to be served, possibly for the prevention of error, perhaps the older traditions may be out of date, and that a much more open attitude ought to be adopted generally?——I think that this is developing already. Indeed, as you will know, the Prime Minister gave a directive some while ago that there should be wider publication of background information relating to policy documents.

3282. If this wider publicity attitude were adopted, it might have the effect of preventing, or of encouraging greater efficiency as a part of that process?——Possibly, yes.

Mr. *Costain*.] I will forgo my normal right of questioning as I have taken the Chair temporarily, although I shall have one or two questions to put at the end.

Mr *Taylor*

3283. Sir Robert, I agree with Mr Crouch that the effect of your answer was to end questioning on the savings in the Southern Region. Of course, this also means that because we ended the questioning about those savings, the heat which the Committee of Public Accounts might have generated on the other regions was taken off. In your letter of 2 May to Mr du Cann you said: 'I am in some difficulty about this as neither the publishers nor the author have been prepared to let us see a copy of the book before publication and I am, therefore, not entirely sure just what points of criticism are to be made'. On the day of publication the *Evening Standard* reported the Department of the Environment spokesman as saying that Mr Chapman's allegations had been investigated and were not supported by the evidence. How do you account for that discrepancy?——This relates, I think, to a memorandum which Mr Chapman sent to the Director General of Organisations and Establishments at the Department of the Environment at the time of his retirement some years before. They dealt with a number of matters, including his own personal position. We did not know, of course, at that point of time what, if anything, further, there would be in the book, and what matters would be covered by the book.

3284. Someone could certainly not have read it by the time that that statement was issued. I bought the book that morning, but here is a statement that Mr Chapman's allegations had been investigated and were not supported by the evidence, and that is referring to the book It is a statement by the Department of the Environment and it is not referring to any memorandum which Mr Chapman may have submitted at the time of his resignation. If that memorandum covered all the allegations in the book, there would have been no need for you to put that sentence in the letter to Mr du Cann?——I had not seen the book at the time when I wrote to Mr du Cann. We asked for a copy from both the publishers and the author, and were refused copies. One of the reasons why I did not write to Mr du Cann – I am not speaking about March, 1977 but of this particular time – earlier, at that stage of the proceedings, was that I was hoping that I might have a sight of the book and to see what other matters were raised. In fact, a copy of the book came into my hands the day after I had signed my letter to Mr du Cann, but, as I say, we had not seen it earlier.

3285. I am suggesting that that statement by the Department of the Environment was the start of another cover up, because there are allegations in this book which we, the Committee of Public Accounts, have now got a duty to investigate with great thoroughness, and I think that these might have been investigated in 1974. I will put to you one or two questions and while I do not expect you to be able to give the answers now——May I say that I have just found the passages that you were referring to? The passage in full was, 'Shortly before his retirement he sent the Department a memorandum making a number of allegations which have formed the basis of the criticism which he has subsequently publicised'. That, I think, was referring to various Press articles which appeared between his retirement and the publication of the book.

3286. I think that that is very helpful. Therefore, the newspapers had left that out, which certainly made another interpretation in my mind. But I still think that it was a very unfair remark which suggests that there is going to be no further inquiry into the allegations in the book. I should like to put one or two questions to you, to which perhaps you would let us have a note of the answers in due course. On page [39] of the book Mr Chapman tells us that the Southern Region had retired men of over 65 years of age, and that they were the first men to be made redundant, which is understandable. Could you tell us whether there are men retained in the other regions who are over the age of 65 at this time? That is one question. The next one refers to the same page. That is, that in 1967 there were over 700 stokers in the Southern Region and by 1973 there were fewer than 50. Perhaps we could have comparable figures for the other regions. On page [40] Mr Chapman says that on sales of land only 5 per cent of the possible reduction had been achieved. Nearly all the other 95 per cent is still there, waiting for the time when the recommendations at the end of his book are implemented. I do not think that we need wait to have the recommendations at the end of the book implemented. We could find out what additional land out of that 95 per cent has been disposed of since Mr Chapman retired. Then more important still is the fact that under Mr Chapman's directorship of the Southern Region the directly employed labour force was reduced from around 4,000 to under 2,000. I think that it would be of advantage to the Committee to have the comparable figures for all the other regions. I think that we have got to make certain that the drive he implemented in the Southern Region does take place right throughout the length and breadth of the country. As you know, Sir Robert, from previous times when you have come before this Committee, in another capacity I often have the opportunity to call at offices of the Property Services Agency, and I am frequently amazed at the number of people who surround the door as I go into an office building and issue me with a pass. The idea is that I should be escorted to the customer that I am going to see. They do not know that I am a Member of Parliament because it is not on my private visiting card. They just tell me to take the lift to the fifth floor or the sixth floor, and they just sit round the entrance to the building wasting time. I think that this is the type of incident which Mr. Chapman put his finger on when he was in command, and I think that we have got to continue this, because, somehow or other, we have got to cut back on expenditure . . .

Mr *Evans*

3295. I was not a member of the Committee at the time and, therefore, have not the benefit of knowing what took place. I have simply read the various documents. I might add that I have not read Mr Chapman's book either, quite deliberately, so that my understanding was not coloured by any other issues. I am receiving an impression that the real issue is that the other regions, or some of the other regions, of the PSA were not as enthusiastic or as determined or as diligent as the Southern Region in pursuing economies, and that they had a vested interest in playing down the original report which showed the Southern Region sticking up like a sore thumb so far as economies were concerned. Therefore they then said, in effect, that there were special reasons for that. Do you accept that?——(Sir *Robert Cox.*) I accept, and I accepted at the time of the 1975 examination, that there were differences in enthusiasm between the different regions, but, certainly, in the case of some regions I would regard the reasons for the difference in performance as being sound and legitimate. There was also another issue that I mentioned. That, of course, was the timing by which this started in the Southern Region, which, of course, brought in economies earlier than the timing of economies through maintenance economy review teams in other regions.

3296. Do you now feel, with the benefit of hindsight, that there was more determination in the Southern Region at that time to pursue economies than there was in other regions?——I think that there was certainly more enthusiasm for this particular technique and probably for maintenance economy in general, but I would not like it to be thought that other regions were not also doing similar things in rather different ways. For example, if I could quote one figure, one of the methods of achieving economies in maintenance is through economies in the use of directly employed labour. In the Southern Region a great part of the economies in directly employed labour was chalked up and recorded as the result of the maintenance economy review team's work. In many other regions the same, or similar, economies were achieved, but they were not recorded in the same way. I think, in fact, that only about 15 per cent of the economies in directly employed labour in other regions was chalked up as a result of the work of these particular teams, and this produced a different balance of results, though, in some respects, similar economies in practice.

3297. You have acknowledged that the officer who prepared the brief for you which somewhat misled the Committee, was the Director of Home Regional Services and that he had previously been the Director of the Southern Region?——Yes.

3298. Were you aware at the time that the man who had written this particular brief for you had been the previous Director of the Southern Region?——I knew that he had been a Director of the Southern Region. What, of course, I was not aware of, was that this particular amendment had been made at his instigation.

3299. On that point, was the then Director of the Southern Region asked for his views about the report that you were presenting to the Committee of Public Accounts?——I do not know; I should doubt it.

3300. Following your evidence to the Committee of Public Accounts, either immediately afterwards or some time later when the tenor of your evidence had become public, did Mr Chapman make any representations to you about your evidence or to anyone within your Department?——I received no representations from Mr Chapman myself, and I do not know of any other representations that went to the Department. We first heard about this, to the best of my belief, through a newspaper reporter.

3301. So that when you gave this evidence in 1975, the first that you knew about Mr Chapman's allegations, or views, or opinions, was the newspaper article?——I am sorry; I may be confusing two things. Certainly I knew about Mr Chapman's representations when he retired from the Department. I did not know about the suggestion that my evidence was incorrect until we heard about this through a newspaper reporter in March 1977.

3302. On that question, in March 1977 did you know that Mr Chapman was writing a book?——No.

3303. You simply heard this via a newspaper?——Yes.

3304. It was at that time that you took the decision not to inform the Committee of Public Accounts that you had erred in your evidence to them. I am always loath to quote people, and I may be wrong, but I think that you said something to the effect that you thought that it was not important and that it would come to light eventually and you could explain it. How on earth would it have come to light if Mr Chapman had not written a book?——It was in the hands of a newspaper and it was our belief at the time that that newspaper was going to go ahead and write a further article on the story.

3305. I should like to get this quite right. You decided to sit tight and do nothing, knowing full well that one day it would all come out, and that you would have to come and explain it?——What we thought was, as I have said, not that it was unimportant, but that it was not critical to the general tenor of the answer that I was trying to give and to the action that we were taking to follow up the Committee's Report, and that the right method of dealing with this would be to deal with the allegation when it was made public.

3306. I find this very difficult, and I am sure that my colleagues find it difficult, because when this matter became public knowledge, with statements in newspapers and television broadcasts you immediately wrote to the Chairman of the Committee of Public Accounts and informed him of the error that you had made in your evidence to this Committee. It seems to me that if there was concern at that stage, you should have informed the Committee – of which, I might add, I was not a member – at the time when you discovered the error?——Yes, I think that this turns partly on our judgement, which may have been wrong, of the importance of this particular statement in relation to our evidence as a whole, and partly on the context in which the matter was coming to light. As I have said, we were anxious to get hold of a copy of the book but this had been refused to us, and one thought in my mind was that it was perfectly possible that I might have made other errors in my evidence or, alternatively, that it might be alleged that I had made other errors in my evidence, and I wanted to deal with any such matters as a package. The last thing that I wanted to do was to be writing a series of letters to the Chairman of this Committee saying 'And there is another thing which has come up'. That was why, at that later stage, not in March, 1977, I wanted, if at all possible, to see what was in the book before I wrote to the Chairman.

3307. So that I am right in assuming that prior to March 1977 you had no idea that you had in any way misled the Committee of Public Accounts in the evidence that you had put before it?——That is so . . .

Mr *Ovenden*

3309. With regard to the error in your evidence which we are discussing, did that arise as far as you are concerned primarily because of what was in your brief on that occasion, or because of your interpretation of that brief?——There must have been an element of both. The brief put me on this track, and this, coupled with other discussion of matters connected with this, led me to use the words that I used before the Committee.

3310. Had you stuck entirely to the brief, I take it that the Committee would not have been misled as seriously as most members now consider that it was?——I think that that may be so, but my intention was to try to bring before the Committee what the brief actually meant, and that is how I arrived at the words that I used.

3311. I certainly do not want to be over-critical in that connection. I see how these problems can arise when you are answering questions off the cuff, of which you have had no notice, and I do not want to be over-critical about that. What does concern me far more, and I think that it concerns most members of the Committee, is the events which occurred after that evidence was given. I for one, like many of my colleagues, find it quite astonishing that it was two years before it came to light that that evidence was incorrect, and that in fact it only came to light because a reporter mentioned it to the Agency. That is absolutely correct? Nobody else in the Agency had mentioned at any stage that there could be anything wrong with this evidence?——To the best of my knowledge that is so.

3312. At that time, of course, this Committee was meeting in private, but as a witness you would have been sent a copy of the draft evidence for your comments. How widely within the Agency would that document have been circulated?——In the ordinary way it would come to me, to anybody who happened to accompany me to the Committee, and to whatever expert area in the Department had been briefing me. The distribution is normally undertaken by the Finance Directorate, and that is, I understand, what happened on this occasion.

3313. The Report of the Committee of Public Accounts, which, of course, includes the whole of the evidence, would be available, I take it, quite widely within the Agency?——That is published. It is a published document available to anybody.

3314. I take it that the Agency does acquire a number of copies and that they are circulated quite widely within the Department?——We acquire a number of copies. I do not know that the circulation is necessarily very wide, because normally only those people who were directly concerned with the issue at the stage of the Committee's hearing would be directly concerned with the outcome.

3315. When the approach was made to the Property Services Agency by the reporter who brought this matter to light, I understood you to say to Mr Evans that there was no mention at any time about the fact that Mr Chapman was publishing a book?——We did not hear about the book – I did not hear about the book – until the late autumn of 1977.

3316. Was anything said by this particular reporter to whoever he spoke to in the Agency about how he acquired this information, where it had come from and in what connection it was being used?——I am speaking at second-hand now, of course, but I believe that he said that Mr Chapman was likely to challenge this part of the evidence.

3317. I am still rather confused after the answers to my colleague, Mr Evans, about why you considered it unnecessary to tell the Committee about this in 1977. I understood that it was on the basis that it was becoming public anyway and that everybody would know, yet, by 1978 you considered it necessary to write to the Chairman before this book was published?——Yes.

3318. I listened carefully to your answer to Mr Evans, but I am still not clear what the difference in circumstances was. Perhaps you could tell me again?——There are two separate points here. One is that it seemed to me to be right that we should deal with the point when we knew fully what it was and what was being stated to be wrong, and, as I said to Mr Evans, certainly at the later stage when I knew that the whole matter was going to be the subject of a book, I had it in my mind that there might possibly be allegations that there were other errors in my evidence which I would want to deal with as a whole rather than as individual items. The second point about the actual timing of my letter to the Chairman was that it came to my notice that he was being interviewed, or that interviews were being sought from him, by television programmes, and I did not want to leave him in the position of undertaking such interviews without knowing that there was an error in my evidence which I was going to acknowledge when it became public. I believe, in fact, that my letter reached him too late for that purpose, but that was the reason why I wrote before I obtained a copy of the book, which is what I should have preferred to do.

3319. Of course the Chairman could have been in that position in 1977 – that the very reporter who approached the Property Services Agency could have made an approach to the Chairman, and he would then have been in the position of being completely ignorant of these facts. Would it not, in retrospect, have been wise to have informed him then?——In retrospect, it would have been, but could I just say that we are trying to exercise judgment on this issue now in the light of the very considerable publicity which has surrounded the book and the television programmes and the Press conferences, and I can only say that things looked very differently to us at that period over a year ago.

3320. Would you accept Mr Crouch's point that the line of questioning at this Committee meeting in April 1975 would have been somewhat different had you answered Question 1318 differently?——Obviously I cannot judge what the Committee might have done. Had there been a different line of questioning, I think that there were general arguments that I would have wished to advance still in support of the general proposition, not that the Southern Region was uniquely placed to deal with this matter in the way that it did, but that it was on a good wicket for this particular type of bowling.

3321. Finally, do you consider that the Committee itself should at least have had the opportunity of deciding whether or not this point was relevant, and of whether it would have liked to re-open the question before this matter became public?——I think, if I may, I would go back to the point made by the Chairman earlier, that it would perhaps have been wiser for me to have taken some informal soundings of the Clerk or of the Comptroller and Auditor General . . .

Mr *Costain*

3325. I have just three questions. I do not want to go back to the question of the error, or otherwise, of judgment, but could you clear my mind on one general point? If a junior civil servant sees that one of his seniors has made a mistake in evidence or in advising, is it not a breach of the Official Secrets Act if he were to go over that senior's head and report it to anybody?——(Sir *Robert Cox*.) I do not know what the technical answer to that question is, but I should certainly expect him in those circumstances to report the matter to me. It not infrequently happens that mistakes are made in evidence, and they are brought to the attention of the Accounting Officer and are corrected. I can remember a case, for instance, on this very matter, when we were discussing the regional car service, when I got into a muddle about car hire charges. Somebody in the Department detected that error and pointed it out and, as a result, we had a footnote put in the evidence.

3326. I did not want to go back to the first issue; I really wanted some general information. Perhaps the Treasury witness can help me. How does the Official Secrets Act affect a civil servant when it comes to reporting if he sees that there has been deliberate misleading? I am not saying that in any way this was deliberately misleading, but could you help the Committee? What is a civil servant tied to – that an ordinary person in a public or a private company could do?——(Mr *Carey*.) I have no expertise of the Official Secrets Act, but my guess is that it does not really come into this. I do not see that the subordinate civil servant is any more inhibited by it than his senior would be.

3327. Could he write to *The Times* about it, or would that be a breach?——I was thinking of the situation of giving evidence to this Committee. Perhaps I misunderstood your question.

3328. It is a general one, because I think that it has a great bearing on the whole issue. Perhaps we could have a note on that at some time.*

* Appendix I V [Appendix 13 below].

Appendix 10

MINUTES OF EVIDENCE TAKEN BEFORE THE COMMITTEE OF PUBLIC ACCOUNTS

Monday 10 July 1978 (pp. 23–39)

Members present:

Mr Edward du Cann, in the Chair

Mr A P Costain	Mr Robert Taylor
Mr David Crouch	Mr John Watkinson

Sir DOUGLAS HENLEY, KCB, and Mr P R GORDON, Assistant Secretary, HM Treasury, called in and examined.

Examination of witnesses

Sir ROBERT COX, KCB, Chief Executive, Property Services Agency, of the Department of the Environment, called in and further examined; Mr G MAY, Principal Finance Officer, Property Services Agency, of the Department of the Environment, called in and examined.

Chairman

3786. Before we begin our discussion with you, Sir Robert, perhaps you would allow me to put a question to the Treasury witness. Mr Gordon, I think that the Treasury is preparing a note for this Committee following a question that Mr Costain asked at our last meeting in regard to the operation of the Official Secrets Act. That is so, is it not?——(Mr *Gordon.*) Yes.

3787. When shall we receive that memorandum?——I have not enquired specifically into progress because I was not sure whether it would be required, but as soon as is convenient to you I will hurry it along.

3788. Thank you very much. The Committee hopes to complete its examination of Sir Robert today, and that means that we shall be considering what reports we wish to write and make to the House, and in the completion of those reports it would be convenient to have that memorandum promptly. If you could ask your colleagues to let us have it this week, I think that would be best?——Yes. Thank you.

3789. Sir Robert, the Committee is much obliged to you for coming back to see us again and at such short notice. Before I begin putting questions to you, perhaps I might make one or two general remarks. The more I consider the Fourth Report of the Committee, which was based, as you know, on the Report to the House from the Comptroller and Auditor General, the more I think that the recommendations in paragraphs 31 and 32 were appropriate and justified. I think that the criticisms that the Committee made then were valid ones. The Committee, as you know, was pleased that the recommendations were accepted, and I think that the chief purpose of our discussion today is to see exactly what has been happening since that time. There is considerable public interest in these matters. It is necessary, and has been necessary, as you know, for the Committee to inquire into them fully and in some detail, and we shall be pleased, if we can, to complete our discussion about them today. We were greatly obliged to you for the memorandum that you sent us, which is marked P A C 61, and which we have before us now.* On Section 1 of the memorandum, on the subject of age, more than half of your men over 65 are in London. Is that because there are particular difficulties about recruitment of younger men in London?——(Sir *Robert Cox*.) That is the position. We have a general difficulty about recruitment in London, and that explains why we feel it necessary to hold on to some of the older men.

3790. Are there any other of those figures in the table at paragraph 4 that you particularly want to draw our attention to? Are there any other places where there are special circumstances?——I do not think so. There is a slightly higher figure in the south east than in other regions. That, I would guess, is probably, as it were, the shadow of London.

3791. Otherwise it is plain that the number of industrial staff over 65 in the United Kingdom as a whole was reduced very substantially.

*Appendix II [Appendix 11 below].

Let me go on to the matter of stokers. The Southern region managed to reduce its complement of stokers by over 90 per cent between 1966 and 1978. Why have the reductions in other regions been so much smaller?——I think that is possibly due to three factors. I cannot be completely certain, but I think that some of this may be to do with the differing degree of automation of boiler plants in different parts of the country which makes it possible to move more quickly in some places than in others. Secondly, of course, there is the question of the starting point. The Southern region started with a rather higher figure than other parts of the country. Thirdly, I think that there may be a complication here in connection with gradings. In addition to stokers, we have plant attendants who undertake certain duties in boiler houses and also certain duties elsewhere. I have not been able to pin this down entirely in the time available, but I do notice that the Southern region has on its strength something like half the national total of plant attendants, so that it is possible that some of the work which in other regions is allocated to stokers is in fact undertaken by plant attendants in the Southern region. I cannot be certain of this, but it seems a possibility.

3792. Are you continuing your examination of this particular matter?——We will take it further and see where it gets to, but I do not know whether the Committee would wish us to do a detailed examination over the whole country. It would be quite a time consuming affair, but certainly I will pursue this point about the plant attendants in the Southern region and where they are being employed.

3793. I do not think that the Committee would wish you for one moment to be engaged in work that is unnecessary or unproductive. On the other hand, the disparities are so great between one region and another, and I think that it would be interesting to hear, within the next week or so, if the examination that you are already making leads you to particular conclusions. Should that be the case, perhaps you would be kind enough to advise us?——Certainly.

3794. Let me go on to the matter of the disposal of surplus land. On reading the Memorandum, it seemed to me that this is a very long drawn out process. What are you doing about the 900 acres or so that are still held in the Southern region, which were proposed by Mr Chapman's teams for disposal?——May I first make a correction to the paper?

3795. Of course.——There is, I am afraid, a factual error in paragraph 8. We said in the second sentence that 476 acres had been disposed of and that these were areas identified in the course of the management economy reviews. I discover on further examination that four hundred and one acres* have been disposed of, which were not specifically identified for disposal as such, though they were, in fact, in establishments covered by management economy reviews. Therefore, they should be added to the remainder outstanding. As for what remains, our difficulty is that we are, of course, not the owners of this land. We are agents for the Ministry of Defence in the case of nearly all of it, and in most cases they are simply unable to agree that the land is fit to be disposed of. They feel that they still require the use of it. These are matters which, of course, we can bring up with them from time to time. We have an estate surveying service which is continually on the look out for opportunities for disposal, not only of land identified in these reviews but of land generally. In fact, in the last five years, we have disposed of about 15,000 acres of surplus land. In the previous five years we disposed of some 21,000 acres of surplus land, and we have also disposed of quite a number of surplus houses. So that this is an activity which is being pursued the whole time, irrespective of, and in addition to, the management economy review teams. (Mr *May*.) The 401 acres actually was not solely in the category of land disposed of. It is 401 acres of land disposed of, or being disposed of, and so, therefore, should be compared with the total of 1,176 and not with the 476 acres.

3796. Sir Robert, however politely you put it, are you saying that in fact your Department are not the arbiters of the land which is to be disposed of, but, none the less, you lose no opportunity to remind departments that land should not be held on to unnecessarily?——That is certainly the case, but, of course, when we have a definite decision that a facility is still required by the service department concerned, then that is a decision which we have to accept. If we think that it is wrong, of course, we can challenge it, but in many cases we have to accept the view of the department concerned.

3797. We were looking particularly at the Southern region. It was on that that we asked you to report, and you have. How much surplus land has been released by other regions in recent years?——I have not got figures region by region, but I was able to give you the global total for Defence land of 15,000 acres over the last five years, and I can, if the Committee wishes, no doubt get a breakdown of those figures into regional terms.

* *Footnote by witness:* Further investigation has shown that the figure is about 500 acres.

3798. I think that it would be interesting to see that, if you would kindly let us have a table. Would you, please?——I think that the table may well reflect the geography of the country, because I think that a good deal of this will be open land rather than urban land, but we will certainly produce that.

3799. If you think it appropriate to explain the table with some notes, pray do so. Let us go on to the matter now of directly employed labour. Reductions in directly employed labour seem to have been fairly consistent throughout the country since 1967, but the Southern region seems to have done rather better than other regions. Why is that?——I think that this is a reflection of the fact that the Southern region did, in fact, do better over this whole field of maintenance economy reviews and maintenance economy than the rest of the country. One of the bigger savings to be made was in terms of directly employed labour and this figure, I think, reflects the greater savings which they made. The only point that I would put on the other side is that there are, of course, some regions which started with a lower total and consequently had, to that extent, a smaller opportunity for reduction.

3800. Do you mind my asking you why it looks as if the South Western region has done so badly?——I cannot be sure about this. The only point that I would make is that it is a very extensive region. In terms of geography, I think, its length is roughly the same as from London to Newcastle, and consequently there are probably pockets of directly employed labour in various places rather than forces which can easily be remodelled, but I am afraid that that is hazarding a guess.

3801. Can we go on to Section II of the memorandum, on property maintenance and operating costs, at paragraph 12? That talks about the achievement of savings by some parts of the PSA 'in other ways'. You will see those words in the penultimate line. Can you tell the Committee what other methods were used? Was any record kept of the savings made?——Except in the manner in which they have been shown in this memorandum. Part of this is simply general control in management terms, part the restricted use of directly employed labour and part, particularly in the later part of the period that we are discussing, the fuel economy campaign.

3802. Are you still using maintenance economy review teams on a regular basis within the PSA?——We have nearly finished the programme. There are still teams operating in London, where we have one full time team, and part of the area management team's energies are devoted to maintenance economy. We have four teams still operating, in Southern region picking up odd pockets that have been left behind or re-doing odd pockets, and, as I think I told the Committee last time, we have teams operating in Germany.

3803. What sort of results are they producing where they are used?——In London, I think that the most recent figure I have seen is a saving of £1 million in annual expenditure, with the possibility of a further million still under examination. In Germany, where we have covered, I think, 15 out of 26 depots, we are hoping to show savings of about two and a half million pounds at a capital cost of half a million pounds. I have not got figures for the last four surveys in the Southern region.

3804. May I take you to Annex B? Since 1973–74 there has been an increase in maintenance expenditure at constant prices in several regions, particularly in the Southern region. What is the explanation for that?——The general explanation is that we were, in 1973–74, operating at a relatively low level, partly because of the determined economy drives that were being carried on throughout the country and partly because of over-heating in the building industry, which was making it difficult for us to get contracts through. This resulted in a certain amount of catching up still to be done. We have also been subject to a certain amount of pressures in both directions from the Ministry of Defence, according to the availability of funds and their priorities. The particular reasons for the increase in Southern region are partly the general ones, which are of application on a nationwide basis as I have mentioned, and, to some limited extent, though I do not wish to argue that this accounts for the full nature of the change, to a boundary change which brought within their ambit one very large Service department which takes a fair bit of keeping up.

3805. I think that the Committee will have read with great interest your comments in Section III of the memorandum which refer to the *Sunday Times* article of 18th June 1978. We were obliged to you for going through that matter so carefully for us. I do not think that I want to ask particular questions about that. It seems to me that the Memorandum speaks for itself, but the first point seems to turn on the exact interpretation of what you said about the Southern region's early start. I think that the point is that you did not lend too much emphasis to that. Second, you are saying that the particular civil establishment referred to was the exception which proved the rule that in general, military installations offered the largest scope for savings. Would that be right?——May I put it in this way? I think that the technique adopted here for savings was particularly valuable in the case of large establishments, typically a large house in large grounds and, perhaps, with a collection of miscellaneous buildings of different ages scattered around it. In such an area there were considerable savings to be made in terms of ground maintenance, possibly dealing with particular buildings that were no longer needed and possibly in relation to the maintenance of the house. I think that the particular establishment referred to was of that type, and it is not a particularly common type among our civil establishments, although it is comparatively commonly found in the Defence estate, where it is not unusual to find extensive grounds and extensive arrays of buildings. On the civil estate, our more normal prospect is of a single office, perhaps a small office in a small town, or a large office block in a city. In such places there is, I think, less scope for this particular type of approach and this particular type of review. Therefore, in saying that this is the exception that proves the rule, what I am really trying to say is that if you take Defence establishments as a whole you tend to find this kind of structure among them. If you take the civil estate as a whole, you tend to find more compact establishments to deal with and therefore, with less scope.

3806. Sir Robert, it seemed important to the Committee that this matter should be taken most seriously and that there should be a searching review of it and, in particular, as I said in the beginning, of what has been happening since we made our original criticisms and recommendations. We shall want to consider everything that you have been kind enough to tell us and we shall write our report in due course, but there are two other things. The first is this. I am sure that I speak on behalf of the Committee if I say how much we are obliged to you for the help that you have given us. Secondly, is there anything else that you want to say to the Committee which you think might be helpful to us in the framing of our reports to Parliament?——I have done my best in this memorandum to bring forward a number of facts which I hoped would be helpful and that I hoped would help to set the whole thing in better perspective. If there is any way in which I can elaborate on that document, either now or in writing, I shall obviously be very glad to do so.

Mr *Watkinson*

3807. Sir Robert, I should like to turn to Section III of your memorandum. I think that running through it is a view which is now commonly accepted. If one turns to paragraph 20 one sees that there 'was greater enthusiasm in the Southern region'. Paragraph 21 says that 'other regions progressed only slowly after they had started', and then in paragraph 22 we find ' "A review in 1969 indicated that the surveys had been generally worth while but there was a marked difference in the results achieved and the efforts made by different Regions" '. How soon did this become observable to you? Was it in 1969?——I am afraid that I cannot answer that personally because I was not in the Department at that time. To the Department I think that it became evident quite early on, in that there were discussions of this problem at meetings of regional directors, and there were discussions about the availability of staff, and advice and instructions were issued.

3808. What sort of instructions were they? Were they to tell the other regions to buck up?——To proceed with these surveys and to return reports of progress, and to exchange ideas about the ideas which had proved successful.

3809. Was there specifically an effort to point out to the other regions what was being achieved in the Southern region?——Yes, certainly, there was indeed.

3810. Was there a marked improvement in the other regions as a result?——There was a gradual build-up I think that part of the problem was one of staffing. I repeat, as I have said before, that there was a difference of enthusiasm for this particular technique. What was also happening at the same time was that other initiatives were being taken to try to achieve economy, notably through the new policy on the employment of directly employed labour. I think that it is fair to say that some savings were being pursued in other regions at the same time that would have come under the general head of maintenance economy reviews in the Southern region.

3811. But if it was apparent very rapidly that the enthusiasm in this one region was producing outstanding results, was it not the business of the PSA to make sure that this enthusiasm was mirrored in other areas?——I think that attempts were made to do this, and the results were of varied quality.

3812. Of varying quality?——Of varying quality, yes.

3813. Is it true to say that thereafter there were continuous reviews in the PSA to bring other areas up to the mark?——Yes; the object was to get the whole of the PSA covered by a series of teams and by a series of reviews. When I came into it, the difficulty that I found was in London, which had not been completed, and there really was a genuine difficulty in manning up teams to do the job, and other methods had to be adopted.

3814. On the matter of enthusiasm, this should have been something which would have been pointed out to other regions and then, if they did not come up to scratch, presumably some action would be taken?——There was a follow through, and progress reports were made and were noted.

3815. It all sounds a very gentle process to me. Is that fair?——I find this difficult to comment on because I was not there at the time, and it is easy for me to sit back here now and say that things should have gone harder and faster. I know that in some parts of the country there were other priorities that had to be dealt with, and there were difficulties about staff. Looking back at it now, I think that we could all wish that this had gone through faster than it did.

3816. So with hindsight – and I appreciate the ease of making statements with hindsight – you would say that other regions were culpable in not pursuing this as fast as the Southern region?——I would not go so far as to say culpable because as I was trying to say just now, and as this Memorandum has tried to say, savings were being pursued, though they were reflected in other ways. I would say for myself that at a time when I was concerned, I was trying to get two teams operating simultaneously in London, and I found that given the competing demands on that particular hard pressed and under-staffed region, I had to concede that they should proceed by way of one and use the local management in addition to support that.

3817. From your study of this issue now, would you say that there was, in fact, resistance, as opposed to just adopting something slowly?——I find that a very difficult question to answer because not only was I not there at the time but many of the people concerned I do not know. It is possible; I do not know, but there is no resistance, to my knowledge, to the idea of maintenance economy. I think that some people were concerned to think that there were other ways of achieving similar results.

3818. Turning to the matter relating to the possible savings and to the comparison between military establishments, army establishments, and others, could you comment on the matter of Bletchley, where, as the

Sunday Times pointed out, there were very dramatic savings, and Bletchley was not a military establishment, as I understand it? Is your argument that Bletchley stands alone?——Not that it stands alone, but that its character is of a kind which is well adapted to this kind of approach and that, on the whole, one tends to find establishments of that character in the Defence estate rather than in the civil estate. This was the point that I was trying to make to the Chairman just now. It is certainly not unique. I would not wish to argue that for one moment, but if you are looking for that kind of combination of circumstance, you are more likely to find it in the Defence estate than in the civil estate.

3819. What you are saying is that Bletchley, from this point of view, from the argument that we are having now, was very similar in kind to a military establishment and not a civil one?——From this particular point of view, yes.

3820. Have you done surveys to establish if there were any other dramatic savings in civil areas?——I cannot recall any myself, but I can think of one or two places which might have been of a similar character but where I do not actually know what the results were.

3821. Because in the memorandum which you have given us we are just given a quotation from Mr Chapman to back up what you yourself have said and it would be interesting to know if there has been a review, monitoring, in the Department to see if other establishments in fact measure up to what you have said?——I am sure that one could find other establishments. What we have done, of course, in the Annexes here, is to try to show the effect over the different kinds of estate as a whole so as to get an averaging out of the types of result, as it were. I would not wish to rest entirely on what Mr Chapman says here, because there are, for example, certain RAF establishments where good and profitable savings can be made, and where I believe, in fact, he did so in his own region.

Mr *Taylor*

3822. Sir Robert, I should like to emphasise my agreement with the Chairman's opening remarks, when he congratulated you on this memorandum. I think that it is first class; it is very helpful indeed. In fact, I think that the replies are really to questions which I put to you at our last meeting, and certainly you have helped me with some of the fears which I had at that time. Going through the various headings, you dealt very explicitly with the question of the sale of land and gave us some additional facts in connection with paragraph 8, but the one question that I have got on that paragraph is on where you say that 'authority has been given to dispose of another 700 acres and action is in hand'. Could you tell the Committee when that authority was given? Has it recently been given as a result of the publicity, or alternatively, was it given some time ago and no action has been taken on it?——I am afraid that I cannot answer that question, but I will let the Committee know what the answer is. The point that I must make is that the disposal of Government owned land is, I am afraid, a lengthy process because of the procedures that we are required to go through. The first stage, obviously, is to get the authority of the owning or using department. We then have to offer it to all other Government departments to see whether they have a prior claim on it. We then have to offer it to the local authority to see if they need to have it. We then, if it is agricultural land or formerly agricultural land, have to go through the Crichel Down procedures in relation to the former owner or owners, and only after that are we in a position to put it on the market. So that I am afraid that it can be a very time consuming process to dispose of any particular parcel of land.

3823. I think that the Committee is aware of the difficulties, because we have similar problems with the disposal of surplus land from the National Health Service, where they have got quite an amount of land which could have been disposed of more quickly, I think, than has been the case, so that I have no doubt that the Committee will want to make some remark on the reply which you have just given. Obviously, if it is going to hold up the process of bringing money to the Exchequer, some action should be taken. If we leave the question of the time factor and go back to the actual acreage, you will correct me if my figures are out of date, in view of your answers to the Chairman, but I made it that only 476 acres had been disposed of out of a total of 2,268?——I wonder if I might offer to send to the Committee a completely re-drafted paragraph 8 for incorporation?

Chairman

3824. By all means.——I am afraid that my explanation was not as clear as it might have been. In reply to Mr Taylor's point, yes, that is correct, but the point is that we had here a series of suggestions for disposal coming from our side. We are in the end dependent upon the user department to say whether or not they are prepared to let the land go. Very often this is a question of whether they can afford to do without a facility altogether, and very often it is a question of whether they are able to find the money to replace a particular facility elsewhere, so that there can be a powerful incentive to them not to release land.

Mr *Taylor*

3825. If there is a clash of opinion between the PSA and the department concerned, would it be possible for you to put in the annual report of the PSA a statement to say that you have recommended, or at least suggested, that so many acres should be disposed of, but that such and such a department wished to retain this acreage, because the House of Commons has got to get to the fundamental point of who is holding up the sale of the land and preventing money coming to the Exchequer?——We are in two different kinds of relationship as far as land is concerned. For the general public service on the civil side, my Secretary of State is the owner of the land, and if we feel that land can and should be disposed of, we proceed. If it is a matter of sufficient importance, we obtain Ministerial authority. For the Defence estate, the situation is different. The title of the land lies with the Secretary of State for Defence, and our relationship is simply that of agent. It is really for the Secretary of State for Defence to decide in the long run whether he wishes to retain land, bearing in mind the points that I have made and, of course, the difficulty of recovering land once it has been allowed to go. We are simply in the position of an estate agent acting on his behalf.

3826. I accept that, but there must be some way in which Members of Parliament can get to the fundamental question as to whether or not the Government is hanging on to land or to accommodation which is unnecessary. You must be aware that over the last two or three years I have put down innumerable questions to the Minister when I have seen that the PSA has taken the lease of an office building in Holborn or in the City or in Southport or in any part of the country. I have always asked in my questions, 'What accommodation is going to be released as a result of the acquisition of the new accommodation for such and such a department?', but I never get any reply telling me that a lease is being surrendered on any alternative accommodation. Therefore, I am suggesting to you that the growth in accommodation which is acquired by the PSA – I accept that you are not the arbiters as to whether you acquire it or not, because it is the demand of a department of the State – is unceasing, and the accommodation which is being acquired by the PSA for the Inland Revenue, for instance, or for the Department of Health and Social Security or for the Department of Defence, is on an astronomical scale. When these buildings are acquired, there is hardly ever a case of a corresponding surrender of accommodation hitherto occupied by the people who are going into the new accommodation. Do you accept that that is a fair criticism?——So far as the Department of Health and Social Security and the Inland Revenue are concerned, I would certainly agree that we have had to acquire a lot more accommodation for them in recent years. So far as the Ministry of Defence is concerned, I am sure that the pattern over the last few years has been one of net decrease, substantial net decrease, in the case of open country. Our problem with departments like Health and Social Security and the Inland Revenue, and Customs and Excise for that matter, is that they have been rapidly growing departments while the rest of the Civil Service has been largely static, or even declining in some areas, and the need has been to acquire premises for them up and down the country to relieve overcrowding and to provide accommodation for new staff doing new work. Where there have been decreases in the Civil Service, they have mostly been in small evenly spread pockets where it has not been so easy to release accommodation in lieu. The big increase which will be taking place for the Ministry of Defence over the next five or ten years is in the dispersal programme, and we are now starting the construction of large new offices in Cardiff and in Glasgow. This is part of the Hardman dispersal programme, as a result of which 30,000 civil service jobs are being moved out of London into other parts of the country. This is going to have two effects which I think will be beneficial from the point of view of points that this Committee has, I know, been concerned with in the past. One is that we are going to be building, as Crown building, most of this new accommodation, and therefore, to some small extent at least, reducing our dependence on leased accommodation. Secondly, it is going to release a fair bit of accommodation in London, and we are starting now on the planning of the re-orientating of the whole of our London office estate so as to allow for these dispersal moves and make the best possible packages that we can for the release of office buildings in central and inner London.

3827. But in Annex C to your Memorandum, where you refer to the maintenance expenditure on the Defence estate, the only places where it has increased substantially are first in the north west and then in London, where it is plus 13 per cent?——In London there have been two big new additions to the Defence estate in recent years. One is the Air Traffic Control Centre at West Drayton and another is the Knightsbridge Barracks in Hyde Park, which have added to the total maintenance bill. There are also barracks on the outskirts of London, at

Hounslow, Caterham and Pirbright, which in whole or in part, were on minimum maintenance standards while their future was being considered and they have now been brought back again into full maintenance.

3828. What about the very substantial office building off Fleet Street? Is it Salisbury Court?——Fleetbank House – for the Procurement Executive.

3829. This was an absolutely enormous development and one which, with respect to you, you did not mention here. This is for the Civil Service, but you have just told me that the intention is for the Civil Service – for the Defence establishment – to move away from London. But we have, as I understand it, just entered into the most enormous commitment for the lease of that building. Again, I had questions down on the occupation of this accommodation, and I said, 'Which accommodation is going to be vacated as a result?', and I could not get a satisfactory answer. Here is a very big commitment for the PSA. It is not your fault at all. I am not blaming the PSA, because you are obviously acting under instructions from the Ministry of Defence. But we have entered into a lease on one of the most substantial office buildings in the centre of London at a very high rent indeed, and you have now told me that the intention is to disperse the Civil Service from the centre of London to the Principality?——Not the whole of the Civil Service.

3830. I am talking about Defence.——No, nor the whole of the Ministry of Defence. The commitment, if I remember rightly, is up to 15,500 to Glasgow and 4,000 to 5,000 to Cardiff, including some elements of the Procurement Executive who occupy Fleetbank House, but not the whole of it.

3831. Let me put the question in a different way. What accommodation was surrendered back to the private sector as a result of acquiring the lease of Fleetbank House?——I cannot answer that question offhand. I would guess that there was probably a very long chain of moves, resulting in the end in the release of some inferior and inconvenient accommodation at the lower end of the scale, which probably took place over a period of time.

3832. Do you think that it would be unreasonable for a Member of Parliament to ask if we could have a memorandum telling us of the number of units of accommodation or the leases which have, in fact, been surrendered over, say, the last three years, and the number which have been acquired by the PSA, because I am very concerned about the amount of accommodation. I repeat, I am not blaming you; I think that it is because of demands that are put upon you by the departments which you have to service. But could this Committee have a note showing what accommodation has been released? Let us exclude anything below, say, 10,000 square feet, so that you do not have to go round Jobcentres, or anything like that. Let us be reasonable about it. Would that be possible?——Is that covering central London, or the whole country?

3833. If you feel that there has been a lot surrendered outside central London, then, fine.——I am sorry. I beg your pardon; I understand your question. I thought you were covering both acquisitions and disposals.

Mr Taylor.] Well, I was. I am obviously more interested in disposals, as I believe that nothing is ever disposed of. That is my view.

Chairman

3834. If I may interrupt Mr Taylor for a moment, I think that there is a significant point involved here in the consideration of maintenance and operating expenses. As I understand it, Mr Taylor is asking you if you will be good enough to let us see a paper showing, in effect, the net growth of the amount of property for which you are responsible. Armed with that information, I think that it is easier for us to put the work that you are doing on the maintenance and operation of these buildings in perspective.——Certainly. If it is in relation to particular buildings, which is what I understand Mr Taylor would like to have, perhaps I could start with London, and see if that would meet his point.

3835. Yes. I think, if I may say so, if Mr Taylor agrees, that we do not really need a tome that thick, but an indication of the footages and, perhaps, the net growth, including the gross figures and the surrender figures, would be of very great interest to us?——May I see how helpful I can be on this? We can certainly provide information about individual premises. I should say to the Committee that I am not satisfied at present with the accuracy of our total estate record and therefore I am slightly dubious about netting off figures. May I do as much as I can to help the Committee on this?

Mr *Taylor*

3836. Thank you, Mr Chairman. The other point that I should like to refer to is the answers to Mr Paul Channon's questions. In the corrected answer to Parliamentary Question 1812, you give the maintenance economy review figures for all the regions in the PSA, which is obviously very helpful, but it would be more helpful if we could have alongside that answer the total Government expenditure of those regions, so that we could relate the maintenance economy reviews to the total expenditure involved. If we look at these figures we see that the Southern region has made a maintenance economy saving of £4,009,875, and then we see that the North-West has only made a saving of £121,725. I am sure that there is justification for these different figures, but if we could have the total expenditure alongside, we could say, 'Well, now, we must pat this region on the back' or 'We must be critical of this other region, which has not been as successful as its competitors'?——I hoped that we had effectively met that point in the Annexes to the paper that we have put in. Annex A shows the effect of the maintenance economy reviews in each region on a constant price basis, and Annexes B and C show respectively the total maintenance expenditure and the Defence expenditure. If there is any way in which we can re-order these figures to make them more illuminating, I will be glad to do so, but the point about these figures is that they are perhaps rather more helpful than the Parliamentary Question answers in that we have got them all down to constant prices.

Mr *Taylor*.] I am looking at those figures now. You have divided them up into recurrent, 'Ministry of Defence' and 'Other', and once-off 'Ministry of Defence' and 'Other'. Perhaps I am not as bright as other members of the Committee, but I should have needed quite a lot of time to work out the totals against the answers that you gave to Mr Channon. But I am quite prepared to have another go, so I will let it rest there.

Mr *Costain*

3837. Sir Robert, in your answers to Mr Taylor on a subject to which I know he has given an awful lot of thought, you emphasised your difference in role – as an agent as far as the Defence Ministry is concerned, and that your Secretary of State is a principal and the owner of Government property, other than Defence property. When you say that your Secretary of State is a principal, in fact, does your Department have any say with the Secretary of State as to what buildings should be got rid of or bought, or are you carrying out instructions from other sections of the Department as an agent?——No, it is our primary function to allocate Government accommodation. Of course, no one Government department has primacy over all others, should there be a dispute, and if there should be disagreement between ourselves and another department about what should happen we might, in the first place, have resort to the Civil Service Department as arbiters or, in the last resort, there is inter-departmental machinery for resolving disputes, which can go up to Ministers, if need be. I mentioned to Mr Taylor the exercise that we are now embarking upon for the re-allocation of accommodation in Greater London after the big dispersal moves take place in the next decade. This is an exercise that we are working out in the first place in consultation with the Treasury and the Civil Service Department, and we shall then move on and consult the individual departments which would be affected by the moves.

3838. When you ask the occupiers of these buildings – and I have done so at previous committees – 'Why has this building, which was very bright and good looking four years ago, got rather drab? Does your staff like working in such a drab building?', they always say, 'It is the PSA's job to maintain it'. This does not happen in private enterprise. Have you say with these other Government departments about the way in which they are maintaining the buildings, or are you only the landlord for the structure, for the fabric?——Perhaps I could put it in this way. They are the housekeepers of the building. They have an accommodation officer. They are the people who look after their own staff and the way they behave in the building, but to the extent that the building needs painting and re-decorating or partitions need moving, that is our business.

3839. There does seem to be a marked difference in general appearance between an office owned by a property company and a Government office after being occupied for a number of years. Do you have any consultations with larger property companies as to what their yardstick for maintenance is, or how they maintain their buildings?—— We are in fact having some consultations with three or four major organisations at the moment, to compare notes with them on maintenance costs and practices.

3840. Most of the property companies have got a yardstick, have they not, as to what the right maintenance is? Have you got a similar one?——We are looking at the yardstick approach. We are not sure that it is going to be all that helpful to us because of the very wide variety of nature of the properties that we have to look after, but we are having consultations, for example, with one of the major banks and with one of the major chains of retail shops to see what they do and what we can learn from their practice.

3841. I was thinking more of the property companies than owner-occupiers of buildings. Large property companies do have a similar problem, because they in fact are landlords as, indeed, you are land-lords. Surely it must be some advantage if you can go to a Government department and say, 'This building has become uneconomical to maintain'. Has that ever happened to your knowledge in the PSA?——Usually the pressures on us are such that we cannot afford to let a building go simply for that reason. There is one standing empty at the moment, a very famous building, Richmond Terrace, which we have had to vacate because it is unsafe and we cannot maintain it. I hope that we can do something about that, but in the ordinary way we have been trying to hold on to some of our older buildings simply because we have the benefit of holding them on long leases at very low rents, and it pays us to spend a bit more on maintenance to keep them going.

3842. Yes, I appreciate that. When it comes to Defence, to get the record right, you are responsible for the care and maintenance of Defence buildings as if they were occupied by tenants. Is that right?——I should distinguish. I am sorry if I have caused this confusion. In so far as the Ministry of Defence are occupiers of offices in central London for civil servants, they are occupiers of the common user estate just like any other Government department. I was talking of the separate capacity of the Secretary of State for Defence in relation to Defence installations, training areas and that sort of thing.

3843. But when there was an amalgamation between the War Department and the Ministry of Works in 1963, I think it was, the Ministry of Works, as it then was – it subsequently became the Depart-ment of the Environment – was responsible for building, erecting and maintaining, and the Army, the sailors and the RAF were responsible for what you call the housekeeping?——There were two stages of amalgamation with the Ministry of Defence. In 1963, as you said, we took over the works organisation of the three Service Departments. These are the people who look after the boilers – the sort of thing that we were talking about earlier this afternoon. Then in 1972, I think it was, we took over the lands organisation of the Ministry of Defence, the people who manage the big estates and Salisbury Plain – those who have the foresters and those sorts of people.

3844. Let us go on to the land situation. At that time there was the Nugent Report on the disposal of Army land. Have you followed that through, as to what land has been disposed of, because the evidence here does not tie up with what the Nugent Report recommended for disposal?——This was a report which made certain recommendations which were for the Government as a whole to accept or reject, and then it was our job to follow through and dispose of the land which it was felt free to dispose of. As I said just now, in the last five years alone we have disposed of 15,000 acres of Defence land.

3845. I think that the situation is improving somewhat on that, but would you agree with me that there is a tendency for it to be nobody's fault or nobody's initiative? Although you are an agent, a number of estate agents would go around the country looking for clients and saying, 'Why do you not dispose of this land?' Do you consider it within your province that you should do the same with the Army?—— We think that it is our business to explain to them what it is costing them to keep maintained buildings or other land which they can perhaps do without. The cost of the maintenance falls on the Defence budget, although it is on our Vote, so that in the last resort it is for them to conclude whether the game is worth the candle. We can go on looking at areas and thinking that a building can be done without or that a piece of land can be disposed of, and I would not want to say for one moment that we get general resistance to this, but there are cases where the military see a need to retain a facility which we simply have to accept as their operational judgment of the situation. I accept, too, in relation to land generally – and I am not just speaking of the Ministry of Defence or, indeed, of the public sector in general – that land is a difficult property to get hold of. It tends to get more expensive as time goes by, and there is a great temptation for anybody holding land who has some doubts whether he may not need it in the future, to want to hold on to it.

3846. Yes, but with cash limits, surely your Department ought to be welcomed now by other departments as a way of raising a bit of ready money for them, should it not?——I am afraid that the Treasury would not allow us to dispose of the proceeds of our disposals.

Mr *Costain*.] May we ask the Treasury? Is there no incentive that we can give these departments to release land? We have had it with the hospitals. Hospitals are releasing more land now because they look as if they are going to get the money allowed to them for developing. Why cannot we do the same with the Army?

Chairman

3847. Before you answer, Mr Gordon, may I amplify Mr Costain's point? This Committee has been – as an earlier question made clear – much exercised at the delays that take place in the release of unwanted surplus land and property by various Government departments. As Mr Costain rightly says, we have had considerable exchanges, as I am sure you will be aware, and I know that the Treasury will be very well aware, with the Department of Health and Social Security on this matter. They have been dilatory in the extreme. This seemed all the more remarkable in view of the fact that the release of land, the sale of land, in this way, would have been beneficial from the point of view of their own accounting. I do not think that there is any doubt that Mr Costain has a very useful point. If there is no incentive for people to get rid of land, they will not get rid of it?——(Mr *Gordon.*) All I can say is that I note the point and will take it back with me. In logic, if the department is going to benefit from disposal of any kind, one would expect that that ought to provide sufficient incentive in itself. I am not at all clear – I am not expert enough to know – what kind of range of incentives one might think of in these circumstances, but, as I say, I am very happy to take the point back and make sure that it is not lost.

Mr *Costain*

3838. I thought that Mr Taylor had an exceptionally good point when he asked whether you could in fact draw attention in your annual report to certain recommendations which other Government departments were not accepting, and which you thought they should. Would you feel that it was telling tales out of school if you were to do that?——(Sir *Robert Cox.*) I might be in some difficulty if I were making an annual report, as part of the Government which, as it were, commented adversely on the decisions of another Government department or of Ministers in general. I am sure that we can – and we will – produce information about our land transactions which will illuminate this question. Whether I would quite like to meet it in this particular kind of way I am not sure.

3849. I think that you have made a most important statement. Do you not appreciate that the reason for Parliamentary Committees now being put to a great deal of work is that each Government department feels that it is rather sneaking to talk about another Government department? Do you think that it is a Member of Parliament's job to knock different departments' heads together, so that we can find out whose fault it really is?——I think that what we can probably do is to produce figures to show how much land we have up as surplus, and are trying to dispose of.

3850. Without criticising another Government department?——I think that that would be the current convention.

3851. Yes, but conventions die slowly. Industry is now bringing in experts such as McKinseys. Is it not time that Government departments did the same? Is it not a fact that the Treasury tried to do it and failed because they had not got the expert knowledge?——I think that the point is really one of substance. The question is whether we fight hard enough to get land disposed of in these circumstances. It is not, I think, just a question of reporting. I think that what we have to do is to make sure that where we believe that there is a case for disposing of land and there is resistance, we carry it through to higher levels, and, if necessary, to Ministerial level, to get a decision on the disposal if this is required. But usually we can either get agreement, or we have to accept, as a matter of plain common sense, that there is a case for retaining the land. In that sense, I am not sure what reporting the disagreement would achieve. It would simply show that there had been two points of view on a particular topic.

3852. When you say that you are not sure about reporting, you might as well say that you are not sure what the reports of the Committee of Public Accounts are all about. Some point of the spiral has got to bring the attention of somebody who can do something. At the moment, surely you must admit from your long experience, Ministers do not have much time to talk about disposing of a bit of land in Chatham. They have got other things to do.——But a thing like the Nugent Report, of course, occupied a fair bit of the time of Ministers; where the thing is on a sufficient scale and of sufficient importance, it does.

3853. Let us go on to the question of direct labour. You have produced figures here. It is difficult for anybody reading the report, and it is difficult for members of the Committee, to appreciate quite what you mean by directly employed labour. Are they people who are actually artisans, and cleaners? There is no office staff at all on this?——I am not speaking about cleaners. These are industrial workers – carpenters and plumbers; people of that kind – who are working on maintenance and minor building work.

3854. If they are definitely doing that sort of work, they are doing the sort of work which normally you would use a day work schedule for, if you were working for an outside contractor. Is that right?——Yes.

3855. What yardstick have you produced to enable you to assess the value of the work that these men have done?——The criteria by which we employ these people were set out in 1969 in a statement made to the House, and three main sets of circumstances were envisaged in which they should be used. The first was where there was fixed plant to be operated, the second was where there were some particular reasons for employing them such as interrupted working or need for on-call staff, and the third was where it could be seen that it was more economic to use directly employed labour for this purpose. At that time there was a directly employed labour force of something like 30,000 and the result of that policy over the last few years has been to reduce it to about 20,000. There are some circumstances where I think we have no practical alternative to the employment of direct labour – for example, at sensitive Defence establishments. There are some places where we cannot rely on getting contractors to do work for us where we need to have it done. We also have to take into account the fact that we did start with a very large labour force, and you cannot just sack them all overnight. But more and more we are trying to cost out the effect of using direct labour, and more and more are trying to make sure that we use them in the most economic circumstances. We have a thing going at the moment known as the Haslar experiment, where we are doing direct comparisons between the cost of using direct labour and contract labour.

3856. Those figures will be available, will they?——Certainly, if the Committee would like to see them.

3857. We did, I think, at our last meeting, rather concentrate on the past, and you quite rightly, I thought, drew the Committee's attention to your disappointment that we had not questioned you on the more modern aspects. I think that you are quite right in that criticism, but can you tell us now, as we are not quite so pressed for time as we were at our last meeting, what is the position about St. John's House, Bootle?
——I am afraid that it has probably deteriorated, even in the last couple of weeks, in that the site is now completely strike-bound. There is a difference with the workers on the site about severance pay. Very large sums are being claimed, which the contractor does not see his way clear to paying, and nor, I think, would we. I would rather not say more than I need about the actual dispute, because we want to get it settled.

3858. It would be wrong for you to give any evidence that made matters worse, and I will not press you for that, but in fact you did say at that time – I agree that it was right at the end of the session and we had overrun our time – that everything else was on target, as far as you could remember. Have you had time to consider that?——No, I am sorry; I said –

Chairman

3859. You said that Devonport was on time?——Yes, that Devonport was on time and was more or less on schedule. But on St. John's House, what I really have to say also is that there has been a further change of plan about the use of the building and that the cost estimates have also gone up, I think, very sharply since I last gave evidence to the Committee on this subject.

Mr *Costain*

3860. What is the revised estimate? How many millions has it gone up by this time?——The last report of the Comptroller and Auditor General on this subject was at 1974 prices. This, I am afraid, imports a certain unreality into the situation. The situation when the Comptroller and Auditor General reported in October, 1976 was that at that time there was an estimate of £7·6 million. Since then it has gone up to about ten and a quarter million, again at 1974 prices. If one were to convert them to 1978 prices, this would take it up somewhere in the range of £17 million to £18 million, and I am afraid that we are not at the end of the road, because we have this strike on our hands. The preliminaries on the site, of course, are still continuing at a pretty high level. I think that it is something like £100,000 a month, so that prolongation of the contract is proving extremely expensive.

3861. So that we are spending £17 million on a building and do not know what we are going to use it for?——No, I would not say that. I am confident that we are going to occupy that building fully but not exactly either for the purpose for which it was originally designed or for the second purpose for which it was designed. We are still going to have, I think, a large number of Inland Revenue staff in there. There is a possibility, to put it no higher than that, that some of the Health and Safety Executive staff being dispersed from London will be able to use part of it. We are hoping that the computer hall that was designed for the Inland Revenue will be used by the Home Office, for whom another one would have had to be built elsewhere in Liverpool, and, as a temporary measure, assuming that we can get the building going again, we are hoping to use it for temporary staff for the 1981 census. That is as far as I can see at the moment, but the building will take something of the order of 3,000 staff, and I hope that in one way or another we will get it fully occupied.

3862. Could you remind the Committee of what this building started out in life as? What was it originally going to be?——It started out as a Schedule E centre.

Chairman

3863. It was to be an Inland Revenue computer centre, if I remember rightly?——It was to be for the Inland Revenue throughout, but the original proposal was for a Schedule E centre, and it was then to be a collection accounts centre. It was this second purpose which was abandoned last autumn.

Mr *Costain*

3864. Are there any other buildings that are behind schedule?——I am afraid that that is a very wide question. I am afraid that the answer to that must be, yes.

3865. Are there any which are a million pounds adrift again?—— There may be some. Certainly if we take inflation into account, there is not the slightest doubt that there will be some that have gone adrift in that sense.

3866. No doubt the Committee will have a chance of seeing those next year?——No doubt.

Chairman

3867. One appreciates that there are difficulties about asking you questions in regard to the works statement where you have not been given notice, but Mr Costain is making a very good point. We have concentrated so much on these particular things that we have not really allowed ourselves very much opportunity to talk to you about building works in general with which you are engaged. May I put one general question to you? You have told us of the appalling difficulties that there have been in regard to the site at Bootle. 'Appalling' is a mild word to describe the position there, where many millions of pounds of taxpayers' money additional to the original estimates and forgetting about inflation, are having to be spent because of consistent and disruptive labour problems. This Committee has examined other projects in the north-west where there have been similar problems, and again, millions of pounds of taxpayers' money have been wasted. Does the PSA take the view in any area where there are consistent problems, that it will not engage in new building projects in those areas in future?——I do not think that we as the building agency for the Government are in a position to take that point of view. From the point of view of our operations, it has obvious attractions. One would obviously wish to avoid difficult areas, but, of course, one primary aim of Government policy at the moment is to bring new employment to the special areas, such as Merseyside, and where this involves new building, it is we who have to undertake the building. What we try to do, of course, is to make the very best arrangements that we can to avoid industrial trouble of this sort, and there are certain ways in which we can help ourselves on this, but they are not always successful.

3868. But there are other areas of the country which are just as deserving as Merseyside and where the need is equally great. Let us take Cornwall as one example. Have you recommended to the Government on any occasion that the PSA should not construct new buildings in an area like Merseyside where you have such difficulty?——No, I have not made such a recommendation because my belief is that Ministers would regard their priorities in relation to the allocation of work as something which we have to follow, rather than to lead upon. The needs of course of Cornwall, as with other parts of the country, are considered, and, indeed, we built a new wealth tax office in Plymouth which is now being made over to the Land Registry. There is Teesside, which is equally in need, and there we are preparing to construct our own headquarters, because we are being dispersed from London. There is, equally, Glasgow, where we have already put up some dispersal buildings, and we are planning two large new buildings for the Ministry of Defence. We have, I think, in this respect, to follow the decisions of Ministers.

3869. Yes, I appreciate that, and I am not asking you to make policy decisions. I am just making the point that this Committee is aware of the additional expenditure, running, I repeat, into many millions of pounds in respect of building projects, some of which the PSA has been responsible for, which seem to us to have involved in the end a waste of taxpayers' money, and an unnecessary waste at that, very much bigger than any of the items that we have been considering which arose out of Mr Chapman's book, for example. I am asking whether the PSA notes this position and whether it makes recommendations to Government departments about these matters which perhaps might mean in future that other areas of the country – I instanced Cornwall; you have, quite rightly, said that there is a very large number of areas in the United Kingdom from which to choose – would get a bigger share of the work, a bigger share of the dispersal, and that an area like Merseyside, which appears to give continuing trouble, might get a little bit less, with a constant saving to the taxpayer's pocket and the attainment of better value for money?——Ministers, of course, well know the difficulties that we are in on Merseyside because they have to some extent been involved in them. I would not want to give the impression that everything we do on Merseyside goes bad. If I remember rightly, although it was before my time, the Giro centre at Bootle went reasonably well in accordance with the schedule and with cost. I will not tempt providence by naming another project that we have going at Liverpool at the moment, but that is well on its way.

Mr *Crouch*

3870. Sir Robert, we have had rather a lot of your Department lately, but I just want to come back to the reason that we are here, namely, your memorandum. A thing that rather concerns me is that we have got a great deal more information out of this memorandum, which was sent to us on the 26th June with Mr May's letter, than we got when we questioned you in 1975, on the 14th April. I have found in Section II, 'Property maintenance and operating costs', a great deal more explanation in the seven paragraphs under that heading of the differences in savings between the Southern region and the other regions, and really it would have been much better for me to have had as much information as that on the 14th April 1975 than the answer that you gave to us then on question 1318. If you recollect, I said, the last time that you were here, that it was that answer and a subsequent answer that you gave to me then that rather blocked off all other questions, because it was almost a simple answer, that the Southern region had special opportunities for saving because of the movement of troops to the north and the closing down of military establishments. If I may say so, this is an observation rather than a question at this stage, as I read this memorandum, it does not reveal so much a cover up as a failure for the Committee to be given enough information about what was happening in detail in all the other regions. Would you, in the light of all the evidence that you have given us, agree that that is the situation?——I accept the criticism of the original answer, as you know, and I have tendered my apologies to the Committee in relation to that and in relation to the delay in revealing it to them. I think what we have done here is to carry the analysis a good deal further than we had at that time, and I think there are concepts in this paper which I do not think we were previously aware of ourselves. What we were working on before were the fairly crude figures of the results of the maintenance economy reviews, which produced basically the pattern of figures in

Annex A, but what we have done here is to try to work out the whole pattern of spending on maintenance, which produces not exactly an even pattern of economy but a much less jagged pattern of figures. I hope, indeed, that it is helpful to the Committee to have this set out.

Mr *Crouch*.] Mr Chairman, you have heard that answer. What strikes me is that in this memorandum – and Sir Robert's answers confirm this – we now have something which is much clearer. It is not just a black and white story that Southern region did well for one reason and that other regions could not do as well because they were not so well placed regionally, because of not having military establishments closing down, and so on. Now we have got the whole story, and my observation to Sir Robert really is that it would have helped us if we had had the whole story then. We, as members of this Committee, have to do quite a lot of homework in a busy life to cope with the very competent people that sit before us, Sir Robert, but we always understand that those who come before the Committee come before it after a great deal of study of the matters being put before them. The study has been revealed after three years; we have got it very thoroughly. I would just say again that it is a pity that we did not have it all then. It does not reveal, as I say, a cover up so much as that there is not so much, as I see it, to cover up. Rather we see the whole story where we did not get it before.

Chairman

3871. I think that it is right to say, as we have said, that this memorandum has been immensely helpful to us, as we have told Sir Robert. I think that what he says in paragraph 12 is very frank, and very fair: 'It has always been acknowledged that Southern region made significantly greater savings through the maintenance economy reviews introduced in 1968 by Mr Chapman . . . than did any other part of the PSA'. That, of course, was the matter that we were inquiring into previously, and that we reported upon. Since that time all of these matters have received a very great deal of publicity and it has been necessary for us to look into them again, and more fully, and to see the extent to which the recommendations that we made, arising out of our criticisms of the PSA, have been followed through, and that is the position today. Sir Robert, is there anything else that you want to speak to us about?——I think not. I hope Mr Crouch thinks that I have responded adequately to his point.

Mr *Crouch*

3872. Indeed.——I do very much regret what has happened in both senses, and I mean that very sincerely.

Mr *Crouch*.] I do, and thank you, Sir Robert.

Chairman

3873. Sir Douglas, is there any point that you want to raise with the Committee?——(Sir *Douglas Henley*.) No, I do not think so. In relation to what Mr Crouch has pointed out, I was just wondering about one point. I think that it is fair to say – it is really for Sir Robert and not for me – that the fact that the PSA always believed that there were other ways of securing maintenance economies, apart from the special maintenance economy reviews, was brought out originally. My understanding is that the various pressures which have resulted from the developments since then have, not unnaturally, caused the PSA to look much deeper into this question and that has produced a great deal more information, but I think that the broad approach has been reasonably consistent throughout. I am subject to correction.

Chairman.] Yes. One matter which does emerge, which I should like to mention to the Treasury witness, is this. We have, as I said earlier, looked on more than one occasion at individual departments and their habit of holding land and not disposing of it. The Committee of Public Accounts has discussed with the Comptroller and Auditor General the possibility of examining certain general subjects during the autumn period, before we begin our work based on the Comptroller and Auditor General's reports, rather analogous to the discussion that we have had with Treasury witnesses about assimilation of cash limits and the Estimates, and it does seem to me that it might behove the Committee to look into this matter as a particular subject of inquiry outside the usual line of discussion. It would be for the Committee, of course, to decide, but all that I hear Sir Robert telling me this afternoon and telling the Committee, leads me to think that this would be a fruitful area for discussion. Sir Robert, thank you very much.

Appendix 11

Memorandum for Public Accounts Committee prepared by Property Services Agency (pp. 45–50)

I. Committee's Questions

PAC Hearing

1. At the Committee's hearing on 12 June the Accounting Officer of the Property Services Agency was asked to give information on four matters arising out of Mr Chapman's book 'Your Disobedient Servant'.

Retention of Men Over 65

2. On page [39] of his book Mr Chapman said that men over 65 bore the brunt of the first reductions in directly employed industrial labour in Southern Region. The Committee asked whether there are men over 65 retained in other Regions.

3. A policy of compulsory retirement of all industrial staff over 65 throughout the Department was introduced in November 1970 as part of a works services productivity agreement. Within the overall policy there is provision for limited exceptions at Regional discretion ie where vacancies exist and cannot be filled or where suitable replacements for particular posts cannot be obtained individual employees may be invited to continue in service beyond 65.

4. The following figures from PSA Headquarters records show the number of industrial staff over 65 in UK Regions (including Southern), Wales and Scotland at March 1969, May 1971 and January 1978:

	March 1969	May 1971	January 1978
Scotland	87	6	4
North West	45	1	0
North East	58	9	3
Eastern	137	24	2
Midland	129	40	1
Wales	50	13	2
South West	145	20	0
Southern	241	54	7
South East	123	23	13
London	420	100	47
TOTAL	1,435	290	79

NUMBER OF STOKERS

5. On page [39] of the book there is a footnote which states that 'In 1967 there were over seven hundred stokers in Southern Region. By 1973 there were fewer than fifty'. The Committee asked for comparable figures for other Regions.

6. Records of numbers of stokers prior to 1972 are generally no longer available at Regional Offices but we have available at Headquarters a June 1966 record. Figures for UK Regions (including Southern), Wales and Scotland from that record and later returns for December 1973 and March 1978 are as follows:

	June 1966	December 1973	March 1978
Scotland	176	148	90
North West	255	167	112
North East	296	135	69
Eastern	345	136	85
Midland	470	226	99
Wales	181	67	34
South West	571	224	87
Southern	613	153	51
South East	177	76	46
London	380	251	163
TOTAL	3,464	1,583	836

SALE OF LAND

7. On page [40] of the book there is a statement that 'Most of the land with which we were concerned was maintained but not owned by

us, and there was a limit to what we could do in the reduction of holdings. As a consequence, although we had our successes, the land disposed of was less than 5 per cent of the possible reduction. Nearly all the other 95 per cent is still there waiting for the time when the recommendations at the end of this book are implemented, especially those relating to the setting up of more effective audit controls'. The Committee asked what additional land of that 95 per cent has been disposed of since Mr Chapman retired.

8. We have identified from the Southern Region review reports proposals for disposing of 2,268 acres of land; occupying Departments agreed to disposal of 112 acres at the time. So far, in fact, 476 acres have been disposed of and authority has been given to dispose of another 700 acres and action is in hand.

SIZE OF DIRECTLY EMPLOYED LABOUR FORCE

9. On page [43] of the book there is a statement that 'In Southern Region, Directly Employed Labour (DEL) was reduced from around 4,000 to under 2,000. Nearly all these reductions had been implemented by the end of 1973'. The Committee asked for comparable figures for all other Regions.

10. The following table gives numbers of all DEL for UK Regions (including Southern), Wales and Scotland as at March 1965, March 1967, December 1973 and March 1978 based on information at present available to us:

	March 1965	March 1967	December 1973	March 1978
Scotland	3,660	3,208	2,475	2,227
North West	2,470	2,343	1,933	1,598
North East	2,624	2,661	2,104	1,696
Eastern	2,939	2,863	2,010	1,765
Midland	2,762	2,929	1,818	1,548
Wales	1,864	1,732	1,367	1,308
South West	5,001	4,835	3,628	3,086
Southern	3,898	3,781	1,794	1,614
South East	4,187	4,082	2,695	2,450
London	5,730	5,615	4,033	3,573
SUB-TOTAL	35,135	34,049	23,857	20,865
London Supplies	1,355	1,187	1,011	838
TOTAL	36,490	35,236	24,868	21,703

Notes:

1. Supplies DEL have been included in the figures because it seems that Mr Chapman included them, although these days they would normally be shown separately.

2. DEL on Ancient Monuments have been included in all years, for comparability, although they were not PSA staff in the latter two years. It has not been possible to make a similar adjustment for the Defence Lands DEL taken over by PSA and shown only in the two latter years.

3. Custody guards, which come under London, have not been included.

II. PROPERTY MAINTENANCE AND OPERATING COSTS

11. It was agreed that the Accounting Officer should add any further relevant material.

12. It has always been acknowledged that Southern Region made significantly greater savings through the maintenance economy reviews introduced in 1968 by Mr Chapman, their Regional Director, than did any other part of the PSA. The economies achieved to date at constant (ie 1977–78) prices are set out in Annex A. Nevertheless, other parts of PSA have also sought to secure economies and have made worthwhile savings, some of them in other ways; and in some places there were special difficulties.

13. The practice was adopted early on of formally logging estimated savings consequent upon maintenance economy reviews. Other savings were not so logged, being regarded as an aspect of normal on-going management. To get a measure of reductions in expenditure consequent upon all techniques a comparison has been made between actual expenditure in various years at constant prices. We are aware that this is not a completely accurate measure of savings (eg during the period they must have been offset to some extent by extra expenditure due to an increase in the size of the office estate, whilst on the other hand the 1973–74 figure was affected by the overloading of the construction industry in that year); it seems however to be the best available means of comparison. Attached at Annex B therefore are figures of Voted maintenance expenditure on the civil and defence estates for the years 1967–68, 1970–71, 1973–74 and 1977–78; Annex C gives the figures relating to the defence estate alone. Percentage changes between 1967–68 (the year before maintenance economy review teams were set up in Southern Region) and 1973–74 (the year during which Mr Chapman retired) are shown.

14. It will be seen that in the combined estate there was, at constant

prices, a £37 million (16 per cent) reduction in annual expenditure as between 1967–68 and 1973–74 on maintenance. In three other Regions besides Southern Region total expenditure reduced by over 20 per cent and in four others expenditure on the defence estate reduced by 25 per cent or more. The overall percentage was affected by the relatively low percentage reduction in London and the increase in North West Region. The low reduction in London was partly attributable to their relatively high proportion of civil maintenance work, ie 70 per cent of 1967–68 Voted maintenance expenditure (defence expenditure is 25 per cent of Voted plus repayment) and to the fact that the civil estate was increasing in size. The North West Region had an increasing Northern Ireland commitment.

15. Mr Chapman says of the reductions in expenditure in his Region that '60 per cent was saved by a different use of DEL'. It will be seen from the table in paragraph 10 that other parts of the PSA had made significant reductions in the numbers of DEL by the end of 1973 (and had started to reduce indeed even before 1967). Southern Region's reductions in DEL seem to have arisen mainly from their maintenance economy reviews but only a small part of the reductions elsewhere were so ascribed. Thus between 1968 and 1973 when there was a reduction of about 8,300 men on maintenance, about 1,660 of the 1,700 in Southern Region came from the reviews, and only 900 of the 6,600 for the rest of PSA.

16. It is not possible to say precisely what proportion of the reductions in expenditure between 1967–68 and 1973–74 were due to maintenance economy reviews as opposed to other techniques. We have however made an assessment of the annual savings from the maintenance economy reviews up to 1973–74 to compare with the reduction in maintenance expenditure between 1967–68 and 1973–74. From this it appears that most of Southern Region's figure of £8·1 million resulted from the reviews whereas threequarters of the £29·1 million for the rest of the PSA arose in other ways.

17. As a result of a new energy conservation policy introduced in 1972–73 by 1976–77 fuel costs had dropped by 23 per cent, despite the increased size of the estate. Most of these savings have been made by technical and other improvements in the control of heating and lighting of buildings. Attached at Annex D is a table showing PSA direct expenditure on fuel for the civil estate at constant (ie 1977–78) prices for 1972–73 to 1976–77. Similar techniques are being applied in the defence estate also.

III. Sunday Times Article of 18 June 1978

18. The Committee wish to have comments on the allegations made in the Sunday Times of 18 June suggesting that 'another serious error' was given in the evidence to the Public Accounts Committee in April 1975.

19. First, the article claims that the Accounting Officer maintains that 'the Property Services Agency as a whole did apply Chapman's methods diligently and that Southern Region's greater savings were due to special local factors'.

20. In fact the Accounting Officer said 'I think that it was not simply a matter of enthusiasm it was also a matter of opportunities and timing'. In saying this he accepted that there was greater enthusiasm in Southern Region for the pursuit of maintenance economy through the review technique introduced by the Regional Director.

21. The Accounting Officer subsequently went on to say '. . . they started sooner before a number of other management initiatives took place which in themselves made economies in maintenance . . .'. The Sunday Times say 'that in fact Southern started only a few months earlier than the other regions. The Property Services Agency's records show that every Region except Wales set up cost saving "survey teams" in the same financial year as Southern – 1968–69. The real difference was that most other Regions progressed only slowly after they had started'.

22. PSA records show that Southern Region started trial reviews in February 1968, set up their first maintenance economy review team in May 1968, the second in September 1968 and the third in June 1969 and as at December 1969 the Region had virtually completed surveys of a third of their depots. It is against this position that the Accounting Officer was speaking when he was trying to give the Committee an idea of the general situation of the other parts of the organisation. They appointed their first review teams mainly between September and December 1968 but two teams were not appointed until sometime in 1969 (in a few cases the team was later disbanded, for a time at least, because of difficulties over staffing); only three of these other parts of the organisation appointed second teams by 1970. Thus the general position was that they started up their teams and reviews later. The fact that better progress on reviews had been made in Southern Region was never in dispute. The Comptroller and Auditor General's published re-

port on the 1973–74 Appropriation Accounts contained the following agreed statement 'A review in 1969 indicated that the surveys had been generally worthwhile but there was a marked difference in the results achieved and the efforts made by different Regions; Southern Region had used three full-time teams, Wales had still to start'.

23. The Accounting Officer did not just say that Southern Region started sooner but referred to other initiatives leading to reductions in expenditure and also to other Regions tending to register less of their savings against the maintenance economy reviews in consequence. Thus, for example, in May 1969 the separate arrangements for more economic employment of directly employed labour were announced in the House of Commons; these had a considerable effect on the number of DEL employed.

24. The Sunday Times goes on to say that the Accounting Officer told the Committee on 12 June 1978 'Southern Region has a high proportion of military estates. Experience has shown, and figures show, that in this kind of estate very considerable savings are to be made'. The article drew attention to one particular civil establishment which yielded particularly large savings. The Accounting Officer said in fact 'This was a part of the country where there was a high proportion of Defence estate, in particular a high proportion of military estate, and experience has shown, and the records show that these are areas where it was possible to make good and profitable savings by this kind of method'. In this connection Mr Chapman circulated a note in 1968 which included the following statement 'It has been found that the type of establishment which yields the biggest economies are the Army ones extending over large areas and that those which yield least are probably the compact purpose-built RAF establishments. It has also been found that the results of detailed examination of small local office buildings do not show a worthwhile return for the time which has to be spent upon them and these are now being put on one side for the most part whilst we concentrate on the more profitable areas'. The PSA has a large number of such local office buildings in its civil estate. In any event the percentage reduction in maintenance expenditure on the civil estate up to 1973–74 appears to have been lower than on the defence estate. Even though there were particular office sites where the maintenance economy review techniques could be used successfully, the general view of the Agency is that taking expenditure on the civil estate as a whole the same proportionate reduction could not be expected from using the maintenance economy review technique as in the case of the defence estate.

IV. GOVERNMENT CAR SERVICE

25. As the Government Car Service was the subject of examination by the Committee also in 1976, it may be helpful to comment also on the statement in the book that delay in reducing the number of cars in other parts of PSA outside London and Southern Region from 172 to 87 led to 'admitted and avoidable losses between £2½ million and £3 million at 1974–75 prices'. In giving evidence in 1976 the Accounting Officer agreed that there had been unsatisfactory delay (Q2382) but the consequent loss is overstated. Thus the cost of the car service outside London is over-estimated; no allowance appears to have been made for other Departments' costs on alternative means of transport, and the delay was less than 6 years. In the view of PSA it was desirable to run down the number of drivers involved over a period to achieve as much as possible by natural wastage and it was not unreasonable to have awaited a report confirming the net savings actually achieved in Southern Region after a year of doing without the car service before going ahead elsewhere. The delay which occurred was nevertheless not satisfactory, as the Accounting Officer has already accepted, but the loss was less than a fifth of the estimate given in the book (and not more than a third even if it is considered that action elsewhere should have started at the same time as in Southern Region).

Annex A

Maintenance Economy Reviews – Savings in each Region – Up to 31 March 1977

The following table shows the savings attributed to Maintenance Economy Reviews under MOD/Other Departments. The figures have been revalued to 1977–78 price levels and rounded to the nearest £10,000.

| | PSA Vote | | | | Client Vote | | | | £'000 Capital Expenditure |
| | Recurrent | | Once-Off | | Recurrent | | Once-Off | | |
	MOD	Other	MOD	Other	MOD	Other	MOD	Other	
Scotland	700	340	50	10	200	70			50
North West	100	60	100		120				10
North East	660	520	10	140		50	50		630
Eastern	640	10			840	20			60
Midland	1,090	80	190		510		2,070		510
Wales	860	90	10		70		60		410
South West	1,460		260		1,060		2,090		820
Southern	7,670	890	670	110	1,280	40			30
South East	1,570	20	480		430				1,270
London	420	780			30	60			170
Total	15,170	2,790	1,770	260	4,540	240	4,270	—	3,960

Notes:

'Recurrent' savings are annual savings (summarised). 'Capital Expenditure' is that necessary to achieve the savings.

ANNEX B

MAINTENANCE EXPENDITURE ON THE CIVIL AND DEFENCE ESTATES (EXCLUDES LANDLORDS MAINTENANCE AND REPAYMENT WORK) AT 1977–78 PRICES

£ million

	1967–68	1970–71	1973–74	Percentage Change 1967–68 to 1973–74	1977–78
Scotland	16·6	18·0	14·7	−11	16·6
North West	13·8	13·2	15·5	+13	17·6
North East	22·4	20·9	17·2	−23	16·8
Eastern	18·3	16·3	14·6	−20	14·3
Midland	23·1	23·7	18·4	−20	17·4
Wales	12·8	11·1	9·9	−23	11·5
South West	31·7	29·6	26·8	−15	27·9
Southern	29·1	26·2	21·0	−28	24·9
South East	22·5	20·8	17·2	−24	22·8
London	39·9	43·9	37·7	−6	39·7
TOTAL	230·2	223·7	193·0	−16	209·5

Note: Between 1967–68 and 1977–78 the price level for maintenance increased about $3\frac{1}{2}$ times.

ANNEX C

MAINTENANCE EXPENDITURE ON THE DEFENCE ESTATE AT 1977–78 PRICE LEVEL

£ million

	1967–68	*1970–71*	*1973–74*	*Percentage Change 1967–68 to 1973–74*	*1977–78*
Scotland	12·6	13·5	10·9	−13	12·1
North West	9·8	8·6	11·6	+18	12·8
North East	17·8	15·9	13·1	−26	12·7
Eastern	16·5	14·0	12·6	−24	12·2
Midland	20·1	20·2	15·1	−25	14·7
Wales	11·2	9·3	8·0	−29	8·9
South West	29·2	26·8	23·9	−18	25·2
Southern	26·1	23·3	18·5	−29	22·0
South East	21·1	18·9	15·7	−26	20·4
London	11·9	14·3	13·5	+13	13·0
TOTAL	176·3	164·8	142·9	−19	154·0

ANNEX D

DIRECT GAS AND ELECTRICITY EXPENDITURES ON THE CIVIL ESTATE

| | £ million at 1977–78 (Provisional) Prices | | | | |
	1972–73	1973–74	1974–75	1975–76	1976–77
Scotland	4·5	4·1	3·7	3·7	3·8
North West	5·2	4·5	4·4	4·1	4·0
North East	5·6	4·6	4·4	4·1	4·3
Eastern	2·4	2·0	2·1	1·8	1·8
Midland	4·3	3·4	3·2	3·0	3·2
Wales	2·2	2·1	2·3	2·0	2·0
South West	3·5	2·7	2·7	2·5	2·6
Southern	3·7	3·1	2·7	2·6	2·9
South East	2·7	2·5	2·5	2·4	2·4
London	16·3	12·3	11·8	11·5	11·6
TOTAL	50·4	41·3	39·8	37·7	38·6

Note: Comparable 1977–78 figure not yet available.

Appendix 12

Letter from the Principal Finance Officer, Property Services Agency, to the Clerk of the Committee (pp. 51–2)

At the hearing of the Committee on 10 July, Sir Robert Cox undertook to let them have information on the following points.

TOTAL DEFENCE LAND FOR DISPOSAL

At the end of February 1978 PSA had about 26,400 acres of Ministry of Defence property to dispose of, equivalent to about 4·6 per cent of the total defence estate in the UK at 1 April 1978. The location by PSA Regions of the land for disposal is given in Annex A.

REGIONAL ANALYSIS OF DEFENCE LAND DISPOSALS

A breakdown of disposals as between Regions is given at Annex B for the years 1974–75 to 1977–78. In the time available it has not been possible to get a breakdown of the over 4,000 acres disposed of in 1973–74.

DISPOSAL OF DEFENCE LAND IN SOUTHERN REGION

Attached at Annex C is a revised version of Paragraph 8 of the PSA's submission, distinguishing between land specifically recommended for disposal in the maintenance economy reviews and other land at locations covered by those reviews. Authority for disposal of the 700 acres was given in the main over the years 1972 to 1978. You will notice that the portion of the 1,176 acres not specifically recommended for disposal has now been identified at about 500 acres.

LONDON OFFICE ACCOMMODATION

Attached at Annex D is a schedule showing office space leased and given up in London over the past three years, listing the individual cases over 10,000 sq ft. In recent years there have been a number of major new hirings in London to meet the needs of Departments; it is not contemplated that hirings on the scale of recent years will be necessary in future. Indeed with dispersal and possibly some new Crown building in the London area the amount of leased accommodation should reduce over the years.

STOKERS AND PLANT ATTENDANTS

The result of further inquiries to date into the position regarding plant attendants is set out in Annex E. This table supplements that in Paragraph 6 of our submission, but we have had to give figures for March 1974 instead of December 1973.

We have not been able to establish how many of the plant attendants at these past dates were working in boiler houses. We have however added to the table figures in brackets to show the numbers employed on boiler house duties recently, in June or July. (The numbers of attendants can fluctuate over short periods as will be seen from the figures for Wales.) These latter figures do, we think, give some idea of the relative dependence of different parts of the UK on plant attendants in addition to stokers for boiler house duties.

DIRECTLY EMPLOYED LABOUR

We will be letting the Committee have in due course figures comparing the cost of work done by the directly employed labour force with that done by contractors in various parts of the country when these have become available.

G MAY

18 July 1978.

ANNEX A

MINISTRY OF DEFENCE PROPERTY WITH PSA FOR DISPOSAL AS AT 28 FEBRUARY 1978

Region	Number of Locations	Number of Acres
Scotland	90	4,587
North West	57	1,965
North East	47	3,347
Eastern	70	3,734
Midland	80	3,637
Wales	31	2,051
South West	66	2,697
Southern	77	1,680
South East	33	2,300
London	33	393
	584	26,391

TOTAL UNITED KINGDOM DEFENCE ESTATE AS AT 1 APRIL 1978

	Acres
Freehold Land	548,939
Leasehold Land	29,536
	578,475

ANNEX B

DEFENCE ESTATE DISPOSALS

Acreage for which sale terms agreed 1974–75 to 1977–78
(plus in brackets transfers to other Government Departments)

Region	1974–75	1975–76	1976–77	1977–78
Scotland	90 (1)	24	64 (6)	583 (3)
North West	15 (2)	92	121	63 (1)
North East	140 (5)	79 (29)	760	875 (45)
Eastern	570 (2)	191 (153)	299 (38)	216 (13)
Midland	215 (14)	530	42 (114)	907
Wales	6 (5)	—	21	380
South West	160 (3)	572	43 (16)	142
Southern	1,167 (56)	363 (5)	149	393
South East	64	291	339	452
London	12	17	130	29 (1)
	2,439 (88)	2,159 (187)	1,968 (175)	4,040 (63)

ANNEX C

REVISED PARAGRAPH 8 OF SUBMISSION TO PAC

8. We have identified from the Southern Region's review reports proposals for disposal of 2,268 acres of land; this consisted of 1,510 acres specifically recommended for disposal, plus 758 acres from two of the other locations where there was a general recommendation to review the land holding. Taking just the 1,510 acres specifically recommended for disposal, we have already disposed of 406 acres and are in process of disposing of about a further 264 acres, leaving around 840 acres (about 56 per cent). We have also disposed of 70 acres and are disposing of about a further 436 acres, at locations covered by the reviews but not specifically recommended for disposal in the review reports.

Appendix 13

OFFICIAL SECRETS ACT

Note by the Treasury (pp. 55–6)

The Committee have asked whether it would be a breach of the Official Secrets Act for an official who believes that misleading evidence has been given to the Committee by one of his senior officers to publicise his opinion of the facts.

Paragraphs 17 and 18 of the Franks Report (Cmnd 5104), attached as an annex, describe the scope of section 2 of the Official Secrets Act 1911. The Government has accepted in principle that the scope of section 2 needs to be narrowed, and intends to issue a White Paper on the subject.

As Sir Robert Cox said in evidence to the Committee, the normal expectation is that any official who saw a significant mistake in evidence to a Parliamentary Committee would draw the attention of his senior officers to it. Ultimately he could report it to his Head of Department.

Normally if there had been a significant mistake it would be rectified. If the mistake were insignificant that would be explained to the officer. If nonetheless the officer without authorisation published the facts (as distinct from his opinion on facts already public), such publication could, depending upon the precise circumstances, amount to a breach of section 2 of the 1911 Act. There would, of course, be no such breach if the sole publication were to the Committee or to the House since the publication would in that event amount to a proceeding in Parliament and would be absolutely privileged.

Prosecutions under the Official Secrets Act require the Attorney-General's consent. The nature of the information disclosed and the appropriateness or otherwise of disciplinary proceedings would doubtless be among the factors the Attorney-General would take into account in reaching his decision. No prosecution has been brought under the 1911 Act in the circumstances that the Committee have in mind.

ANNEX

CHAPTER 2

THE MAIN FEATURES OF SECTION 2

16. Although we have been concerned with only one section of one Act of Parliament, this section has extensive ramifications. Section 2 is short, but it is in very wide terms and it is highly condensed. It covers a great deal of ground, and it creates a considerable number of different offences. According to one calculation over 2,000 differently worded charges can be brought under it. It is obscurely drafted, and to this day legal doubts remain on some important points of interpretation. The section forms an integral part of the Official Secrets Act 1911–1939, and its relationship with section 1 of the 1911 Act is of particular importance. The starting point in any examination of section 2 is to understand it. The text of sections 1 and 2 is set out in full in Appendix I, which also explains their meaning and summarises related provisions of the Official Secrets Acts.

Section 2 is a catch-all

17. The main offence which section 2 creates is the unauthorised communication of official information (including documents) by a Crown servant. The leading characteristic of this offence is its catch-all quality. It catches all official documents and information. It makes no distinctions of kind, and no distinctions of degree. All information which a Crown servant learns in the course of his duty is 'official' for the purposes of section 2, whatever its nature, whatever its importance, whatever its original source. A blanket is thrown over everything; nothing escapes. The section catches all Crown servants as well as all official information. Again, it makes no distinctions according to the nature or importance of a Crown servant's duties. All are covered. Every Minister of the Crown, every civil servant, every member of the Armed Forces, every police officer performs his duties subject to section 2.

The dispensation from the catch-all: authorisation

18. Nevertheless governments regularly reveal a great deal of official information. These disclosures do not contravene section 2. A Crown servant who discloses official information commits an offence under the section only if the information is disclosed to someone 'other than a person to whom he is authorised to communicate it, or a person to

whom it is in the interest of the State his duty to communicate it'. The Act does not explain the meaning of the quoted words. We found that they were commonly supposed, by persons outside the Government, to imply a fairly formal process of express authorisation. Actual practice within the Government rests heavily on a doctrine of implied authorisation, flowing from the nature of each Crown servant's job. In the words of the Home Office, 'the communication of official information is proper if such communication can be fairly regarded as part of the job of the officer concerned'. Ministers are, in effect, self-authorising. They decide for themselves what to reveal. Senior civil servants exercise a considerable degree of personal judgment in deciding what disclosures of official information they may properly make, and to whom. More junior civil servants, and those whose duties do not involve contact with members of the public, may have a very limited discretion, or none at all.

Appendix 14

SECOND SPECIAL REPORT

INQUIRY INTO EVIDENCE GIVEN TO THE COMMITTEE OF PUBLIC ACCOUNTS OF SESSION 1974–75 BY THE PROPERTY SERVICES AGENCY OF THE DEPARTMENT OF THE ENVIRONMENT RELATING TO MAINTENANCE AND OPERATING EXPENSES (pp. vii-x)

The Committee of Public Accounts have agreed to the following Special Report:

1. The Committee of Public Accounts of 1974–75 examined the Property Services Agency (PSA) on the subject of property maintenance and operating expenses. The Committee's examination, based on a report by the Comptroller and Auditor General, was mainly directed to the PSA's methods in achieving more economical maintenance of the Government-owned property estate, both military and civil, with special reference to the comparison between the performance of the Southern Region of the PSA and other regions. The Committee's report was critical of certain aspects of the PSA's performance, including the time which had been taken to secure in other regions the substantial economies which had been achieved in the Southern Region.

2. On 2 May 1978 the Accounting Officer of the PSA, Sir Robert Cox, wrote to inform the Chairman of the Committee that he had unwittingly made a factual error in his evidence to the Committee on 14 April 1975 when he referred to redeployment of military resources from the Southern Region. This letter and the Chairman's

reply of 5 May 1978 are printed at Annex A of Appendix I. Subsequently the validity of this evidence was questioned in a book by a former PSA official and it was suggested in two TV programmes and in the Press that the Committee had been misled by it. We therefore thought it necessary to enquire into this and related matters and report to the House.

3. At our request the Comptroller and Auditor General investigated how the particular error in the PSA's evidence came to be made and submitted a Memorandum to us, Appendix I. We took evidence from Sir Robert Cox, and he submitted two further Memoranda to us, Appendices II and III, which answered specific questions we had put to him on certain aspects of building maintenance and land disposals, and also commented more widely on other points which had been raised, including some raised in the Press.

4. Sir Robert Cox stated in his letter that in answering Question 1318 on 14 April 1975 he had sought to accept that there had been greater enthusiasm for maintenance economy reviews in some regions than in others; to say that the early timing of the initiative in Southern Region had affected the way in which cost savings had been recorded; and to make the point that Southern Region had offered good opportunities, including those arising from a substantial redeployment of military resources from that region to the North. This last statement about redeployment had been incorrect. There had however been some reduction in military strength in the Aldershot area due to a general rundown in the size of the Forces, and Sir Robert stood by his general judgment that the nature of the estate being managed by Southern Region and the circumstances at the time were well suited to the type of initiative that was launched there.

Appendix I, Annex A.

5. On this particular issue, we think it possible that if Sir Robert had not produced so telling a point regarding the redeployment of military resources as part explanation of the scope for greater economies in Southern Region the Committee of 1974–75 might well have pressed

him further on the respective opportunities open to the various regions. We have carefully re-examined this aspect of the subject in the light of Sir Robert's further evidence and the PSA's Memoranda. These Memoranda, which we found useful and informative, gave up-to-date figures of developments and progress in all the PSA's regions since the late 1960s as regard employment of men over 65, the use of directly employed labour, disposals of land and property and fuel economy. The first Memorandum, Appendix II, also dealt with some further allegations which had been made in the Press about the original 1974–75 evidence; and provided more general information about the timing and approaches to the problem of securing economy in maintenance expenditure which had characterised the PSA's operations over the period in question.

6. We consider that this additional information substantiates and expands the general picture presented to the Committee of 1974–75 in the Comptroller and Auditor General's Report and Sir Robert's evidence at that time: that Southern Region were pre-eminent in the achievement of economies in maintenance through the use of independent review teams, partly because this method was particularly suitable for the military estate which predominates in the region; and that although other regions were slow to follow Southern Region in using the same method they also in time secured sizeable savings, though of lesser extent, particularly in directly employed labour and in fuel consumption. We must add that the Committee would have been assisted in their enquiry in 1975 if the PSA had expanded their oral evidence at that time with additional information of this kind, as up-to-date as possible.

7. So far as it is possible to reconstruct the basis for past judgments we believe that had the Committee pursued their questioning on the comparison of the results between Southern Region and other regions, their Fourth Report of 1974–75 would have included a critical comment on the slowness of other regions to secure similar savings in maintenance expenditure. How-

ever, the Committee's main conclusions and criticisms in that Report, reproduced at Appendix V, were directed mainly towards the PSA's objectives for the future rather than to the reasons for their uneven performance in the past. Those conclusions still seem to us to have been well based and we do not believe that Sir Robert Cox's incorrect statement, read in the context of his evidence as a whole, had any material effect upon them. We are glad to see that the Committee's suggestions for improvement are still being implemented as reflected in the further evidence now before us.

8. As regards the reasons for the incorrect statement, Sir Robert told us that it was his interpretation, in what he thought was straightforward language, of information in his brief which referred to

Appendix I, para. 9.

'a trend during the relevant period for the Ministry of Defence to concentrate its facilities elsewhere than in the South which made the time for review in Southern Region most opportune.'

This phrase had been substituted for a statement in an earlier draft of the brief, which Sir Robert did not see, to the effect that Southern Region had more scope for economy than other regions because of the directly employed labour and under-occupation of buildings associated with Army establishments. Both the Comptroller and Auditor-General and Sir Robert Cox confirmed that this earlier draft was more consistent with the facts than was the final version of the brief.

Appendix I, para. 11, Q. 3212.

9. The alteration to the draft brief was made at the suggestion of a senior PSA official, on the strength of his own recollection of knowledge gained during his previous tenure of the post of Regional Director, Southern Region. The PSA are of the opinion that this official, who has since retired, believed his recollection to be correct and did not suggest the alteration from any ulterior motive. The PSA had the usual opportunity to check the accuracy of Sir Robert's statement to the Committee, based on the altered brief, when they received a proof copy of

Appendix I, para. 9.

Qs. 3218–9, 3266–7.

Q. 3215

Q. 3226 his evidence. Sir Robert said that, because the statement
Q. 3225 represented the belief of those within the Agency who
were concerned with the matter, they would have had no
reason to undertake a further check at that point, though
he was himself surprised when the error came to light.

10. We accept unreservedly that Sir Robert Cox believed his evidence to be correct and that he had no intention of misleading the Committee. On the evidence
before us we are unable either to accept or to reject the
PSA's opinion that the alteration to the earlier draft of
Sir Robert's brief was made in good faith, but we consider that as proof one way or the other is unlikely to be
forthcoming it would serve no useful purpose to pursue
this line of enquiry further.

11. The Comptroller and Auditor General's investigation raised further points on which we think we should
comment. First, while recognising the difficulties of an
Appendix I, Accounting Officer attempting to give oral answers to
para. 12 numerous questions, often on complicated subjects, we
must stress the importance we attach to the responsibility
of witnesses before the Committee of Public Accounts for
ensuring that the evidence they give is factually accurate
and complete in all material respects. This requires among
other things that the proof copies of evidence should be
carefully checked to ensure that any significant mistakes
or inaccuracies are brought to our attention and rectified
before we produce our Report.

12. Second we learnt from the Comptroller and
Appendix I, Auditor General's Memorandum that the PSA had
para. 8 discovered the error in Sir Robert Cox's evidence in
March 1977 after being warned by a newspaper reporter
that it was likely to be questioned. They decided however
to defer dealing with the matter until they were challenged
Q. 3229 publicly because they did not consider the error to be of
Q. 3318 great significance and also because they preferred to wait
Qs. 3302-4 until they learnt the full extent of the possible allegation.
The public challenge was eventually made in a book
rather than in a newspaper article, and 14 months
Q. 3229 elapsed before the Committee were notified of the error.
Sir Robert admitted to us that, with hindsight, it would

have been sensible for him to have consulted the Committee Clerk or the Comptroller and Auditor General as soon as the PSA were aware of the error. We agree; and we expect the normal practice to be that a material error in evidence should be notified to the Committee upon its discovery.

13. Finally, we asked the Comptroller and Auditor General about his own approach to the scrutiny of evidence given to the Committee. We recognise that he has no formal responsibility for verifying evidence other than his own, but we note that he and his staff use their knowledge of, and access to, Departments' records to satisfy themselves as far as possible that the Committee are not misled in any important particular. We regard this as a helpful service to us, and we endorse the Comptroller and Auditor General's view that such verification should continue to be confined to statements in the evidence which he and his staff judge to be likely to influence our conclusions or recommendations.

Appendix I, paras. 12 and 13 Qs. 3231–2

Main Conclusions

14. Having investigated the allegation that the Committee was misled by Sir Robert Cox's earlier evidence, we conclude that although there was an inaccuracy in his evidence, it did not materially affect the conclusions set out in their Fourth Report for 1974–75, and that there was no attempt on his part deliberately to mislead the Committee. However, we believe that the error should have been drawn to the Committee's attention when it was first discovered and we stress the importance we attach to the accuracy of evidence given to the Committee of Public Accounts and to the responsibility of witnesses to ensure this.

More about Penguins and Pelicans